ON THE GROTESQUE

Critical Studies in the Humanities
Victor E. Taylor, Series Editor

This open-ended series provides a unique publishing venue by combining single volumes issuing from landmark scholarship with pedagogy-related interdisciplinary collections of readings. This principle of cross-publishing, placing scholarship and pedagogy side by side within a single series, creates a wider horizon for specialized research and more general intellectual discovery. In the broad field of the humanities, the Critical Studies in the Humanities Series is committed to preserving key monographs, encouraging new perspectives, and developing important connections to pedagogical issues.

Proposals for submission should be directed to the Series Editor, Victor E. Taylor, Department of English and Humanities, York College of Pennsylvania, York, PA 17405-7199.

Sander L. Gilman, *Nietzschean Parody*
Sharyn Clough, Ed., *Siblings Under the Skin: Feminism, Social Justice and Analytic Philosophy*
Dominick LaCapra, *Emile Durkheim: Sociologist and Philosopher*
Gregg Lambert, *Report to the Academy*
Michael Strysick, Ed., *The Politics of Community*
Dennis Weiss, Ed., *Interpreting Man*
Jonathan Culler, Flaubert: *The Uses of Uncertainty*
Geoffrey Galt Harpham, *On the Grotesque*
Steven Connor, *Samuel Beckett: Repetition, Theory and Text*
Gragg Lambert, *The Return of the Baroque in Modern Culture*

ON THE GROTESQUE
Strategies of Contradiction in Art and Literature

Geoffrey Galt Harpham

Critical Studies in the Humanities
Victor E. Taylor, Series Editor

The Davies Group, Publishers
Aurora, Colorado USA

opyright © 1982 by Princeton University Press.
Copyright © 2006 by Geoffrey Galt Harpham.

All rights reserved. No part of the contents of this book may be reproduced, stored in an information retrieval system, or transcribed, in any form or by any means — electronic, digital, mechanical, photocopying, recording, or otherwise — without the express written permission of the publisher, and the holder of copyright. Submit all inquiries and requests to the publisher.

Address all requests to:
 The Davies Group, Publishers
 PO Box 440140
 Aurora, CO 80044-0140
 USA

Library of Congress Cataloging-in-Publication Data

Harpham, Geoffrey Galt, 1946-
 On the grotesque : strategies of contradiction in art and literature / Geoffrey Galt Harpham. -- 2nd ed.
 p. cm. -- (Critical studies in the humanities)
 Includes bibliographical references and index.
 ISBN-13: 978-1-888570-85-4 (alk. paper)
 ISBN-10: 1-888570-85-7 (alk. paper)
 1. Grotesque. 2. English fiction--History and criticism. 3. Grotesque in literature. 4. Fiction--History and criticism. 5. Grotesque in art. I. Title. II. Series.
 BH301.G74H37 2006
 823.009'15--dc22
                            2006011020

Printed in the United States of America
Published 2006. The Davies Group Publishers, Aurora CO 80044-0140

1 2 3 4 5 6 7 8 9 0

To the memory of my father,
John Wood Harpham
1919–1981

Contents

List of Illustrations	ix
Preface to the Second Edition	xi
Preface to the 1982 Edition	xxi
Acknowledgments	xxix

Part One		1
Chapter one.	Formation, Deformation, and Reformation: An Introduction to the Grotesque	3
Chapter two.	Grotesque and *Grottesche*	27
Chapter three.	Grotesque and Grotto-esque	71
Part Two		103
Chapter four.	Walking on Silence: The Lamination of Narratives in *Wuthering Heights*	105
Chapter five.	Permeability and the Grotesque: "The Masque of the Red Death"	135
Chapter six.	Metaphor, Marginality, and Parody in *Death in Venice*	153
Chapter seven.	To Make You Sea: Conrad's Primal Words	179
Chapter eight.	Conclusion: Doodles, Dragons, Dissonance, and Discovery	213
Notes		247
Index		279

Illustrations

1. Lucas Cranach, "Der Papstesel," 1523. Forschungsbibliothek Gotha, Theol. 4° 231/2 (3) Rara.
2. Erhard Schön, "Der Teufel mit der Sackpfeife," 1535. Schlossmuseums Gotha.
3. Nicolas Ponce, engraving from Domus Aurea designs, in *Descriptions des bains de Titus* (Paris: Ponce, 1786), pl 37.
4. Nicolas Ponce, engraving from Domus Aurea designs, in *Descriptions des bains de Titus* (Paris: Ponce, 1786); detail, pl 45.
5. View of Vatican Loggia, decorated by Raphael and Giovanni da Udine.
6. Detail, engraving of pilaster in Vatican Loggia by Marcello Ferrari, in *Les ornaments de Raphael* (Paris: J. Marie, 1860).
7. From The Luttrell Psalter; The British Library, Ms. 7952104.
8. Initial from Incunabula, Paris-Lyons, 1485–1499.
9. Initials by Lucas Kilian, from *Newes ABC Buchlein*, Augsburg, 1627.
10. Luca Signorelli, detail from the Chapel of the Madonna of St. Britius, Orvieto Cathedral.
11. Agostino Veneziano, ornamental engraving, before 1520.
12. Marco Dente, ornamental engraving, 1525.
13. Cornelius Bos, ornamental engraving, 1546.
14. Peter Flötner, ornamental metal etching, 1546.
15. Lucas van Leyden, ornamental engraving, 1546.
16. Cornelius Floris, ornamental engraving, 1556.
17. Christoph Jamnitzer, ornamental engraving, 1610.
18. Nicasius Rousseel, ornamental engraving, 1623.
19. Jean-Marie Delattre, ornamental engraving, last quarter of 18th century.
20. Raphael, *The Transfiguration*, Vatican Museum.
21. The "Sorcerer" of Les Trois Frères; watercolor and ink redesigning of cave painting by Abbé H. Breuil.

Preface

Like many first books, *On the Grotesque* began as a dissertation, which was completed at UCLA under the direction of John Espey and Robert Martin Adams, both of whom were more troubled than impressed by it. Dissertations are demonstrations of competence in a small compass; my dissertation was the opposite.

None of us really understood why I had picked such a topic in the first place. My original choice, something on black American novelists from Wright to Baldwin, had been rejected by all the professors I had approached. "If you actually completed such a dissertation," one said, "and if you were hired, which you would not be, when it was announced that you were to teach a course in your field, the Black Student Caucus would be in your office in ten minutes, demanding your removal from the course. And," he added, "all your friends would be on their side." Then, softening, he gave me some counsel: "Don't just look for an interesting topic. Ask what's interesting about you." Nothing could have been more disheartening.

Months of inactivity followed. When I finally determined to write about the grotesque, I avoided the professor who had given me this advice lest he ask me what I had settled on.

In truth, I wasn't sure why this subject seemed right for me, especially since, once I got into it, it proved to be almost impossible to make orderly progress. I had no idea how or where to begin, what to read first, or what to read at all. The subject kept slipping away, always seeming to be in my peripheral vision, but never squarely in my sights.

A long, long time passed during which, if I were asked to say what field I was working in, all I could come up with was "the grotesque." Not "Renaissance non-dramatic literature," "Romantic poetry," "the history of the novel," or "American prose romance." Just the one off-putting word, a word that raised questions about one's motivations or character. Even worse, I could not say exactly what I knew about this word. I had no facts that seemed central. All the critical approaches that I had dutifully learned — psychoanalytic theory, myth criticism, formalism — and some that I hadn't learned but had only heard about — Gestalt theory, game theory — seemed equally valid, equally productive, equally necessary. I could not even say whether the grotesque was a feature of history (aesthetic, literary, intellectual) or a feature of mind. The world was full of instances of the grotesque, but I could not fix the thing itself. The major work on the subject, Wolfgang Kayser's *The Grotesque in Art and Literature*, exemplified the problem. The grotesque was located "in" something — a work, a genre, a period — which was then analyzed and described from this point of view. But what was the thing itself that was presumed to be in these other, more definite things?

I tried to create some order by limiting myself to a time period and a textual field, calling the dissertation "Cultural Degeneration and the Grotesque in H. G. Wells, Jack London, and D. H. Lawrence." I thought I could link these three — a nice number, three — almost contemporaneous writers by creating a cultural context in which images of apocalyptic monstrosity accompanied a general sense of cultural and historical deterioration and decay. At first, this worked, because I could study expressions of cultural despair by figures such as Henry Adams, Cesare Lombroso and Max Nordau; and I could include such factual episodes as the formation of the Boy Scouts in the wake of the British defeat in the Boer War.

With this historical focus, I found that I could write easily but not well. I began to produce pages, but everything I wrote seemed even to me to miss the point, the "it" that was "in" something else. The dissertation was beginning to resemble its subject, a mass of unsorted and ill-formed details adding up to nothing coherent. I showed a 125-page shambles of a chapter to a sympathetic professor, and he returned it mostly unread with a shrug: "You've done a lot of work." Later, when I sent a chapter to Espey, this kindest and gentlest of men drove from Los Angeles to my apartment in Santa Barbara, where I had taken an adjunct job, and handed me my chapter, unmarked, with the words, "I just wanted to tell you this simply won't do." Ah. Well — would he stay for lunch? "I have to go." Robert Martin Adams, evaluating another chapter, did not make the trip. Neither kind nor gentle, but surpassingly brilliant, subtle, incisive, and capacious — "our Kermode," as he has been described — he wrote a long letter whose point was difficult to avoid, since it included the sentence, instantly engraved in my memory: "The impression is of wandering, almost out of control, through the nineteenth century." Not even the uncharacteristic compassion of that "almost" could soften the blow.

Daunted but driven, I worked away. When I completed the section on H. G. Wells, Espey suggested that I simply drop the Lawrence chapter and pronounce the dissertation finished. I had the thing typed and drove to Los Angeles to hand it in, two days before the deadline, after which I would have to pay a dissertation fee for the next term. To my dismay, Adams and my third reader were out of town and unreachable. What to do? Espey scratched his head and speculated that they would probably sign the thing — by which he may have meant that they had no belly for further revisions — and so it was probably all right. While I was wondering what he meant, he took his pen and signed his name, and then, with his left hand, signed the name of my third reader so the two would not look as if they had been done by the same hand. He handed the pen to me. I knew what I had to do. I signed my name, and then, with a trembling left hand, signed for Adams. Espey and I took the bundle of paper over to the Graduate School office, where I gave it to a woman famous for her biting screw of an eye, who inspected it fiercely for margins and typos — but not for forgery. Espey and I exchanged a look, and I felt that with this gesture I had at last done something with the dissertation that had earned his respect.

The degree I had obtained did me little good on the job market — it seemed that a "specialist" on a marginal subject as it occurred in certain instances lying on the cusp of the nineteenth and twentieth centuries in England and America was not in great demand — and I found myself in a one-year position at the University of California at San Diego. I mention this only because of what happened in the course of my U-Haul move. In one of those lucky disasters in which great misfortune turns out to conceal even greater fortune, I somehow lost my dissertation. I had no copy, no carbon, nothing at all. I could have gone back to UCLA and Xeroxed the whole thing, but I was very busy, and so even though I felt miserably exposed, I let time pass, and — gradually stopped grieving. By December 1975, when I conducted my fourth annual job quest at the MLA convention, this time in San Francisco, I had decided that losing that thing was a liberation. And when the University of Pennsylvania offered me a position for the following year, I began the project once again, from the beginning, which was, I realized, where I had always been anyway.

That year was Fredric Jameson's last at UCSD before moving to Yale. I found the atmosphere of the campus almost suffocating in its moralizing thickness, intellectual smugness, and spirit of political conformity. But Jameson himself (who was not altogether responsible for this atmosphere) had gotten onto a book that had been recently translated, Mikhail Bakhtin's *Rabelais and His World*, and the word was spreading. People were saying that this was the authentic voice of the revolution, an amalgam of the 60s and actually existing Marxism from the pre-Stalinist era; and while I didn't find this persuasive, Bakhtin did provide an extraordinarily appealing and powerful view of the grotesque, one that was as far removed from the abyssal gloom suffusing Kayser's book as could be. What Bakhtin gave me was not just the feeling that my subject could be constructed differently, but that it could be constructed in a multitude of ways, could take on any tonality or thematic emphasis. In one sense, I was farther away from the "it" than ever, but I was beginning to feel that I could at least articulate my problem in a way that interested me, and perhaps others.

But a problem is not the same as a book. After two years at Penn, I got an NEH fellowship, and went to work for a year at Clare Hall, Cambridge. Faced with acres of free time, I confronted once again the old bewilderment. Everything was relevant, nothing essential. Settling in at a desk high up in the massive university library, I asked myself each morning what I was going to read that day between visits to the cafeteria for cheese scones. I wandered, almost out of control, through the library, searching for the right books — they had to be there somewhere — and began to pick books that seemed merely interesting, books I'd wanted to read but had never gotten around to. One was Gibbon. I found myself oddly excited by the account in his diary of the genesis of his project, the sight of the monks passing by what was once the temple of Jupiter. This image of the spatial superimposition of two different worlds, so full of meaning for Gibbon, also seemed highly significant for me, although I couldn't say why until, meditating on another book plucked from the cavernous stacks, Vasari's *Lives of the Painters*, I read about the event that gave birth to the Renaissance, the late fifteenth-century discovery in the middle of Rome, beneath tons of rubble and a millennium and a half of urban life, of the ruins of Nero's Golden House, or Domus Aurea.

Since this bizarre structure was the site of the first objects to be called grotesque, or grotto-esque (*grottesche*), I felt that if I understood them, I could make some headway towards understanding the still-elusive "it." The Domus Aurea, I realized, was another structure in the middle of Rome in which two radically different world-views, two entirely different contexts, were not simply juxtaposed but crushed into a single space. I pored over the two large books about this site authored by Nicole Dacos, and several others as well, and came to realize that the charming decorative designs on the walls of this building, designs that excited everyone in the artistic community at the time, themselves represented two distinct systems in the same form — typically, the human and the animal, or human and vegetable. Perhaps the word grotesque originally referred to forms in which species were crossed. But — and here I made a conceptual leap — beneath any given blended or mixed form there might be two distinct ways of understanding the world, one in which such mergings and minglings made sense, and one in which they did not.

How to describe these systems? Pursuing the contingent fact that the Domus Aurea designs had been discovered underground and as a consequence were described as grotto-esque, I began to think about grottoes, and so I was led to Lévi-Strauss, Lévy-Bruhl, Leroi-Gourhan, and other students of mythic thinking, in which stars marry, people turn into flowers, and humans mate with woodland animals and learn their ways. I was also excited by Mary Douglas's *Purity and Danger*, with its compelling account of the concept of "dirt" as a function of things being out of their assigned places. And so, I began to realize, grotto-esque forms constituted echoes of the ancient, mythic world that were heard in a modern context. Our confusion in the presence of such forms reflected the fact that they suspended us between "worlds."

It is almost as embarrassing to confess that I had never so much as taken an art course in college as it is that I forged my director's name on my dissertation. But it is true. I now began to read art history driven exclusively by my interest in its most marginal, exotic, and underconceptualized aspects. I read everything I could get of Ernst Gombrich, whose book on ornament, *The Sense of Order*, was just about to be published; when he came to Cambridge, I cornered him for a 45-second conversation from which I inferred his approval of my project. With cathedrals all around me, I reread Ruskin on the Gothic, and tried to imagine the state of mind of stone carvers operating high above ground level, fashioning gargoyles that might have given expression to an older folk paganism. I read Bernard of Clairvaux, and began, when in cathedrals, to look in such places as the underside of the seats in the choir stalls, where little worlds of monstrosity flourished unnoticed. At the same time, I began to search for literary instances of bi- or multi-temporality — the crumbling griffins above the doorway to Wuthering Heights, for example, which led me into the grotesque in that book as they led Lockwood into the house itself — as well as of other features of the "it" that seemed to me relatively constant.

I was beginning to get a grip on the subject, but was doing so at the cost of any pretense to expertise. An Ivy League professor wholly committed to passionate amateurism, I was devolving into an autodidact. And much of my Cambridge experience was extra-academic — the social scene, travel all over England, theater, music, sports, brief but memorable little encounters with Queenie Leavis, Frank Kermode (the English one), Christopher Ricks, Marilyn Butler, Raymond Williams, and a youthful Allon White, who was beginning to think through the material that would become *The Politics and Poetics of Transgression*. A missed opportunity with I. A. Richards still haunts me. After delaying for months, I wrote to Richards introducing myself and asking if he would consent to having coffee with me some day. He was alive when I sent the card, but dead when it arrived. One drizzly night, the details of which are irrelevant, I found myself with Stephen Hawking cradled in my arms as I negotiated a stretch of slippery wet paving stones, the destination — his car — some fifty feet away. As history records, I accomplished my mission.

I forged on. That summer, I headed south, and made a point of visiting, in addition to every cathedral in my path, El Escorial, where artists from Italy had decorated the immense palace in the style then fashionable in Italy, the style derived from Nero's Domus Aurea. I hiked from the train station up the hill to Orvieto, and somehow managed to get a gesticulating, fast-talking photographer out of his shop and over to the cathedral to take pictures of Signorelli's frescoes in the cathedral. In Rome, I visited the Golden Palace myself, straining to recapture what it might have looked like both five hundred and two thousand years before. And, in a halcyon month spent in a palazzo-turned-pensione on the Piazza Santo Spirito in Florence, I walked the city with Vasari in my pocket, studying pilasters, margins of paintings, ceilings, anywhere except the obvious center of attention. And, in my high-ceilinged room overlooking the piazza — once a chariot-racing oval and now the center of the Florentine traffic in street drugs — I began to assemble the whole thing into a sequence of arguments, laying out the chapters and establishing the architecture of the whole.

I was now convinced that my subject, my one-word mystery, should not be considered as a bounded or even as a stable category. It was not a formal property that could be isolated, identified, and described without begging the question. Nor, as the conjunction of Kayser and Bakhtin demonstrated, was it a particular feeling, an affective tonality. Nor was it associated with a consistent set of meanings. All methods discovered it, all approaches approached it. It — "it" — was . . . a species of confusion, a phase in a sequence of understanding, a moment of partial comprehension provoked by certain forms or works in certain contexts. I can still recall the moment in the palazzo, nearly ten years after having begun my dissertation, when I typed what I knew would be the first sentence of the book: "When we use the word grotesque, we record, among other things, the sense that though our attention has been arrested, our understanding is unsatisfied." *The New York Times Book Review* used to have a feature called "Noted with Pleasure," in which a number of quotes from recently published books were cited, with wry comments. A year after my book appeared, this sentence was quoted, with an appreciative comment on its innocent pedantry. Anyway, with this sentence behind me, I passed out of my own extended period of partial comprehension, and began in earnest to write a different kind of book than the one I set out to write, a theoretical inquiry into a traditional aesthetic category. An immense mass of material and possibilities sorted itself into Chapter 1 (a great labor, and a strong sense of wandering, almost out of control, through the centuries), Chapter 2 (a great pleasure; a cascade of lucky discoveries), and Chapter 3 (a great sense of original and deepening insight); and I was off and running.

I am deeply grateful that my absorption in my own struggles delayed and blunted my encounter with the form of theory that was then flooding into the United States. Except for a couple of fumbling references to Derrida and de Man, *On the Grotesque* discovers its own methodology and terms of analysis. If I had really gotten hold of the concept of *différence*, or it of me, I might well have written a more sophisticated and timely, but really more conventional book.

Back in Philadelphia, my tenure clock began to intrude on my awareness like the clock in "The Masque of the Red Death" (the subject of the first chapter actually composed, and it shows in its amateur structuralism). In the fall of 1980, I submitted the book to Jerry Sherwood, the longtime editor at Princeton University Press. As it will, time passed. And then, while on a research trip to Venice in the spring of 1981, I received a telegram at the American Express office on the Piazza San Marco. At the time, my father was gravely ill, and I feared that this telegram would summon me back to the United States. Instead, it read: "Manuscript accepted. Joy. Sherwood." I had somebody take my picture holding the telegram,

Venice behind me; that photograph, placed in a frame with the telegram itself, has hung on my office wall ever since. I was made.

Or so I thought. In fact, I was unmade. *On the Grotesque*, dedicated to my late father, was published in fall 1982, on my wife's and my first anniversary. We went to a little restaurant in south Philly, and proposed a toast to the book, propped up on a chair between us, and to our rosy future. Two days later, however, I received word that I had been denied tenure. As I was later to discover, the reason for the denial was the book you now hold in your hands. In the eyes of a small subcommittee through which my case had to pass, *On the Grotesque* represented a dangerous practice in which a scholar trained in one field was presuming to work in others. My ventures into art history were particularly reprehensible — not bad in themselves, just bad policy. Amateurs getting into art history "mess up the field," as one member of this subcommittee put it in an indiscreet comment to a friend of mine, who relayed it to me. Soon, this practice would be called interdisciplinarity and pronounced a good thing.

And, through the cunning of history, it was a good thing. By flinging me out into the world, *On the Grotesque* permitted me to live in Boston and New Orleans, two of my very favorite cities in the country. If I hadn't messed up the field, I might have settled in to an Ivy League existence, with its assurances, its complacency, its self-importance, and who knows what other dire academic and moral consequences.

The book also took me to Paris. In the fall of 2001, I received an email inquiry from a young composer named Edmund Campion, who wished to know if I was the author of the book that had, he said, inspired his composition for piano and vibraphone, which was having its premiere in Paris. If I was the author, he could get me a tape of the occasion. Tape, shmape, I said; I'm coming. And so, amid a sea of black leather and black turtlenecks, I heard "my" piece, "Domus Aurea," performed at the Centre Pompidou on November 4, 2001. The connection between the music and the book was not immediately apparent to me, but it sounded great.

At the time, or times, I wrote this book, I was simply trying to bring some order to the chaos I had chosen to work on. But with the passage of time, I can see more clearly what I was doing even without knowing I was doing it, and these things are to me now as interesting as the things I knew I was doing. First, I was taking an interest in the concept of the margin. Margins, paradoxes, mixed forms, disorder — all these, gathered into the concept of the grotesque, opened out onto a capacious view that included both norm and exception. I was very excited by the sentence of Edgar Wind's quoted at the end of the first chapter: "Both logically and causally the exception is crucial, because it introduces (however strange it may sound) the more comprehensive category." With the publication of Derrida's *Margins of Philosophy* in 1984, the margin became the settled home of critical thinking — so much so that it rapidly crystallized into a new center, with all the features of centrality, including social hierarchy, that had driven marginalized critics to promote the virtues of the margin in the first place. I bear no responsibility for this because I was trying to direct attention not to the margin as such, but to the more radically ambiguous or ambivalent space between the margin and the center. This space, or phase, was where one could find not an inverted and re-authorized center but "the more comprehensive category" that included both.

Second, I was attempting to locate a fundamental concept informing all contingent instances, the "it" that troubled me for so long. This is a difficult but worthy task, and could be applied to other fields with profit. Some ten years after this book was published, I was, in fact, undertaking the same project with respect to ethics, asking what was the "ethics" that was confidently attributed to Aristotle, Hegel, Spinoza, and others? It was a relatively easy matter to talk about, for example, Kantian ethics, but a far more difficult thing to talk about or even to identify ethics itself, the thing that takes these various forms. But this is the only way to get at fundamental issues in any field. Asking about the identity of any "it" that has become taken for granted in scholarly discourse is a way of scraping off the accretions of scholarly practice and beginning again. This task generally falls to beginners who mess up the field and suffer the consequences, but even if a few hapless individuals fall by the wayside, all fields need such rejuvenation from time to time.

Third, by treating the grotesque as an interval of understanding rather than a formal feature, *On the Grotesque* suggested an argument that was shortly to be developed more fully by many others, that even formal features were imputed rather than merely described. Accounts of the aesthetic generally stress the co-implication of subject and object, but this co-implication was difficult to realize in critical practice, where the integrity of form as a describable aspect of the aesthetic object continued to be presumed if not explicitly defended. Many scholars, especially those working in hermeneutics, narrative theory, and the new field of reader-response theory, were trying to work their way beyond this understanding of form by approaching the problem deductively, often in a spirit of quasi-political commitment. In this book, I was beginning with an interval in a dynamic process of understanding and going from there.

Last, I would like to draw attention to one feature of the book that, considered as the product of my youth, gives me special pleasure. Many scholars, disciplined by the experience of the dissertation, begin their careers in a spirit of solemn professionalism. As I've said, this book is in no way a professional production. But neither is it solemn. Reading it over two decades after it first appeared, I am struck by a keen responsiveness to qualities of vitality, openness, curiosity, diversity, fertility, and complexity. Something of the joy of discovery, of unstructured curiosity, has been captured and inscribed here. From the epigraph from Deleuze at the beginning (which represented the totality of my knowledge of Deleuze) to the unpunctuated ending, *On the Grotesque* is informed by the spirit of beginning and by faith in the proposition, which I still hold to today, that, as William Carlos Williams says,

> Dissonance
> (if you're interested)
> leads to discovery

Preface to the 1982 edition

This book is neither a history of the grotesque, nor an exhaustive inventory of its modes, nor even an extended definition. It is a series of linked essays that explore the resources of a single protean idea that is capable of assuming a multitude of forms. The first thing to notice about these forms is that they are not purely grotesque; rather, the grotesque inhabits them as an "element," a species of confusion. In our time this element has been detected in the work of Bosch, Dante, Poe, Hitchcock, Bellow, Mann, Piranesi, Flannery O'Connor, Alban Berg, Kafka, Swift, Joyce, Felicien Rops, Sterne, Anthony West, Ravel, Henry Miller, T. S. Eliot, Flaubert, Huysmans, Beardsley, Carlos Fuentes, Crashaw, Waugh, José Donoso, Gogol, Nabokov, Shakespeare, Conrad, Bartok, Schoenberg, D. H. Lawrence, Dali, and — as I am certain to have left out somebody's favorite — others. In some inconceivable spot where the vectors of these artworks intersect, we are to infer, there lies the grotesque.

It is always difficult to think clearly about confusion, but the grotesque presents special problems to those who would study it. What can possibly be "in" all these things? How can "it" be strained out so it can be observed by itself? And what is to be made of the fact that the grotesque is by no means confined to art, but can be experienced as a psychological event for which works of art may create a favorable climate, but which can occur outside their sphere of influence altogether? Should it be approached indirectly, through its various incarnations; or, through an undeflected effort of mental penetration, as a *Ding an sich*, an "essence"? The question running through the entire book is, What is the character of the grotesque, what kind of thing is it?

As a practical matter we commonly adhere to several tacit assumptions about ideas: that they can be clearly expressed; that they have kernels or cores in which all is tidy, compact, and organized; and that the goal of analysis is to set limits to them, creating sharply defined, highly differentiated, and therefore useful concepts. We assume that, however complex an idea may be, it is essentially coherent and that it can most profitably be discussed in an orderly and progressive way.

The grotesque places all these assumptions in doubt. Whether considered as a pattern of energy or as a psychological phenomenon, it is anything but clear. Whereas most ideas are coherent at the core and fuzzy around the edges, the grotesque is the reverse: it is relatively easy to recognize the grotesque "in" a work of art, but quite difficult to apprehend the grotesque directly. Curiously, it remains elusive despite the fact that it is unchanging. Although it appears in various guises, it is as independent of them as a wave is of water, for it is somehow always recognizable as itself. Most curious of all, it has no history capable of being narrated, for it never began anywhere. In the second chapter I take up this problem, discussing the work of the first generation of artists (in the late fifteenth century) who consciously employed a newly discovered ornamental style they called *grottesche*. Their work would seem a natural jumping-off point. As we poise to leap, however, the ground crumbles beneath us, for this style was copied from recently excavated buildings from ancient Rome; there we must go in order to begin. But Rome proves to be a false bottom, for it had borrowed the style from older cultures Before long we find ourselves back in Asia Minor looking for antecedent, and nearly unrecognizable, forms of "it." And from there back to cave paintings and the origins of art. Even this conscientious process permits many fish to slip through the net. Bosch, for example, was innocent of the concept and of the word; all his "grotesques" were created *avant la lettre*. These problems are typical: a study of the subject in any of its forms is always threatened by an endless receding and dissolving, the essence filtering through formulae like vapors through a mesh.

Even if we regard the grotesque as pure essence which, like recently created perfumes designed to smell different on each person, has a unique influence on each artifact in which it participates, we have merely discovered a new kind of problem. For how can the meaning-in-form of a thing be defined when the forms under consideration have no common structure and the range of possible meanings approaches the random? A model for any student of essence is Paul Frankl's *The Gothic: Literary Sources and Interpretations through Eight Centuries*.[1] Like the grotesque (with which it overlaps in the area of gargoyles and chimeras), the Gothic resists precise conceptualization; in fact, after an 830-page survey of all the relevant historical documents, Frankl concludes that not one of them has ever captured its essence. Still the task is not hopeless because the Gothic form is so well defined and its origins so undisputed. In a subsequent book, *Gothic Architecture*,[2] Frankl restricts himself to the form of the Gothic; one is immediately struck by his sense of relief at finding himself on terra firma as he begins this book with the following pithy and authoritative one-sentence paragraph: "The Gothic style evolved from within Romanesque church architecture when diagonal ribs were added to the groin-vault." Thus the Gothic is contained within fixities of time and place, form and function: definable architectural style, coherent symbolic significance, clear origin and terminus, and a limited number of instances. Although the smoky essence had escaped eight centuries of interpretations it is absolutely confined to a definite individual world of concepts and ideas that is historically unique. And these restrictions are what had at last enabled Frankl to crack the code. "The essence of church Gothic," he had said at the conclusion to *The Gothic*, "is the form of the churches of the twelfth and thirteenth centuries as the symbol of Jesus."[3]

None of these helpful limitations applies to the grotesque.

Given such a commotion, how does one, for example, "master the field"? Or "narrow the topic"? Or even compile a bibliography? How does one qualify oneself to speak? What does one read first? Athanasius' *Life of St. Anthony? Paradise Lost? The Tin Drum? Gothic Architecture?* Leslie Fiedler's *Freaks?*

In the absence of a "field," one's first and giddy impression is that nothing is irrelevant, and that all methodologies are justified, from depth psychology to communication theory, from the study of visual perception to cultural history. Even if we confine the study to aesthetic problems and methodologies, we still confront a dizzying variety of possibilities: the decadent, the baroque, the metaphysical, the absurd, the surreal, the primitive; irony, satire, caricature, parody; the Feast of Fools, Carnival, the Dance of Death — all tributary ideas funneling into a center at once infinitely accessible and infinitely obscure.

It is perhaps inevitable that great confusion should prevail among the scholarly works intended to elucidate the subject. Wolfgang Kayser's *The Grotesque in Art and Literature* and Mikhail Bakhtin's *Rabelais and His World* are deservedly considered the two most important. Both are prodigiously well informed, carefully argued, persuasive accounts. And they manage to contradict each other utterly on the most basic premises. Authority is even more widely dispersed among the lesser lights, so that, in mastering the field, one watches it atomize into fine mist.[4] One reason for this confusion is that the grotesque is so omnipresent that nearly any theory at all can be supported by a judicious choice of examples. Indeed, the very use of examples, however necessary to thought and argument, seems (to one who has read most of them) prejudicial, a way of stacking the deck, almost an impurity in the theory. For no example is truly exemplary, and there can be no inevitable progression from the observation even of a great number of particulars to the formulation of a general comprehensive theory. It is the business of theoreticians in all fields to disagree, but such disagreements usually concern the arrangement or interpretation of the material; at least that is the pretense. The field of the grotesque is exceptional in that although there is almost no agreement among critics, there is almost no real disagreement either. It is nearly impossible to argue about the subject because nobody has yet authoritatively ascertained or delimited the material so that it can be arranged, much less interpreted.

A properly methodical approach would begin by accumulating instances and extracting common features. But in this case, bias plays an unusually large role in the decision as to what constitutes an "instance." It is historically demonstrable that no single quality is constant throughout the range of generally accepted grotesques. Most people today would think that ugliness would be a minimal prerequisite, but, as the illustrations to this book should demonstrate, this is a modern prejudice: the *grottesche* of the Renaissance was primarily intended to be, simply, beautiful.

It is possible to compile a history, if not of the grotesque, at least of the documents that discuss it. But there is no historical certainty to be won by doing so, for these documents consist largely of statements relating the grotesque to such touchstone but historically inconstant concepts as reality or nature. The Renaissance, for example, regarded *grottesche* as pure fantasy; their term was *sogni dei pittori*, the dreams of painters. But over the centuries the grotesque somehow negotiated a separate peace with reality. In the eighteenth and nineteenth centuries we find the word associated with caricature in discussions of such artists as Rowlandson, Hogarth, Goya, Daumier, Gavarni, Grandville, Cruickshank, and Tenniel, most of whom we would not associate with fantastic art. By the beginning of the twentieth century the grotesque had outflanked an unvigilant reality: Thomas Mann commented, in *Meditations of a Nonpolitical Man*, that the grotesque was "properly something more than the truth, something real in the extreme, not something arbitrary, false, absurd, and contrary to reality." Since Mann's time even this difference has evaporated. One critic wrote recently of *The Great Gatsby* that Fitzgerald "wove the grotesque so firmly into the real that their textures, however improbable the *Gestalt*, are thread by thread indistinguishable."[5] Flannery O'Connor has remarked that Northern readers think all Southern writing is grotesque "unless it is grotesque, in which case it is going to be called realistic."[6] For us in the last days the sense of a blending is widely shared. How often have we read sentences beginning something like, "Given man's freakish and absurd nature, and the nightmarish malignancy of the modern world...."? Gahan Wilson, striking a particularly modern note, has reported that even his imagination is routinely outdone by the newspapers. He cites one instance from among thousands: in the early days of heart transplants, doctors attempted to transfer the heart of a pig to a man. In the middle of the operation, the story goes, the anesthetized pig woke up and ran squealing around the room with the doctors in pursuit as the man died on the operating table.

A recent book, on *The Grotesque in Photography*,[7] completes this progression, displaying not only artificially distorted or rearranged images, but also technically uncomplicated photographs of hangings, murder victims, Che Guevara's staring corpse, and the famous picture, almost a modern icon, of the televised pistol execution of a Viet Cong. *Sogni dei paparazzi*.

In short, whereas the grotesque had once seemed the very opposite of the real, recent commentators have seemed unable or unwilling to extricate the two from each other, and have even encouraged an identification between them. The same could be said of the relation between the grotesque and the "natural." From Thomas Browne's assertion that "There are no Grotesques in Nature" (*Religio Medici*, 1643) to Theophile Gautier's that "Le grotesque a toujours éxistée dans l'art et dans la nature" (*Les Grotesques*, 1853), we can trace a steady line of advance. By the end of the nineteenth century, it was more common than not to speak of the "naturalness" of the grotesque. Ruskin had listed both "Naturalness" and "Grotesqueness" among the attributes of the Gothic, implying that they could coexist in the same entity. And he had conceded in *The Stones of Venice* that the grotesque sometimes gave "evidence of deep insight into nature."[8] Walter Bagehot and G. K. Chesterton agreed, arguing that Browning's grotesqueries demonstrated his fidelity to nature. Chesterton put it vigorously:

> Energy which disregards the standard of classical art is in nature as it is in Browning. The same sense of the uproarious force in things which makes Browning dwell on the oddity of a fungus

or a jellyfish makes him dwell on the oddity of a philosophical idea.[9]

Definition is the last refuge of a scholar. But if the grotesque cannot be defined formally, thematically, affectively, or even by relation to other concepts, then what hope for clarity is left? What is left to define? What makes a work grotesque? In the presence of such reasonable and, for the moment, unanswerable questions, it is cold comfort to recall Karl Popper's recommendation that all "what is" questions should be avoided because they lead only to sterile verbalism. It is only the imprecision of language, he suggests, that enables us to use it at all. Even granting Popper's point, we must feel some apprehension concerning the alarming loss of precision in the concept since the Renaissance. If the usage of that time (see Chapter Two) seems to us far too narrow and restricted, contemporary usage is so loose that the word is in danger of losing all meaning and passing out of critical discourse altogether.

That the grotesque exists has always been a given. But it is up to the culture to provide the conventions and assumptions that determine its particular forms. Culture does this by establishing conditions of order and coherence, especially by determining which categories are logically or generically incompatible with which others. Despite the accelerating acceptance of the grotesque as a "mode" in contemporary art, this book appears at a time when the grotesque is becoming less and less possible because of the pervasive, soupy tolerance of disorder, of the genre mixte. When the television talk shows present the casual viewer with "in-depth" interviews with, for example, transvestites and transsexuals, how can we continue to call the hermaphrodite grotesque? More to the point, with the emphasis, especially in literature, on non-closural and heterodox works that deliberately skew traditional forms, how can any given point of mixed-mode confusion be called merely an "element"? The most conspicuous forms of our culture contribute to this process: in more innocent times it was possible to create a grotesque by mingling human with animal or mechanical elements; but as we learn more about the languages of animals, and teach more and more complex languages to computers or robots, the membranes dividing these realms from that of the human begin to dissolve, and with them go the potentiality for many forms of the grotesque. In short, the grotesque — with the help of technology — is becoming the victim of its own success: having existed for many centuries on the disorderly margins of Western culture and the aesthetic conventions that constitute that culture, it is now faced with a situation where the center cannot, or does not choose to, hold; where nothing is incompatible with anything else; and where the marginal is indistinguishable from the typical. Thus the grotesque, in endlessly diluting forms, is always and everywhere around us — and increasingly invisible.

This moment of crisis in the history of the term is also, however, an appropriate time to try to establish the nature of the grotesque, before it hides itself from us completely. We should not contribute to its elusiveness by pretending that it exists in some positive form. It is, as I said at the beginning, a "species of confusion" — that is, it is defined and recognized in common usage by a certain set of obstacles to structured thought. The grotesque is that sort of thing in the presence of which we experience certain methodological problems. Attempting to account for this experience, the first chapter begins with a discussion of the grotesque as a confusion in language categories. The word itself is a storage place for the outcasts of language, entities for which there is no appropriate noun; and this accords with the sense of formal disorder we perceive in grotesqueries, in which ontological, generic, or logical categories are illegitimately jumbled together.

Chapters Two and Three seek to develop formulae or "master codes" for the entire range of the grotesque by exploring the conditions under which it came into being. The concept is easy enough to trace, for it came into being, as I have already indicated, in the late fifteenth century when the word *grottesche* was applied to certain ornamental designs modeled on recently excavated Roman frescoes. These designs were primarily decorative in character but they differed from most traditional ornament in that not only were they capable of filling a space all by themselves with no help from any central subject, but they also incorporated interpretable, frequently human, elements into the design, and so they were ambivalently meaning-bearing as well as decorative. Chapter Three, the most speculative chapter in the book, attempts to trace the origins of the designs themselves, exploring the relation between our sense of the grotesque and the earliest forms of "grotto-esque," Paleolithic cave art. Chapters Four through Seven are devoted to literary texts and are intended not to "apply the theory" but simply to extend the ground of a consistently theoretical inquiry to include literature. Each of these chapters, therefore, is intended to serve to some extent as a model argument. The final chapter discusses the function of the grotesque in the theories of representation of Kant, Hegel, Ruskin, and others. Noting that the grotesque has frequently been conceived as a figure either for a "pure" art or for the impurities and ambiguities of art, I argue that the grotesque appears to us to occupy a margin between "art" and something "outside of" or "beyond" art. In other words, it serves as a limit to the field of art and can be seen as a figure for a total art that recognizes its own incongruities and paradoxes.

The book thus spirals out from a single point-the word itself-to take in a great deal of territory. In this movement it is faithful to its subject, which has had a similarly centrifugal lifeline. The only justification really needed for such an extension is not that it is proper, or true, or necessary, but simply that it is possible.

Acknowledgments

In preparing this edition of *On the Grotesque*, I benefited from the expertise and generosity of Eliza Robertson, Barbara Mormile, Caryn Koplik, Joel Elliott, and Lee Sorenson. I would like to thank the following publishers and photographic agencies for supplying the following illustrations or permitting me to use them in this book: 1, 2: Insel-Verlag Anton Kippenberg, from H. Meuche ed., *Flügblatter der Reformation und des Bauernkrieges*, Leipzig, 1976, pl. 16 in the *Textband*, and no. 16 in the *Portfolio*, respectively; 3, 4, 6, New York Public Library; 5, 10, 20, Photo Alinari; 7, Janet Backhouse, ed., *The Luttrell Psalter*, by permission of Ivan R. Dee, publisher; 21, H. Bégouën and H. Breuil, *Les Cavernes du Volp* (Paris: Arts et Métiers Graphiques, 1958), pl XX. Plates 11-19 are from Rudolf Berliner, *Ornamentale Vorlageblätter des 15. bis 18. Jahrhunderts*, 4 vols. (Leipzig: Klinkhardt and Biermann, 1925): 11: I.38; 12:I.46; 13:I.152; 14:I.176; 15:I.75; 16:I.163; 17:II.242; 18:II.271; 19: III.446.

Grotesques: Pictures wherein (as please the Painter) all kinds of odde things are represented without anie peculiar sence, or meaning, but only to feed the eye.
— R. Cotgrave, *A Dictionnairie of the French and English Tongues*, 1611.

PART ONE

True theory does not totalize, it multiplies.
— Gilles Deleuze

CHAPTER ONE

Formation, Deformation, and Reformation
An Introduction to the Grotesque

1. *Betweeen Nullity and Justice: Perceiving the Grotesque Form*

When we use the word "grotesque" we record, among other things, the sense that though our attention has been arrested, our understanding is unsatisfied. Grotesqueries both require and defeat definition: they are neither so regular and rhythmical that they settle easily into our categories, nor so unprecedented that we do not recognize them at all. They stand at a margin of consciousness between the known and the unknown, the perceived and the unperceived, calling into question the adequacy of our ways of organizing the world, of dividing the continuum of experience into knowable particles.

Fittingly, the word itself betrays an irreducible queerness. As an adjective it has no descriptive value; its sole function is to represent a condition of overcrowding or contradiction in the place where the modifier should be. This place can never be occupied by any other single adjective but only by a number of adjectives not normally found together. The grotesque is concept without form: the word nearly always modifies such indeterminate nouns as *monster, object* or *thing*. As a noun it implies that an object either occupies multiple categories or that it falls between categories; it implies the collision of other nouns, or the impossibility of finding a synonym, nothing more. Before we can ask how the grotesque "functions" or how it is "used," we must recognize that grotesques have no consistent properties other than their own grotesqueness, and that they do not manifest predictable behavior. The word designates a condition of being just out of focus, just beyond the reach of language. It accommodates the things left over when the categories of language are exhausted; it is a defense against silence when other words have failed. In any age — this one, for example — its widespread use indicates that significant portions of experience are eluding satisfactory verbal formulation.

The anthropologist Edmund Leach has proposed a theory of taboo and nameable categories that bears directly on this problem. Leach argues that the physical and social environment of a young child does not contain any intrinsically separate "things" but is perceived as a seamless fabric, a flow. With training the child develops and imposes on the world a discriminatory grid that isolates a large number of separate things, each with its own name. Inevitably, the grid fails to account for or identify a certain segment of reality, which therefore appears as a series of "non-things." Our suppression of the objects in the interstices of consciousness takes the form of taboo, so that the sacred flourishes only in the gaps, where we find incarnate deities, virgin mothers, supernatural monsters that are half-man and half-beast. Susan Stewart has made useful distinctions among types of nonthings: "The anomalous stands between the categories of an existing classification system.... The ambiguous is that which cannot be defined in terms of any given category.... The ambivalent is that which belongs to more than one domain at a time."[1] Primitives worship the taboo, but modern secular adults are so indebted to and dependent upon their discriminatory grids that they find the taboo mostly a source of anxiety, horror, astonishment, laughter, or revulsion. Witness, for example, our strong but ambivalent feelings toward those exudations of the human body that mediate between self and non-self, the magical outcast ingredients of witch's brews such as feces, urine, semen, menstrual blood, nail parings, and spittle.

As its peculiar linguistic status indicates, "grotesque" is another word for non-thing, especially the strong forms of the ambivalent and the anomalous. The mind does not long tolerate such affronts to its classificatory systems as grotesque forms present; within an instant of its being exposed to such forms it starts to operate in certain ways, and it is these operations that tell us that we are in the presence of the grotesque. The "temptations" that engulf and torment St. Anthony in representations by Schöngauer, Bosch, Breughel, Grünewald, Ensor, and countless others activate such characteristic responses, which are revealed as we try to describe the non-things attacking the saint. Typically, the "temptations" cannot be gathered into a single noun, for they are composed of parts of different species, including, sometimes, human parts. One can only describe them in parts, despite the manifest inadequacy of a description that gathers but does not cohere or synthesize. The whole of a "temptation" is, if not more than, at least very different from the sickening jumble of its parts. Temptations are grotesque not because they are hideous — dragons and gorgons and terrible beasts are not necessarily grotesque — but because, in the midst of an overwhelming impression of monstrousness there is much we can recognize, much corrupted or shuffled familiarity. Knotting the alien whole with more or less familiar parts, these creatures simultaneously invoke and repudiate our conventional, language-based categories. Perceiving them in bits, the mind moves toward a level of detail at which those categories are adequate, at which we can say for certain, "This is an ear," "This is a claw," "This is a wing," and so forth.

This response, of breaking down the strange into the recognizable, is often accompanied by another: enlarging the context, considering the particular figure as a member of a class of such things. Many grotesqueries seem to fit only into the class of "grotesqueries," but in the case of the iconology of St. Anthony, we have another class: "temptations." When the horrifying non-things are regarded as "temptations," they are not only moralized, they are de-grotesqued. The grotesque form is one that is apprehended at a certain level of generalization; it can always move out of the category of the grotesque by being broken down or by being absorbed into a larger group.

The "temptation" is an ambivalent being belonging to no real class of objects, but whose reality is difficult for the saint to deny; his fortitude, indeed, is measured by his ability to make this denial. Grotesque figures test us in a similar way, for they seem to be singular events, appearing in the world by virtue of an illegitimate act of creation, manifesting no coherent, and certainly no divine, intention. This is why the grotesque is embraced by "aesthetic" artists who insist on the non-mimetic character of artistic creation: as Aubrey Beardsley said, "If I am not grotesque, I am nothing." And it is also why the grotesque, and those who indulge in it, frequently encounter a backlash that takes the form of genealogical abuse, with accusations of illegitimacy, bastardy, or hybridization, terms that indicate structural confusion, reproductive irregularity, or typological incoherence. Genre, genus, and genitals are linked in language as in our subconscious.

This kind of abuse informs many religious satires. Figures 1 and 2 date from the Reformation and demonstrate how naturally its arguments assumed grotesque form. The first, Lucas Cranach's *Der Papstesel* (1523), is supposedly a representation of a creature that had washed up on the banks of the Tiber; it bodies forth the degeneracy of Rome by portraying the Pope as a horror of ambivalence, with donkey head, fish-scales over that part of the body that is not human and female, the nether extremities a cloven hoof and buzzard claw, a querulous human face for rump, and bearded, predatory bird for tail. Cranach has taken a meaningless horror, the creature, and cross-bred it with the Pope, to produce a grotesque that comments on both.

Figure 2 is from the other side, an anti-Lutheran blast by Erhard Schön. It is called *Der Teufel mit der Sackpfeife* (1535) and portrays the devil using the functional part of a cleric, perhaps Luther himself, as a kind of bagpipe. Is Luther the devil's "organ"? The formal confusion here is more riotous than in the Cranach: not even the Tiber could harbor such a creature. How to describe it? Where to begin? There is a priestly head — awake, obliging, content to be a bladder; and the devil itself — partly vertebrate with strong suggestions of fowl from the neck up, except for the small tusks; and, in the lower belly and genital region, a semi-autonomous, one-eyed grinning male face. The quality of grotesqueness arises not so much from the specific contents of the image as from the fact that it refuses to be taken in whole because it embodies a confusion of type. If we did not have the word devil, a category which, like temptation, serves as a storage-place for demonic non-things, we would have no word for it at all. Nor could we describe it easily in its parts, for "chest," "belly," "torso," and so forth do not apply here, although we have no others to substitute for them: the figure is more like a vertebrate than anything else, but of course it is not like a vertebrate. "Grotesque" is a word for this paralysis of language.

Behind these serious plays with form lies the idea that soul is form and (to use Spenser's phrase) doth the body make. "Soul" here means an organizing spiritual principle, the source of structure and order. Grotesque forms are material analogues or expressions of spiritual corruption or weakness. Their parts are in a state of anarchy, producing an impression of atrocious and inappropriate vitality. Such vitality is the emblem of sin which, as Lavater said, is the same as the destruction of order. In his biography of Michelangelo, Giorgio Vasari describes sketches made by the artist for a treatment of The

Last Judgment, noting the awesomeness ("*terribilità*") in the groups of nudes "as they rain down from heaven to turn into demons of weird and frightening appearance on reaching the center of the earth: certainly a strange flight of the imagination."[2] Stranger still that Vasari should consider it so strange, for most representations of such "falls" portray the damned, or the rebels, as being distorted even as they topple, having surrendered their structural integrity and formal coherence in the act of transgression.

For the artist, such forms must be a great temptation. "Heaven," with its order galvanized by the Creator, has no details at all, really; it is commonly represented, as by Doré in his illustrations for the *Paradiso*, as a swirl of sparkling dots, a convention E. H. Gombrich calls the "etc. principle."[3] The damned, on the other hand, announce and suffer their singularity; their clotted and degraded shapes, seen throughout Western art, are entirely their own, or those of their sins—all highly individualized, with a feeble or confused formal principle. Considered as a class, the damned resist family grouping. They suffer the torments appropriate to them, while the blessed enjoy a common bliss. Like Dickens heroines, angels are hard to tell apart. No matter how many of the damned are assembled, others cannot be inferred from them. Unlike conventional forms—a sonnet, a flatworm, a dodecahedron, a Corinthian column — they cannot be described generically, in the abstract. All form and many virtues are the result of limitation, and the figures of Schöngauer, Cranach, and Schön manifest a superabundance of detail that mounts to the demonic in its rejection of restraint.

The grotesque often arises in the clash between the "virtuous" limitations of form and a rebellious content that refuses to be constrained. *In Speak, Memory*, Nabokov describes his creation of chess problems in precisely these terms:

> Deceit, to the point of diabolism, and originality verging upon the grotesque, were my notions of strategy; and although in matters of construction I tried to conform, whenever possible, to classical rules, such as economy of force, unity, weeding out of loose ends, I was always ready to sacrifice purity of form to the exigencies of fantastic content, causing form to bulge and burst like a sponge-bag containing a small furious devil.[4]

1. Lucas Cranach, *Der Papstesel*, 1523

Formation, Deformation, and Reformation

2. Erhard Schön, *Der Teufel mit der Sackpfeife*, 1536

Nabokov's originality consisted neither in his problems' "purity of form" nor in their "fantastic content," but rather in his devilishly ingenious marriage of the two. Grotesque forms place an enormous strain on the marriage of form and content by foregrounding them both, so that they appear not as a partnership, but as a warfare, a struggle. To return to Michelangelo's figure, we could say that, although the grotesque is more comfortable in hell than in heaven, its true home is the space between, in which perfectly formed shapes metamorphose into demons. This mid-region is dynamic and unpredictable, a scene of transformation or metamorphosis.

Within the space of ambivalence or ambiguity, energy is confused, incoherent. Accordingly, Hugh Kenner describes Wyndham Lewis's paintings as a "trammeling of energy": "A grotesque is an energy which aborts, as if to express its dissatisfaction with available boundaries, as a dwarf may be nature's critique of the tailor's dummy. Lewis's earlier pictures announce an energy art cannot accommodate."[5] These sentences agree with Baudelaire's conception of the grotesque, which is based on its utter unorganizability, its refusal to submit even to hell's hierarchy. Cruickshank's special merit, Baudelaire says in "Some Foreign Caricaturists," is his "inexhaustible abundance in the grotesque":

> I should say that the essence of Cruickshank's grotesque is an extravagant violence of gesture and movement, and a kind of explosion, so to speak, within the expression. Each one of his little creatures mimes his part in a frenzy and ferment, like a pantomime-actor.... The whole of this diminutive company rushes pell-mell through its thousand capers with indescribable high spirits, but without worrying too much if all their limbs are in their proper places.[6]

Depending upon the circumstances, trammeled energy can be fearsome or exuberant, or both. Grotesque forms in fact almost always inspire ambivalent emotional reactions. But Chesterton was right to give sheer energy its epigrammatic due, writing in his 1903 study of *Robert Browning* that "Energy and joy are the father and mother of the grotesque."[7]

Consider by contrast the circle, the simplest, most perfect, and least energetic form. The circle is not merely a shape, but nearly an ideology. The form, as Georges Poulet says, "of the perfection of being,"[8] round is the primal totality, the unbroken unity of the cosmos. Plato's original man was perfect — bisexual and spherical. Origen prophesied that we would roll into heaven, meaning that once out of nature we would naturally gather into spheres to meet our maker. Gaston Bachelard concludes — rounds off — his study of *The Poetics of Space* with a chapter, "The Phenomenology of Roundness," citing van Gogh's statement that "Life is probably round," and altering a formulation of Jaspers' to read: "*das Dasein ist rund*," being is round.[9] Round is, in short, what we have emerged from, will return to, and fail to achieve in the meantime. It is the most formal form, the shape most ideal. The idea is Idea itself, total coherence and unity.

The grotesque is the opposite, the least ideal form. The circle's tension is perfectly controlled, but the grotesque is always a civil war of attraction/repulsion. I once heard a lecturer make what he condescendingly called a "grotesque comparison" between Titian and the Pre-Raphaelite painter Holman Hunt. Titian can be compared without violence to Tintoretto or Velasquez, and cannot be compared at all with my cat. But bring him together with Holman Hunt and we have a "grotesque comparison." The lecturer's point, as I recall it, was that they drew feet the same way; so that, despite a great dropoff in subtlety, taste, richness of conception, imaginative and intellectual penetration — all that constitutes quality — the two artists have a genuine point of similarity; and therein lay (for him) the grotesqueness of the comparison. Although the mind struggles to prize them apart, almost with a sense that the proximity of Hunt, even in our thoughts, even in this sentence, contaminates Titian, we are compelled to admit a humiliating resemblance in the feet.

Most grotesques are marked by such an affinity/antagonism, by the co-presence of the normative, fully formed, "high" or ideal, and the abnormal, unformed, degenerate, "low" or material.[10] (The ingredients' of witch's brews, for example, are not themselves grotesque until they are described to a skeptic as having healing powers.) The "grotesque heads," with misshapen noses and pre-modern dental formations, in Leonardo's notebooks were given their name long after they were created because they exhibited such torsions. Barely but recognizably human, they grade toward some species lower down on the evolutionary or ontological scale, toward a principle of formlessness, primitivism, or bestiality. The result is a compromise, a taboo, a nonthing.

Dante, writing in the golden age of the grotesque before it became self-conscious, provides an especially vivid example of this combinatory de-grading. We are deep in hell, on the seventh bowge, where thieves are punished:

> Lo! while I gazed, there darted up a great
> Six-legged worm, and leapt with all its claws
> On one of them from in front, and seized him straight;
> Clasping his middle with its middle paws,
> Along his arms it made its fore-paws reach,
> And clenched its teeth tightly in both his jaws;
>
> Hind-legs to thighs it fastened, each to each,
> And after, thrust its tail betwixt the two,
> Up-bent upon his loins behind the breech.
>
> Ivy to oak so rooted never grew
> As limb by limb that monstrous beast obscene
> Cling him about, and close and closer drew,
>
> Till like hot wax they stuck; and, melting in,
> Their tints began to mingle and to run,
> And neither seemed to be what it had been....
>
> Two heads already had become one head,
> We saw two faces fuse themselves, to weld
> One countenance whence both the first had fled;
>
> Into two arms the four fore-quarters swelled;
> Legs and thighs, breast and belly, blent and knit
> Such nightmare limbs as never eye beheld;
>
> All former forms wholly extinct in it,
> The perverse image—both at once and neither—
> Reeled slowly out of sight on languid feet.[11]

Blake attempted to render this "perverse image"; appropriately, the work was left unfinished.

Dante's image qualifies as grotesque not only because of its skewing of logical or ontological categories, but especially because of its confusion of hierarchy: one of the most grotesque features of Dantean demons is that they do not respect the proprieties of high and low. It is in this context that we should consider the use of the term by D. H. Lawrence. With his elaborately metaphysical notions about love, he was continually embarrassed by the act itself: "To have created in us all these beautiful and noble sentiments of love, to set the nightingale and all the heavenly spheres singing, merely to throw us into this grotesque posture, to perform this humiliating act, is a piece of cynicism worthy, not of a benevolent Creator, but of a mocking demon."[12] Sex dramatizes the incongruity of the human: straining for sublimity, we ape the beasts. The embrace of Agnello by the Worm points to a number of other couplings that exploit and develop the affinity between sexual love and the grotesque: Beauty and the Beast, Caliban and Miranda, Othello and Desdemona, Quasimodo and Esmeralda, Quilp and Little Nell, Humbert Humbert and Lolita. In the more simplistic of these pairings the principles of high and low are distributed one to a person in order to clarify, however crudely, the structure of amalgamation that characterizes human love, and humanity, in general.

In all the examples I have been considering, the sense of the grotesque arises with the perception that something is illegitimately in something else. The most mundane of figures, this metaphor of co-presence, in, also harbors the essence of the grotesque, the sense that things that should be kept apart are fused together.[13] Such fusions generate the reaction described clinically by Freud, who noted that when the elements of the unconscious "pierce into consciousness, we become aware of a distinct feeling of repulsion."[14]

Some grotesques, however, are not true hybrids at all in the sense that, in them, generic lines are not crossed. Bakhtin discusses one such instance, certain terra cotta figurines of laughing, senile, pregnant hags. These figurines manifest a "grotesque conception of the body" by embodying the poles of the biocosmic cycle: "There is nothing completed, nothing calm and stable in the bodies of these old hags. They combine a senile, decaying, and deformed flesh with the flesh of new life, conceived but as yet unformed."[15] These figures can best be described as images of instantaneous process, time rendered into space, narrative compressed into image. In his chapter on shells in *The Poetics of Space*, Bachelard talks about grotesques of this type, medieval engravings of creatures emerging from coiled shells. Since the creature "does not come out entirely," he says, "the part that comes out contradicts the part that remains inside. The creature's rear parts remain imprisoned in the solid geometrical form." Several of these creatures "have discarded their shells and remain coiled in the form of the shell. Heads of dogs, wolves and birds, as well as human heads, are attached directly to mollusks. And so, unbridled bestial daydream produces a diagram for a shortened version of animal evolution. In other words, in order to achieve grotesqueness, it suffices to abridge an evolution,"[16] to attach a creature to another phase of its own being, with the intervening temporal gap so great that it appears that species boundaries, and not mere time, has been overleaped.

In an age of rapid evolution we are everywhere confronted with such abbreviations or shortcuts. We can spot them even in our fictions. They are what Kenner refers to when he speaks of random-number tables, "computer-generated because it is so difficult for the mind to avoid unwilled patterns":

> These books, and the intricate rules by which the machines that print them out must be instructed (for by what laws may we specify the lawless?), are among the idiosyncratic curiosities of our age. A great order, paradoxically, underlies them. Thus embedded in a random sequence in one such book we find the pentad "44844." It is in place there because to forbid a symmetry of 4's would be to impose a trimness alien to the very concept (concept!) of the random. The order that underlies *Gravity's Rainbow* (Pynchon) or *The Recognitions* (Gaddis), an order achieved by the writer specifying for himself laws like a programmer's, has a not dissimilar feel. Any momentary resemblance to older fictions is like that symmetry "44844," permitted because it would be over-tidy to forbid it.[17]

The presence of older fictional modes embedded in programmer's prose explains and justifies Gaddis's subtitle: "A Grotesque Novel."

The issue of titles or naming can be crucial to the grotesque. An analysis like Kenner's, in fact, undercuts Gaddis's subtitle: it short-circuits the text's grotesqueness by prying it loose from the category of "novel" and slotting it into another category, occupied not by *Vanity Fair*, *Tom Jones*, and *War and Peace*, but by random-number tables. It follows from this that we can deform an image, creating a grotesque by slotting it into the wrong category, or even by applying the wrong kind of conceptual scheme altogether. T. S. Eliot implied as much in a remark in *The Sacred Wood*: "The ordinary intelligence is good only for certain classes of objects; a brilliant man of science, if he is interested in poetry at all, may conceive grotesque judgments."[18] He may — and distinguished poets may do the same on politics and culture, by applying a method of analysis and mode of expression to a "class of objects" unsuited to them.

But we would be wrong to consider such methods as mere confusion, for they can sometimes achieve striking insights. Metaphors, which I will discuss more fully in Chapter Six, work in this way, through the application of what Aristotle called a "foreign" name, or what Gilbert Ryles has called a "category mistake." Eliot knew how illuminating such mistakes could be; and this is why, in another essay in that volume, he referred to Baudelaire as "a deformed Dante." Certain features of Baudelaire's emerge only when he is seen through Dante's grid; the deliberate deforming of the image is an essential step in the process of reforming it.

Sometimes the gap between systems of understanding can produce the grotesque, as when representations produced in one historical era or cultural system are apprehended through the lens of another. We can see this in the case of a 1465 painting that depicts an aged and emaciated couple, standing side by side, miserably nude, their bodies festering with open sores, enormous toads feasting on genitals, vipers twisting in and out of wounds, gigantic flies and spiders crawling over gashes and scabs. The title by which it is sometimes referred to in English is "Pair of Lovers," a name that is not merely perverse, but something far more profound: it is grotesque, not only because it is so horribly wrong, but also because, as we slowly realize, it fits. In their solitude and nudity these figures may remind us (although we may dismiss the resemblances as meaningless) of Adam and Eve. Pondering that title, our minds may stray to Dante's Paolo and Francesca, or to

Romeo and Juliet, or Tristan and Isolde, all associations we may try to reject as accidental. But (as the mind may insist on realizing) what these pairs of lovers have in common is transgression and death. How easily (as we now see) these golden lads and lasses melt in the imagination into the *danse macabre* tradition; how they virtually summon up images of mocking skeletons heaving wailing belles and beaux into the cauldron-jaws of hell. The toads hanging from the mouths of sinners or attached to breasts and genitals as emblems of lust in many medieval depictions are kissing cousins to those crawling over these lovers. Love and death, we see, can entwine themselves as intimately as shade and serpent. From this point of view, "Pair of Lovers" is an indirect but highly effective title. The Musée de Strasbourg calls the painting *Les Amants Trépassés*, which, making explicit the moral recognition that "Pair of Lovers" enabled the viewer to grope toward, converts the painting into an orthodox *momento mori*, ensuring that the point is made, but robbing us of the experience of watching the vision of the grotesque dissolve into a Vision of Justice.

If a name can make a grotesque, it can also unmake one. The Viennese court painter Arcimboldo (1527-93) is known for a series of paintings that demonstrate this fact. If we look closely at one of his paintings, we see only a mass of fish; then as we move back from the painting, that mass begins to gather into the suggestion of a human face, a suggestion that increases in intensity the farther back we move, until finally, at a considerable distance, we see no fish at all, just a side portrait of a man. From the close-up view, "Fish" appears an appropriate designation and "Man" a mistake; from far away, the reverse is true. But there is a point in the middle distance, the point of the grotesque, when there appears to be equal evidence for both titles, which is to say, when neither title by itself is adequate as a referential description. At this point our understanding is stranded in a "liminal" phase, for the image appears to have an impossible split reference, and multiple forms inhabit a single image. We struggle to make sense of this grotesque, searching for ways in which the concept of humanity overlaps with that of fish. And at this point, the name "*Wasser*" (water) appears, like a genie from a lamp, a nonreferential name that, suggesting an abridged evolution, a common origin in the sea, accommodates all possibilities.

Arcimboldo's painting, as well as the others I have been using as examples of the grotesque, equally justifies multiple interpretations.

For this reason they are "liminal" in the sense that anthropologists use the word to describe the middle phase of primitive initiation rituals, when the celebrant is "between two worlds." In a liminal image, opposing processes and assumptions coexist in a single representation.[19] Broadly and basically speaking, we apprehend the grotesque in the presence of an entity — an image, object, or experience — simultaneously justifying multiple and mutually exclusive interpretations which commonly stand in a relation of high to low, human to subhuman, divine to human, normative to abnormal, with the unifying principle sensed but occluded and imperfectly perceived.

2. *The Grotesque as Interval*

It is common usage to call "monster" an unfamiliar concord of dissonant elements: the centaur, the chimera are thus defined for those without understanding. I call "monster" all original inexhaustible beauty.

— Alfred Jarry, "Les Monstres"

No definition of the grotesque can depend solely upon formal properties, for the elements of understanding and perception, and the factors of prejudice, assumptions, and expectations play such a crucial role in creating the *sense* of the grotesque. It is our interpretation of the form that matters, the degree to which we perceive the principle of unity that binds together the antagonistic parts. The perception of the grotesque is never a fixed or stable thing, but always a process, a progression.

To illustrate this progression I would like to return for a moment to the lines quoted above from the twenty-fifth canto of the *Inferno*. In these images Dante claimed to have out-metamorphosed Ovid. He certainly created a more powerfully grotesque impression than any in the *Metamorphoses*. Transformation is the central principle in Ovid's mythic world, but Dante is from our world and sees with our eyes: in the moment of apprehension he can have no more than an inkling of the unity and character in the midst of the overpowering strangeness of the form. As any commentary will inform us, this unity lies in the fact that, as thieves had made no distinction in life between *meum* and *teum*, so are they here rewarded by a hellish parody of theft. Without access to exegesis, we may suspect that Dante is only conscious of beholding the co-optation of one being, a man called in life Agnello, by another being loathsome and wholly alien. But he must also be conscious of beholding the execution of a rough but exact justice. That is what hell is all about, as the sign above its gates ("Justice made me, and eternal love") had informed him. So in fact he sees a metamorphosis from one form to another which a worldly view tells him is repellent to it, but which is, by a circuitry of logic he only dimly apprehends at the time, intimately related to it. If there had been no justice at all, no reason for the merging, no analogue between Agnello and the serpent, the confusion would be absolute and the object "simply null." But if Dante saw only and clearly justice (as Virgil, accustomed to such sights, would perceive), then there would be no confusion, and no sense of the grotesque, but simply more of the schematic perfection of the Law. The grotesque occupies a gap or interval; it is the middle of a narrative of emergent comprehension.

The sense of an "interval" of the grotesque is developed by George Santayana in one of the few nineteenth-century discussions of the subject that remain fully persuasive. In *The Sense of Beauty,* he suggests that we can consider a given object that registers with us as grotesque either as a distortion of an ideal type or as a new kind of object with its own "inward possibility." If we take the first approach we enter a state of confusion at the initial encounter, but then retreat with categories intact. But if we take the second approach we break through confusion to discovery, and what had at first appeared impossible or ludicrous "takes its place among recognized ideals":

> And the grotesqueness of an individual has essentially the same nature. If we like the inward harmony, the characteristic balance of his features, we are able to disengage this individual from the class into which we were trying to force him; we can forget the expectation which he was going to disappoint. The ugliness then disappears, and only the reassertion of the old habit and demand can make us regard him as in any way extravagant.
>
> What appears as grotesque may be intrinsically inferior or superior to the normal. That is a question of its abstract material and form. But until the new object impresses its form

on our imagination, so that we can grasp its unity and proportion, it appears to us as a jumble and distortion of other forms. If this confusion is absolute, the object is simply null; it does not exist aesthetically, except by virtue of its materials. But if the confusion is not absolute, and we have an inkling of the unity and character in the midst of the strangeness of the form, then we have the grotesque. It is the half-formed, the perplexed, and the suggestively monstrous.[20]

This purgatorial stage of understanding during which the object appears as "a jumble and distortion of other forms" would seem to be a rare occurrence; in fact, it happens all the time, but the interval is generally so brief, and so easily bridged by memory and anticipation, that we do not recognize it.

Once our perceptual habits begin to be established we see the present as a modified version of the past, and perception becomes a matter of ceaseless and slight adjustments to our working hypotheses about the world. When we encounter something new we ask, "What's it like?" which can be translated as, "What familiar forms can you recognize in it?" Eventually we discover the proper place for the new thing, and recognize it not only for what it is like but also for what it is, in itself. We have followed this process in learning to call mouse-birds bats, horse-men centaurs, and women-bosses chairpersons. The interval of the grotesque is the one in which, although we have recognized a number of different forms in the object, we have not yet developed a clear sense of the dominant principle that defines it and organizes its various elements. Until we do so we are stuck, aware of the presence of significance, or of certain kinds of formal integrity, but unable to decipher the codes. Resisting closure, the grotesque object impales us on the present moment, emptying the past and forestalling the future. An identical force sustains the knower and the known, for this interval is the temporal analogue of the grotesque object, with its trammeling of energy and feeble or occluded formal principle.

Ovid provides an example. Scylla makes an enemy of Circe, who poisons the pool where Scylla bathes:

There Scylla came; she waded into the water,
Waist-deep, and suddenly saw her loins disfigured

> With barking monsters, and at first she could not
> Believe that these were parts of her own body.
> She tried to drive them off, the barking creatures,
> And flees in panic, but what she runs away from
> She still takes with her; feeling for her thighs,
> Her legs, her feet, she finds, in all these parts,
> The heads of dogs, jaws gaping wide, and hellish.
> She stands on dogs gone mad, and loins and belly
> Are circled by those monstrous forms.[21]

Scylla had entered the pool having settled beyond dispute that all of her parts were "parts of her own body." When she is suddenly transformed she cannot at first accommodate the new evidence to the old belief. But having experienced the paradox of running both *from* and *with*, she is experiencing the grotesque, suffering the logically impossible though undeniable recognition that "her loins" are also "dogs gone mad." She may go mad herself, or she may cope with her situation; but in either event the entire sequence could be framed as the death of the theorizing mind, the temporary reign of the senses (and the confounding of theory), followed by a resurrection of theoretical certainty.

Confused things lead the mind to new inventions. This is true for Scylla, for whom this knot or clumping of normal theorizing will, if she does not go mad, engender larger categories, freer thought; it is true in scholarly work as well. It is especially and most famously true in science, where the logical rigor necessary for research fosters a hypersensitivity to anomaly or ambiguity, to instances that seem to break the rules. Thus Darwin, for example, was led to his revolutionary theory of the chance emergence of new characteristics by attending closely to the quirks in the breeding of domestic plants, in which "odd, exotic, and quite useless or even detrimental characters were preserved by artificial selection."[22] In a larger sense, an interval of confusion lies at the heart of all scientific discoveries of a revolutionary character. This is the position of T. S. Kuhn, who opened up an extremely fertile area of inquiry by exploring the time of transition when scientists shift from one explanation of a given set of phenomena to another. This pregnant moment is a "paradigm crisis," when enough anomalies have emerged to discredit an old explanatory paradigm or model so that one can no longer adhere to it, but before the emergence of a generally accepted new paradigm.²³ The paradigm crisis is the interval of the grotesque writ large.

The process of confusion generating new insight applies to the understanding of the "data" of art as well, but especially to representational art that invokes the categories and paradigms of what Alfred Schutz calls the "commonsense life-world." Only within these categories can this kind of confusion occur. It was one of the central tenets of Gombrich's *Art and Illusion* that ambiguity as such could not be perceived, that the famous reversible duck-rabbit figure could be seen either as a duck or a rabbit, but not as both, for the mind switches categories instantaneously. This argument has been attacked, most notably by Leo Steinberg, who has cited the entire career of Picasso as a refutation.²⁴ But Gombrich demonstrates how the mind substitutes one naive interpretation for another: the figure appears first as a representation of one or the other; only later do we discover the alternate possibility. Steinberg's example of Picasso's art does not really rebut Gombrich's argument because the perceptual process involved is reversed: the pictures appear first as ambiguous and only later as representational. Steinberg demonstrates, for example, how a certain line in a one-plane, non-illusionistic composition may be understood to designate both a spine and a frontal median. What Steinberg is actually saying is not that the mind is capable of holding alternate readings in suspension, but that a given design harbors many representational possibilities. When we perceive Picasso's ambiguity clearly, we say to ourselves that if we viewed this picture representationally, which we do not, it would be ambiguous. We perceive the illusion of ambiguity, but do not experience ambiguity, or illusion, itself.

The grotesque is a naive experience, largely contained within the context of representational art, art in which, however temporarily and provisionally, we believe. Obviously, the more naive and intense our belief, the more violent will be the transition from one interpretation to another, and the stronger our experience of the grotesque. Fragmented, jumbled, or corrupted representation leads us into the grotesque; and it leads us out of it as well, generating the interpretive activity that seeks closure, either in the discovery of a novel form or in a metaphorical, analogical, or allegorical explanation.

However beneficent the effects, the experience does not come cheaply. Baudelaire described the response to the "absolute comic" as an agony, a paroxysm, a swoon; G. Wilson Knight says that the "demonic grin of the incongruous and absurd" in the "grotesque comedy" of *Lear* "wrenches, splits, gashes the mind till it utters the whirling vapourings of lunacy."²⁵ These are descriptions of the mind poised between death and rebirth, insanity and discovery, rubble and revelation.

3. *Interpretation and Deformation*

The phrases of Baudelaire and Knight remind us that what is commonly conceived of as an opposition between the sublime and the grotesque is often a mere difference of point of view: as Shaw said of flower girls and duchesses, the difference is not so much in what they are as in how they are treated. When we try to imagine the form of the *mysterium tremendum*, we conceive either of airy nothings, a swirl of sparkling dots, or of grotesqueries. In the words of Christian Morgenstern, "God's material form is grotesque."²⁶ Sometimes only the context enables us to decide between devil and deity. Dante places the Minotaur and the centaurs in Hell, but the griffin is stationed at the highest point in Purgatory as a symbol of Christ.

Christ requires this symbol because unpurged human eyes are incapable of beholding divinity directly. In the words of Ruskin, the fallen human soul can be compared to a diminishing glass,

> ...and that a broken one, to the mighty truths of the universe around it; and the wider the scope of its glance, and the vaster the truths into which it obtains an insight, the more fantastic their distortion is likely to be, as the winds and vapours trouble the field of the telescope most when it reaches farthest.²⁷

The implication here is that the more grotesque the image appears, the more exalted the reality it may betoken; and that, as Edmund Burke said, a clear idea was another name for a little idea. Many grotesques, Ruskin acknowledged, were simply debased or degraded, but the formal confusion of the "terrible" grotesque was an intimation of an idea too large for any form: "if the objects of horror in which the terrible grotesque finds its materials were contemplated in their true light, and with the entire energy of the soul, they would cease to be grotesque, and become altogether sublime." In other words, when we call such forms grotesque we betray our own fallen condition, and the limitations of our vision: "it is some shortening of the power, or the will, of contemplation, and some consequent distortion of the terrible image in which the grotesqueness consists."[28]

Our ability to perceive images as grotesque may be the emblem of original sin, marking our once and future intimacy with the divine, and our present alienation from it, but if we resign ourselves to life in a fallen world, we can see that grotesque forms present great opportunities for the imaginative intellect, for they are pre-eminently interpretable. "A fine grotesque," Ruskin said, is "the expression, in a moment, by a series of symbols thrown together in a bold and fearless connection, of truths which it would have taken a long time to express in any verbal way."[29] The delight of interpretation is the puzzling-out of this truth, which is implied just as strongly by what is left out as by what is included. It is "the gaps, left or overleaped by the haste of the imagination"[30] that form the grotesque character; and the mind, which hates gaps as nature hates a vacuum, leaps to fill them in through interpretation to the point where the grotesqueness vanishes and the image appears, if not as a "Gospel" (as Ruskin said) at least as a compressed allegory. Cranach's "*Papstesel*" can be read in this way: as little as the head of a donkey belongs on this creature, so does the Pope belong at the head of the Church.

If the grotesque can be compared to anything, it is to paradox. Paradox is a way of turning language against itself by asserting both terms of a contradiction at once. Pursued for its own sake, paradox can seem vulgar or meaningless; it is extremely fatiguing to the mind. But pursued for the sake of wordless truth, it can rend veils and even, like the grotesque, approach the holy. Because it breaks the rules, paradox can penetrate to new and unexpected realms of experience, discovering relationships syntax generally obscures. This sense of revelation accompanying a sudden enrichment of our symbolic repertory accounts for our experience of depth: it is very nearly synonymous with profundity itself. But while we are in the paradox, before we have either dismissed it as meaningless or broken through to that wordless knowledge (which the namelessness of the grotesque image parodies), we are ourselves in "para," on the margin itself. To be in "para," then, is a

preludial condition that dissolves in the act of comprehension: like the grotesque, paradox is a sphinx who dies once its riddle is solved.[31]

Victor Hugo and his followers advanced *le grotesque* as the epitome of then-modern art, the antithesis of a decorum-defined classicism they called *le sublime*. Hugo and conventional wisdom notwithstanding, the grotesque is often, like the experience of "para," an augury, rather than a negation of a new, even a "sublime" awareness. It is one characteristic of revolutions, whether literary, political, or scientific, that they liberate, dignify, and pass through the grotesque. A shift in vision, often from literal to symbolic, and suddenly the deformed is revealed as the sublime.

Paradox is simply an extreme form of a common case, for all interpretation entails such a shift of vision. This is pointed out by Frank Kermode, who argues in *The Genesis of Secrecy: On the Interpretation of Narrative*[32] that texts should be regarded as having both a "carnal" or literal sense, on which readers can generally agree, and a "latent or spiritual sense" accessible only to those who look beyond the literal. Carnal readings, he says, are much the same, but spiritual readings are all different, as they depend upon the reader's filling in the text's gaps in signification.[33] Kermode's model for the spiritual reader is the early Christians, "insiders" who could understand the mysteries of Christ's teachings, which seemed but harmless riddling nonsense to the nonelect. We might add that the early Christians developed the notion that "discordant figures uplift the mind more than do the harmonious,"[34] and so provided us with an even more specific model for reader-text interaction: our confrontation with the most discordant of all figures, the grotesque. In a carnal reading, the grotesque is no more than the sum of its synonym — ludicrous, wildly formed, absurd, disgusting, etc. But transcategorical hybrids also offer endless and compelling temptations to interpretation. Confused, unresolved, unstable, and apparently filled with great but uncertain significance, such images seem to demand that we rescue them from absurdity, that we make them complete, as Martin Luther "completed" the "Mönchskalb," a terribly deformed man in whom he read allegorical witness of the "signs of the times."

The test of any stylistics, or any theory of reading, is how well it accounts for the phenomenon of incompatible, variable, or switching interpretations.[35] This phenomenon is presided over by the grotesque, which sustains *only* such interpretations. As all fictive texts require some kind of interpretive "completion," students of interpretation might do well to consider the grotesque. They might begin by attending to nonnons. These are described by Nabokov in *Invitation to a Beheading* as absurd objects, shapeless, pockmarked, mottled, knobby things which, when placed before a distorting mirror become handsome and sensible. The nonnons have been interpreted to death by the commentators but I do not recall ever seeing the following interpretation, which seems to me at least as justified as any parable reading. The nonnons could be said to stand for the text, or the artifact itself; the mirror is the act of interpretation. All interpretation disfigures the artifact by rearranging it, taking elements out of their contexts and placing them in new juxtaposition to one another; but it takes a nonnon to enable us to see that distortion. The handsome and sensible form we see in the mirror is, quite simply, meaning — a recreation of the text according to the demands of design or pattern, formal qualities which are prerequisites for any sense of significance.

At the conclusion to his study of *Pagan Mysteries in the Renaissance*,[36] Edgar Wind describes Raphael's use of grottesche ornament in the Vatican Loggias in terms that recapitulate and complete this line of thought:

> Addressing the devout in a foolish spirit, these calculated freaks represented to perfection what Pico della Mirandola had defined as the Orphic disguise: the art of interweaving the divine secrets with the fabric of fables, so that anyone reading those hymns "would think they contained nothing but the sheerest tales and trifles," *nihil subesse credat praeter nugasque meracissimas.*[37]

This study is informed by the conviction that serious attention to the grotesque can unlock many secrets. In this spirit, I have assumed throughout that all the aberrant and atypical aspects of the grotesque described in the Preface and in this chapter, all the ways in which it deviates from normal practice, are simply nonnon-versions of the conventional. I argued, for example, that the grotesque was unusual in that instances could support nearly any theory and that there was no inevitable progression from particular to general. Grappling with this problem, I have come to understand Karl Popper's point, at first so counterintuitive, that theory always precedes observation, and that induction simply does not exist. I mentioned, too, that it was extremely difficult to determine what a fact was when dealing with the grotesque. Increasingly, we find a troubling and destabilizing awareness of the problematic nature of the facts growing in virtually every area of study as scholars come to a greater understanding of the ways in which "fiction" and "interpretation" are intertwined with "the objective" and "the real." Even history, so recently demythologized, has lately been de-realized and de-factualized by the metahistorians. In the next chapter I will be discussing the grotesque as a form of ornamental art that co-opts the center by incorporating interpretable elements. At the present moment a virtual war is being fought within literary studies between those who, broadly, would retain some notion of a central core of meaning and those who focus on hitherto ignored reservoirs of meaning on the margins — in the ulterior, the secondary, the unstressed, the repressed.

The grotesque provides a model for a kind of argument that takes the exceptional or marginal, rather than the merely conventional, as the type. We can, by the logic of this approach, infer the conventions of, for example, the novel better from such fringe works as *Tristram Shandy*, *Alice's Adventures in Wonderland*, and *Ulysses* than we can from *The Scarlet Letter*, *Henry Esmond*, or *A Farewell to Arms*. That all the marginal-typical, thought-enlarging examples are rich in grotesquerie should be no surprise. For, as Wind says at the conclusion of his discussion of Raphael, "Both logically and causally the exceptional is crucial, because it introduces (however strange it may sound) the more comprehensive category."[38]

A topic, clearly, for the times — and not only because of our dilapidated physical environment, the unrelenting strangeness of our culture, man's freakish and absurd nature, etc. — but also because the necessary way of thinking about it presents difficulties and opportunities that are painfully congenial, distinctively our own.

CHAPTER TWO

Grotesque and *Grottesche*

1. *Excavating the Origins*

As the grotesque is a mental event as well as a formal property, its history is impossible to narrate. The case is very different when we consider the word itself, of whose development and applications we can form a very clear account, at least of its formative years. This story is worth telling because through it we may be able to get some idea of how the disorderly concept with which we moderns have to struggle grew out of, and is still genealogically linked to, concrete particulars.

The first things to be called grotesque were dainty, innocuous frescoes decorating the walls of Nero's Domus Aurea, or Golden Palace. Despite their inaugural status in this respect, these frescoes did not represent a new or original style, for they derived from designs and ways of thinking much older than Rome. Nor were they immediately recognized as "grotesque." This recognition had to wait until the Golden Palace had been buried underground for nearly a millennium and a half. The Palace was rescued from oblivion around 1480, when antiquarians began the excavation of an enormous structure in the center of the city, across the street from the Colosseum. Of all the recoveries of classical Rome made by the Renaissance, this was to be the most exciting, influential, and confusing. In these ruins, scholars and artists beheld the ancient past suddenly revealed in the form of an awesome enigma, a vast labyrinth of passageways, rooms, and supporting pillars to structures that no longer existed, and a great mass of utter junk. The site inspired the imagination as it resisted comprehension, and in fact for decades no visitor knew exactly what he was looking at, for although it was generally known that the Baths of Titus had been erected in that area, popular tradition had placed the Domus Aurea at the Lateran, the Quirinal, or the current site of the Vatican.

Their confusion is understandable, for the site consisted of several structures crushed into a single area. The most interesting parts actually belonged to the earliest structure, Nero's palace. The story of this unique building, so grandiose in its conception and so important in its decay, was described at the time of its construction by Pliny, Tacitus, and Suetonius, and has been studied recently by Giuseppe Lugli, H. P. L'Orange, Axel Boëthius, Nicole Dacos,[1] and others, whose diligent labors enable us to understand what the Renaissance could not.

Historical movements great and small pivot on this monstrosity. After the great fire of 64 A.D. had devastated most of Rome, a popular rumor spread that Nero had ordered the conflagration so that he could found a new city named after himself; moreover, that while the blaze consumed Rome, Nero had appeared at a window, performing a recitation on the fall of Troy. To distract the people and redirect their suspicion from himself, Nero began the persecution of the Christians, ostensibly as punishment for arson. Despite this entertaining spectacle, doubts persisted, based now on Nero's reconstruction of the city. With the land cleared and old Rome extinct, Nero began to fancy himself a Sun-God, sweeping his hair forward and up to resemble a wreath of flames;[2] and he built an imperial villa so enormous that Tacitus was moved to remark that the whole of Rome had been reduced to one house.[3] Nero had created a huge central building, lakes, pastures, vast woods, and, on the spot where the Colosseum was later to be built, a man-made pond surrounded by buildings devised to resemble a seaport. All this occupied an area roughly twice the size of the present Vatican City. In the central building Nero's guests could bathe in sulphur water piped from Tivoli while contemplating walls inlaid with mother-of-pearl and gems. Or they could feast in a manner that can be inferred from Trimalchio's banquet in Petronius' *Satyricon,* in rooms with fretted ivory ceilings fitted with pipes through which scents could be sprayed. The rooms included a *cenatio,* or round hall, that revolved perpetually in emulation of the sky. Horses pulling a capstan beneath the floor helped accomplish the transformation of the round hall into an image of the heavens, a notion that complemented the prevailing metaphor of the Domus Aurea, of Nero as Sun-God. According to H. P. L'Orange, Nero had looked to the East for his models, drawing on a Hellenistic-Oriental tradition epitomized in the palace of Nebuchadnezzar in Babylon in the sixth century B.C. in which the king is enthroned in his palace as God is enthroned in the heavens.[4] And Paul Frankl has argued persuasively that the very concept of a cathedral in the Middle Ages derived from this tradition of a palace for a god, especially as exemplified in the Domus Aurea.[5] Before occupying his neo-Hellenistic proto-cathedral, Nero commented that he, a god, scarcely deigned to live as a man in this house.

He did not have to endure it long. He joined his true company the immortals by suicide in 68, after which the Flavian emperors sought to regain popular favor by demolishing the villa, by then a symbol of tyranny. Vespasian began the reclamation of the land; following him, Titus built *thermae,* or baths, opposite the Colosseum, leaving the main palace remaining, where Pliny saw it in 79 A.D. A large fire in 104 hastened the destruction and permitted Trajan to build his huge *thermae* on the site. During this project many openings were bricked up for greater structural stability, and the rooms filled with debris.[6] Renaissance excavators, looking for statues, had to sift through a very considerable muddle: Nero's passageways, intricate enough to begin with, were now confused with the substructures of the Baths of Titus in a matrix of dirt and rubble. To Quattrocento eyes, many parts showed every effect of nearly 1500 years of subterranean decay; other parts — wall designs, for example — were almost perfectly preserved. What a sight this must have been, a circus of formidable but uncertain significance. At the time of its disinterment the very place was an architectural palimpsest, an optical jumble much like objects we have learned to call grotesque.

While the scholars were trying to solve this puzzle, artists were studying the frescoes of Nero's walls, which were decorated in a style largely lost since the fall of Rome — walls preserved through the barbarian sack because they had already been sacked by the Romans themselves. These frescoes were the work of an austere nonentity providentially named Fabullus, one of the few Roman artists whose names we know.[7] Charged by the emperor with the interior decoration, Fabullus devoted himself to the project so utterly that the Domus Aurea became known as the "prison" of his art;[8] but, in Lugli's words, "it does not seem as if this *Fabullus* brought any notable novelties to the style of his times, nor does he seem to have felt the grandioseness and the new form of the rooms he was to decorate."[9] We can be grateful for Fabullus' failure to grasp Nero's new forms, for with his dutiful pedestrianism he provided the finest example we have of a style that had appeared in Rome about 100 B.C. This style consisted of graceful fantasies, symmetrical anatomical impossibilities, small beasts, human heads, and delicate, indeterminate vegetables, all presented as ornament with a faintly mythological character imparted by representations of fauns, nymphs, satyrs, and centaurs. The designs are now so badly deteriorated through exposure to the air that we cannot see much. But at the end of the eighteenth century the French engraver Nicolas Ponce made a series of engravings that reveal the character of Fabullus' decoration in great detail[10] (Figures 3, 4).

On its appearance in Rome, the new style had immediately drawn fire. Horace took it as a model for artistic absurdity, beginning his *Ars Poetica* by demanding what one could possibly make of a figure with a man's head, a horse's neck, the wings of a bird, and a fish's tail.[11] Before long it inspired one of the most important denunciations in the history of aesthetic criticism, Vitruvius' attack in *De Architectura* (ca. 27 B.C.) on designs like those in the Domus Aurea:

> On the stucco are monsters rather than definite representations taken from definite things. Instead of columns there rise up stalks; instead of gables, striped panels with curled leaves and volutes. Candelabra uphold pictured shrines and above the summits of these, clusters of thin stalks rise from their roots in tendrils with little figures seated upon them at random. Again, slender stalks with heads of men and animals attached to half the body.
> Such things neither are, nor can be, nor have been. On these lines the new fashions compel bad judges to condemn good craftsmanship for dullness. For how can a reed actually sustain a roof, or a candelabra the ornaments of a bagle, or a soft and slender stalk a seated statue, or how can flowers and half-statues rise alternatively from roots and stalks? Yet when people view these falsehoods, they approve rather than condemn.[12]

We can be grateful, too, for Vitruvius' misapplication of the canons of representation to ornament, for this schoolmasterish passage has proved enormously useful. E. H. Gombrich has demonstrated that all the labels learned by undergraduates tracking the progress of art — Classic, Romanesque, Gothic, Renaissance, Mannerist, Baroque, Rococo, Neo-Classical, and Romantic — are easily reducible to two terms, Classical and Non-Classical. The point of discrimination, he asserts, is the passage quoted above. For example, Vasari described the Gothic style ("which could well be called Confusion or Disorder instead") in phrases that closely follow Vitruvius', and at the end of the eighteenth century Winckelmann censured what has come to be called "Rococo" on the grounds that it had "no more of Nature about it than Vitruvius' candelabra, which supported little castles and palaces." Winckelmann, Gombrich notes, objected to this style "possibly because of its association with the grotto, a place which favoured excesses of irregularity and whimsy."[13] Bearing Vitruvius in mind, Vasari, Winckelmann and others could divide the non-classical style into two parts, "Gothic being increasingly used as a label for the not-yet-classical, the barbaric, and *barocco* for the no-longer-classical, the degenerate."[14] In other words, the style Vitruvius attacked, which had no descriptive name and violated all categories, has provided the means of distinguishing all our major stylistic categories and so has contributed crucially to the study of art history as it is generally conceived.

It was left to the Renaissance, digging up its own past, to christen the style. Many of the masters who had gathered in the city to participate in the construction and decoration of the Vatican and St. Peter's came to the site. In the 1480s, only the upper parts of a few of the walls were visible at all, and access to these was extremely hazardous. One by one, artists and antiquarians, bearing provisions for what might be a long day and accompanied by ill-informed but agile guides, crept down into the ruins, crawling for hours through tunnels to the rooms designated the *volta dorata* and the *cryptoportico*. There they were lowered on a sling to gaze at the designs on the walls by torchlight, frequently scratching their names on the walls and ceilings before returning to the upper world. Through a study of these graffiti Nicole Dacos has reconstructed the progress of the excavation itself, so that we now know which rooms were unearthed at what time, as well as who saw them.[15]

Fabullus's frescoes were among the first sights to be made available. More because of the setting than because of any qualities inherent in the designs themselves, a consensus soon emerged according to which the designs were called *grotesche*, of or pertaining to underground caves. Like Vitruvius' judgment, this naming is a mistake pregnant with truth, for although the designs were never intended to be underground, nor Nero's palace a grotto, the word is perfect. The Latin form of *grotta* is probably *crupta* (cf. "crypt"), which in turn derives *etymology of grotte/sche/grotesque*

from the Greek Κρύπτη, a vault; one of the cognates is Κρύπτειγ, to hide.[16] *Grotesque,* then, gathers into itself suggestions of the underground, of burial, and of secrecy.

2. Margins and Centers

As I was considering the way a painter I employ went about his work, I had a mind to imitate him. He chooses the best spot, the middle of each wall, to put a picture labored over with all his skill, and the empty space all around it he fills with grotesques, which are fantastic paintings whose only charm lies in their variety and strangeness. And what are these things of mine, in truth, but grotesques and monstrous bodies, pieced together of divers members, without definite shape, having no order, sequence, or proportion other than accidental
— Montaigne, "Of Friendship"

Those artists who, like Filippino Lippi, Pinturicchio,[17] Perugino, Signorelli, and Ghirlandaio,[18] came to the Domus Aurea excavations immediately saw in Fabullus' designs a vocabulary that could be adapted chiefly to ornament or marginal decoration. The humble concept of ornament is manifest even in the grandest achievement of Renaissance *grottesche,* the decoration of the Vatican Loggias. This enormous project is a major event in the Renaissance and in the career of its creator, the Chief Architect and Prefect of Antiquities at the Vatican, Raphael. Athough Raphael's interests and genius did not run to ornament, he was greatly interested in antiquity, having accumulated a vast knowledge of sarcophagi, gems, statues, coins, and archeology; he permitted himself to be led through the ruins — by then more accessible than they had been several decades earlier at the time of their discovery — by one of the most gifted members of his "school," Giovanni da Udine, an exceptional painter of animals and vegetation, and a man whose talents certainly did run to ornament.[19] Under Raphael's direction, Giovanni was to become the acknowledged master of *grottesche.*

This Dantean descent initiated an extraordinary series of creative insights. Deeply impressed by the underground frescoes, which he considered a form of ideal art,[20] Raphael decided to use them in the decoration of the Loggias, the vaulted passageways in the palace of Nicholas III, which he finished in 1519 (see Figure 5). Turner has recreated this moment of painterly inspiration in a huge canvas hanging in the Tate Gallery in London, "Rome, From the Vatican. Raffaelle, Accompanied by La Fornarina, Preparing His Pictures for the Decoration of the Loggia" (1820). Actually, Raphael himself applied little paint, applying himself instead to the conception and planning of the whole, which was to portray nothing less than the history of the world as revealed by the Bible. The entire design is sometimes referred to as "The Raphael Bible." The story was to be told through a series of four panels on the vault of each of the thirteen bays, with twelve depicting scenes from the Old Testament and one from the New. The pilasters, walls, and spaces between panels were to be taken up with ornamental designs.

If creativity involves the juxtaposition of dissimilar or unlike elements, real creation occurred here. The method of depicting the narrative line of history through a series of pictures was no recent invention.[21] But Raphael's idea of uniting a sublime Christian message and *grottesche* pagan designs — in an insubordinate position — was a bold stroke. Although others had, for the most part, simply incorporated ancient elements into their own decorative vocabulary, Raphael transfigured them, recreating the ancient style according to his own designs. Impressively, he did so despite the strictures of Vitruvius, whom he had read closely, having sponsored his own translation.[22] Even more impressively, he had been able to appropriate this style in so distinctive a way that, although it had seemed to Vitruvius to embody the spirit of decadence and absurdity, it now seemed the mark of vitality, confidence, mastery, and inspiration. Such a plan could have been conceived only by a genius, in Rome, at that time, when not only were major Christian edifices being constructed, but Pope Leo X was encouraging Church participation in the recovery of the classical past. It was a remarkable moment, when collective inspiration was nourished by the underground past and applied to the mighty labors of the celestial hereafter. From couplings of incongruities such as these, discovery is born: Gibbon reports in his diary that the idea for *The Decline and Fall of the Roman Empire* came to him as he sat one day observing a group of monks singing vespers in a ruined Temple of Jupiter.[23] In fact, as the Renaissance itself can be characterized by the fusion of antiquity and Christianity under the amalgamative pressures of its master spirits, the application of *grottesche* to the Vatican Loggias provides a way of looking at the entire epoch from the viewpoint of one of its more idiosyncratic products.

Raphael assigned the decoration largely to Giovanni, who, given a free hand, created a system of design based on what he had seen in the "grottoes" that filled their space so entirely, and were so independent of any center, that they rivaled the main panels themselves, effecting the liberation of ornament from the domination of the center. Never before had *grottesche* been applied to such a large or important surface area; never before had ornament stood so independently.

To an artist like Giovanni, vague instructions are life itself, as his lively assimilation of the pagan style attests. In so far as we can tell, the Domus Aurea designs were not distinguished for their detail or their delicacy of execution, but the pilasters of the Loggias are remarkable for both. Unfortunately, they too have deteriorated badly, so, as with the Domus Aurea designs, we can recapture the fullness of their detail only through engravings made in later centuries.[24] These redesignings by Giovanni Volpato, Marcello Ferrari and others enable us to see the exacting attention paid to the figures, each one articulated with a precision that anticipates the detailed botanical and scientific drawing techniques of the following century (See Figure 6). In them the eye is continually soothed by the balance and proportion of the figures, and continually reassured that nothing means or coheres, nothing signifies. All is lively and symmetrical, with figures alternating in subtle rhythms from architectural to human to animal to foliate forms. For all the animation and activity on the pilasters, there is almost no narrative interest at all: the figures give the impression that their postures and attitudes express nothing, but merely fill the available space, the space left by the other figures. Vasari, who decorated the ceiling of the main hallway of the Uffizi with *grottesche,* exclaimed of Giovanni's work, "And what should I say of the various kinds of fruits and flowers without number that are there, in all the forms, varieties, and colours that Nature contrives to produce in all parts of the world and in all seasons of the year? What, likewise, of the various musical instruments that are there, all as real as reality?"[25]

One thing we can say is that Giovanni has married a purely non-representational, stylized, and fantastic mode with a technique of the most scrupulously illusionistic accuracy and fidelity to naturalistic detail. It is significant that the discovery and development of *grottesche* occurred just as artists were acquiring the techniques necessary to produce a nearly perfect form of visual realism. The Greek division of art into *fantasia* and *mimesis* was ingeniously overturned by the new ornamental style, which provided artists with a scene for the exhibition of pure technique, an occasion for the display of taste, in which the methods of representation and the principles of design could be judged on their own terms, liberated from their secondary status as implements of imitation. This liberation was unpalatable to Ruskin, who digressed from his discussion of the "Grotesque Renaissance" in Venice to attack Raphael's work as "an elaborate and luscious form of nonsense...a poisonous root; an artistical pottage, composed of nymphs, cupids, and satyrs, with shreddings of heads and paws of meek wild beasts, and nondescript vegetables." It is, Ruskin marvels, "almost impossible to believe the depth to which the human mind can be debased in following this species of grotesque."[26] What particularly appalled Ruskin was the misuse of superb technique, the abuse of skills acquired with much labor. Giovanni's patterns represent a vivid example of what happens when "great minds" are "degraded to base objects":

> The care, skill, and science, applied to the distribution of the leaves, and the drawing of the figures, are intense, admirable, and accurate; therefore, they ought to have produced a grand and serious work, not a tissue of nonsense. If we can draw the human head perfectly, and are masters of its expression and its beauty, we have no business to cut it off, and hang it up by the hair at the end of a garland. If we can draw the human body in the perfection of its grace and movement, we have no business to take away its limbs, and terminate it with a bunch of leaves.[27]

It is waste that Ruskin condemns, and triviality. The capacity, matched with the unwillingness, to inspire "Divine terror" or to teach "noble lessons" seems to him a violation of the right order of things, and Raphael's grotesque is therefore "an unnatural and monstrous abortion."[28]

But the artists of the Renaissance did not see it this way. They recognized a division of labor between the main panels and the ornament: the panels may draw their programs from the Bible, may teach, guide, and inspire; but in the contemplation of these designs, Vasari implies, the soul or intellect is intended to play no part. Giovanni's work is scarcely to be contemplated at all, but merely observed. It is pointless to try to extract any lessons from *grottesche,* or even to describe it, for its formal arrangement of elements repels translation into syntax, much less into paragraphs. Here on the borders, it was assumed, is a place for the eye alone, where it can wander at will, luxuriating in the delights of unencumbered design.

This is a tempting position, but we should not be too quick to dismiss Ruskin, who is worth listening to even in his most narrow-minded and intemperate moments. Ruskin was no foe of ornament itself — he praised Ghiberti's leaf-borders lavishly — but he did have strict notions about its proper function. What offended him in the Loggia designs was the trivialization of the eloquent human form, the corruption of meaning. He is responding to the semiotic ambivalence of *grottesche,* not its perfect emptiness of significance. In this he may be closer than Vasari to the sympathies of the Rohrschach age, which has been taught by Mondrian, Escher, and others that even perpendicular lines and geometrical swirls can spur the search for meaning, can activate interpretation. The ambivalent presence of meaning within the ostensibly meaningless form constitutes the real threat, and the real revolution, of *grottesche.* This effect, however, was not immediately apparent to those who saw in the new style simply a more sophisticated form of ornament.

By ornament we generally signify art with a decorative rather than a significative function; we mean art that does not represent existing or possible objects, and so does not generate the kind of meaning that is made by connecting art to reality, representations to things represented. In Montaigne's terms, ornament does not occupy the "best spot," but rather fills up "empty space"— a border, a frontispiece, a table leg, the surface of a musical instrument, a pilaster. Our ways of defining ornament do not so much characterize the art itself as they reflect an attitude toward it, or to the space it occupies.

Ornament is universal and its motivating impulses primitive and profound, but Western attitudes toward it have been greatly affected by the Christian attitude toward images. Specifically, our views have been significantly shaped by the history of the interpretation of Exodus 20:4, which explicitly forbade the making of "any carved image, or any likeness or anything that is in heaven above, or that is in the earth beneath, or that is in the water under the earth." Pope Gregory beveled the edges of this uncompromising dictum by granting in a famous pronouncement that images could serve the same didactic function for those who could not read as words for those who could. This concession had the effect of establishing a distinction between godly or "readable" images, and non-signifying or "unreadable" ornament. By this means two systems of art were codified: the art of the center that had a subject and signified in an intelligible and coherent way with recognizable images arranged according to traditional and conventional schemata, and an art of the fringe that, at least in terms of the center, had no subject, yielded no meaning, and represented things that were not, nor could be, nor had ever been.[29]

The art of the fringe could achieve this meaning-vacuum by one of two means: either through the unprecedented strangeness of its forms or through its utterly conventional nature. Both means allow the images to escape our categories (and thus official censure). With regard to the latter method, Henri Focillon observed in his *Vie des Formes* that "It lies in the essence of ornament that it can be reduced to the purest forms of intelligibility, and that geometrical reasoning can be applied without hindrance to an analysis of its constituent relationships...."[30] Even in those border designs not purely geometrical, no attempt is made at significance, but rather at a triviality that persuades us easily by its simplicity and familiarity that we are not being challenged in any way. As Kenneth Clark says in *The Nude,*

> Decoration exists to please the eye; its images should not seriously engage the mind or strike deep into the imagination, but should be accepted without question, like an ancient code of behavior. In consequence, it must make free use of clichés, of figures that, whatever their origins, have already been reduced to a satisfactory hieroglyphic.[31]

We will turn in the next chapter to the problem implied in Clark's phrase "whatever their origins." We must now consider the class of ornament into which the grotesque falls — the "rough," or strange.

When an absence of meaning is created by unprecedented strangeness, so that we know that our experience has not adequately prepared us to interpret or read the design, the ornament not only soothes, but stimulates as well. It awakens our senses, rousing them into readiness so the central figure of the painting, or the text, can perform its task of edification. In an important work *On the Picturesque* (1794) Uvedale Price commented that

> Almost all ornaments are rough, and most of them sharp, which is a mode of roughness.... But as the ornaments are rough, so the ground is generally smooth; which shows, that though smoothness be the most essential quality of beauty, without which it can scarcely exist-yet that roughness...is the ornament, the fringe of beauty, that which gives it life and spirit, and preserves it from baldness and insipidity.[32]

In many instances this "roughness" is achieved by strikingly direct methods. Michelangelo speaks for an ancient tradition when he defines the pragmatic function of a certain kind of rough ornament:

> One may rightly decorate better when one places in painting some monstrosity (for the diversion and relaxation of the sense and the attention of mortal eyes, which at times desire to see what they have never seen before or what appears to them just cannot be) rather than the customary figures of men or animals, however admirable these may be.[33]

Michelangelo's description applies to the kind of decorative art that had flourished for centuries in the margins, the neglected or unstressed areas of Christian architecture and manuscripts. Gargoyles, marginal "drolleries," and misericords carved on the perches beneath the seats in choir stalls have a common function of providing a charming place for mortal eyes and other parts to relax while one appears to be paying attention. Fanciful or monstrous beasts had virtually always been a feature of ornamental art, so that the late Middle Ages could look back on a long tradition of such ornament, even in a Christian context.[34]

By itself, however, tradition could not always reconcile text with context, or text with ornament. Such tensions inspired a denunciation that rivals Vitruvius' in urgency and historical importance, a letter from Bernard of Clairvaux condemning the more vigorous forms of early twelfth-century decoration:

> But in the cloister, in the sight of the reading monks, what is the point of such ridiculous monstrosity, the strange kind of shapely shapelessness? Why these unsightly monkeys, why these fierce lions, why the monstrous centaurs, why semi-humans, why spotted tigers, why fighting soldiers, why trumpeting huntsmen? You can see many bodies under one head, and then again one body with many heads, here you see a quadruped with a serpent's tail, here a fish with the head of a quadruped. Here is a beast which is a horse in front but drags half a goat behind, here a horned animal has the hindquarters of a horse. In short there is such a variety and such a diversity of strange shapes everywhere that we may prefer to read the marbles rather than the books.[35]

Bernard's complaint did not go unheeded; in fact, it was frequently repeated. An early thirteenth-century tract, *Pictor in Carmine,* inveighed against the "criminal presumption of painters" who decorated with "sports of fancy, which the church ought not to have countenanced so long."[36] But by this time the situation was clearly beyond control, for painters had discovered a marvelous new mode, the human-animal hybrid. Animal-vegetable forms had appeared in the late twelfth century, derived primarily from the Bestiaries. But, as Margaret Rickert points out, "the animal-human grotesque is a different creature. Its basic idea is the application to animals (sometimes rendered naturalistically, sometimes as monsters) of the attributes of human beings, usually with the intention of caricaturing or even satirizing human types or their occupations."[37]

This form of drollery appeared in the thirteenth century (Bernard had died in 1152), suddenly opening up spectacular new, and problematic, possibilities for marginal art. Taste was routinely threatened by the violations of decorum, probability, and logical categories presented by human-animal hybrids, and the triumphs and shortcomings of this form reflect the poles of exhilaration and disgust implicit in the concept of "bad taste."

As we have seen, ornament was intended to augment piety, not to undermine it. But especially with the advent of human-animal forms, ornament was beginning to present a potential rival to the central message, a competing text. With elaborately worked initials, with figures twisting in and out of the lines of the text, and other ingenious methods, artists made an aggressive claim for the reader's attention. One figure in the Rutland Psalter, for example, shows a kind of merman lying on his back, holding up a single finned foot, exposing his anus to the penetration of an arrow, the terminus of the descending stroke of the letter p.[38] This style, Rickert points out, achieved "a height of vulgarity and ridiculousness in the East Anglian style,"[39] the foremost example of which is the Luttrell Psalter, in which the marginal monstrosities achieve an extraordinary conspicuousness. In Figure 7, from this work, vegetal forms utterly without interpretable significance are merged with or attached as tails to human or animal forms. But what kind of animal is that on the top? Not even all the parts can be named, much less the wholes. In another depiction from this work (not shown), a fantastical bird has a human face where its breast should be. The problem of the relation between center and border is raised in miniature by this figure: which is within which? Which is the dominant principle and which the subordinate element? In yet another image from the Luttrell Psalter, we see a figure — or perhaps two figures — with a single ludicrous head and a body — or two bodies? — that splits off from either side. The body is scaled, like a snake, but has a shell like a tortoise, and webbed feet like a duck. We cannot even call the tail a tail, for it crosses out of the animal realm and into the floral Most puzzling is perhaps the odd beauty of the monsters that populate this work, the elaborate attention to form and coloration they betray, an attention that does not seem to sort well with the absurdity of the whole design. The impression is often so incongruous as to provoke versions of Bernard's criticism even in our time: Rickert complains that "too often even a reasonably good initial and border...are spoiled by a repulsive grotesque";[40] and a modern editor of the text calls the designs "a serious disfigurement," adding that "The mind of a man who could deliberately set himself to ornament a book with such subjects...can hardly have been normal."[41]

To impious modern tastes, this commentator seems to have missed the point. To many of us, psalms are psalms, readily available for those who want them, and the only interest this manuscript has derives from the prodigious hyperbole of its ornament. What he has caught, however, is the threat these drolleries represent to the center by inviting the eye, and perhaps even the "reluctant" soul, to "wander."[42] Augustine said that all sensory sins were essentially "sins of the eye," and these designs almost taunt the earnest believer through their invitation to distraction, to nonsensical play.

Lilian M. C. Randall's massive inventory of *Images in the Margins of Gothic Manuscripts*[43] is a great treasure-trove of such art, collecting not only the truly great monuments of English, French, and Netherlandish border ornament, but also hundreds of lesser examples. These include a torrent of parodies, caricatures, obscenities, scenes of daily life, jokes, sporting events, and a wealth of what can only be called sheer play with form. In an appreciative review of this book written in 1970, Meyer Schapiro gave an eloquent and generous description of the whole assemblage:

> They are a convincing evidence of the artist's liberty, his unconstrained possession of the space, which confounds the view of mediaeval art as a model of systematic order and piety. There is also in these images a sweetness and charm which seem to arise from the truly miniature scale.... The humans here play, fight with, and dwell among tiny creatures whose minuscule size they assume without loss of their own essential humanity.... This art is a boundless reservoir of humor, spirited play, and untamed vitality. The ape is everywhere, inviting the viewer to recognize the animal core of human behavior in the easy translation of all the higher forms of social life — learning, religion, law — into simian games.... No other art in history offers so abundant an imagery of the naked and clothed body as a physical engine. Free from classic norms, the artist experiments with the human frame as the most flexible, ductile, indefatigably protean, self-deforming system in nature.[44]

What are we to make of such an art; what can it mean? Despite "the unprogrammatic effect of its design," Lilian Randall believes that "the possibility of an unrecognized underlying scheme still exists."[45] Schapiro thinks this a likely guess, but suggests that it would "help the search for meanings if one recognized that we are not limited to the alternatives: symbolic or decorative. There are other kinds of meaning (as in metaphor, parody, and humor) which need not be symbolic in the coded manner of mediaeval religious symbolism" even when there appears to be an obvious connection between the text and its "illustration." The connection may be made by allusion to something outside the text that bears on the text's message. This may be the case, for example, with the bowman who shoots the arrow into the merman in the Rutland Psalter,[46] or in the apes Schapiro appreciates, both of which draw on motifs established elsewhere.[47] Or the connection may be made by analogy, whose meaning cannot necessarily be puzzled out by examining the religious commentaries. As Schapiro says, such possible analogies "call for another and essentially poetic approach."[48]

The problem with much border ornament is not that it has no point, but that it makes many conflicting points, performing a number of tasks at the same time. Gargoyles and chimeras, which fall into the same class as drolleries, are intended to ward off demons, on the assumption that demons, being only human, will be frightened by the same things that frighten us. But they also represent the demonic forces themselves, contrasting with the divine order of the cathedral. They serve as "rough" ornaments, exciting and defeating interpretive attention, almost cohering into intelligible patterns, so that, roused, our ruffled sensibilities move on to images that are more ennobling; these include the sculpted saints and kings standing in more stately postures, and the architectural order which, by itself, would be too vast to comprehend.

Gargoyles scale the cathedral down to human size; they may even be felt to represent the human element itself. They demonstrate that incoherence and disorder, too, have been attended to, and that motley has a place in the grand scheme. Ruskin based his description of the emotional ambivalence of the grotesque on such forms:

> …it seems to me that the grotesque is, in almost all cases, composed of two elements, one ludicrous, the other fearful;

that, as one or the other of these elements prevails, the grotesque falls into two branches, sportive grotesque, and terrible grotesque; but that we cannot legitimately consider it under these two aspects, because there are hardly any examples which do not in some degree combine both elements; there are few grotesques so utterly playful as to be overcast with no shade of fearfulness, and few so fearful as absolutely to exclude all ideas of jest.[49]

The doubleness of the gargoyles puts us in mind of the doubleness of the cathedral, which, although it honors God, was built by mortals.
It is possible through such an analysis to discover a metaphorical relationship between the ornament and the edifice it decorates. It may appear that the interpreter courts blasphemy in seeking affinities between stone monsters and the Word, or between marginal drolleries and the text, but this is not necessarily so. Gerard Manley Hopkins was far from blasphemy when he meditated on "Pied Beauty":

All things counter, original, spare, strange;
    Whatever is fickle, freckled (who knows how?)
    With swift, slow; sweet, sour; adazzle, dim;
He fathers-forth whose beauty is past change:
Praise him.

If we cannot say precisely how this "fathering-forth" is accomplished, we can at least recognize that the basis for a "poetic" reading has been intuitively established. The efforts of scholars to discover the "unrecognized underlying scheme" indicates a long-standing hunch that the ornament, especially the grotesque ornament with human elements, can be interpreted, that it can contribute to or even encroach upon the center. If this is true, and the margin and center are equally and mutually readable, and equally mysterious, then the text may become the ornament for the illuminations, the cathedral for the gargoyles. When this possibility arises, all images split, assuming incongruous double functions; and everything is thrown into doubt. These pre-*grottesche* designs are today called grotesque not only because of certain formal characteristics, but also because they throw the reader/viewer into that intertextual interval described in Chapter One. Looking for unity between center and margin, the interpreter must, whether he finds it or not, pass through the grotesque.

From a technical point of view, *grottesche* represented a great advance. It served all the traditional functions of ornament while submitting gracefully, in a way that drollery sometimes did not, to the demands of symmetry and the limitations of available space. More flexible and frequently less conspicuous than drollery, *grottesche* was incomparably suave, elegant, and subtle. We can measure the contribution of *grottesche* by looking at Figure 8, an initial from the very end of the fifteenth century, just before the new Italian form was to be made available, and Figure 9, from a book of initials executed in the early seventeenth century by Lucas Kilian, a Netherlandish master of *grottesche*. In the Kilian engravings a certain rude force is lost, but a wild elastic fancy has replaced it, a playfulness not at all primitive. Kilian's forms are not simply crushed into each other, but are melted, worked like molten glass, and stretched, so that, for example, the curl through the middle of the central stroke of the W appears to be a tongue, although it is identical to many other such curls that seem not to represent anything. Even in this baroque example there is a memory of lightness, grace, a conscious design to be lovely—and a sly play with the process of representation; the artist knowingly teases us with forms that are both/and, neither/nor, forms that we, despite ourselves, cannot help recognizing as human.

One salutary effect of *grottesche* is to provide an alternative center that does not threaten the viewer with damnation for "reading" it. Its play is purer; that is, it plays not only with things but also with the act of representation. It invites a search for meaning at the same time that it calls attention to the act of artistic creation. It suspends belief, and therefore takes reading out of the shadow of dogma. As Schapiro points out, Christian hermeneutics, no matter how dependent upon analogy, is a closed or bound system, with a determined teleology according to which "the universe — nature and history — is saturated with Christian finality, everything points beyond itself to a formal system evident in the analogical structure of things, due to a divine intention working itself out in time." The play of analogy in Christian thought, "while seeming poetic and unconstrained, has a systematic, constructive character"[50] that makes a Christian interpretation of *grottesche*

simply impossible: the material resists it. Moreover, the new style was known to be an old style, already a meaningless cliché in Nero's time. From the point of view of *grottesche,* ornament is appreciated for its representational feats, but the central figure, as if relieved of a portion of the responsibility for signification, can be more fully appreciated for its aesthetic qualities. *Grottesche* issues not a temptation but an invitation to appreciate craft, to consider alternative possibilities. It has, therefore, a distinctive place in the development of the humanistic culture of the Renaissance.

Two examples will demonstrate the effect of *grottesche* on the reading of a composition. The first (not shown) is a detail from the vault of the church at Santa Maria del Popolo by Pinturicchio that shows the Sibyl, reclining, surrounded, in their separate spaces, by *grottesche.* The surrounding design has achieved such weight and integrity that it can fairly be considered a separate creation from the central figure, which is not merely a painting within a border but a painting within a number of other paintings; the ornament is mixed up with "business." The mysteries surrounding the cult of the Sibyl encourage the suspicion that there may be in the margin some clue to the center — or even that the center may provide some clue to the margin. Some thirteen strata of geometrical patterns separate the spatial center from the *grottesche,* an arrangement that actually reinforces the margin's claim to centrality, for it, too, is framed by meaningless ornament. Four human-like faces mixed in with the *grottesche* impart a psychological aspect to the margin: their aggressive expression is, we assume by irresistible force of habit, motivated by something they have witnessed. We look for the source of their outrage—perhaps Ruskin or Bernard could tell us, but whatever hypotheses we form will already constitute a narrative, a plot; and the entirety is now a fiction within a fiction.

The second (Figure 10), from the Chapel of the Madonna of St. Britius in the cathedral at Orvieto, by Luca Signorelli, represents the philosopher Empedocles gazing at one of the walls of the chapel portraying scenes of his prophecies of the end of the world. But this description is center-oriented and overlooks Signorelli's elaborate play. Empedocles is looking across an empty space to a scene above him to the left, but the initial impression is that he is simply looking in frank wonderment at the prodigies that encompass him, the creations of his creator. Liberated from marginality, this boiling mass of dream-creatures acquires an indefinable but powerful, even apocalyptic, sense of significance — which is at the same time undercut by the "masking" effects of perfect bilateral symmetry. They engage our attention with their promise of profundity, their formal affinity with representations of ancient sacred mysteries. No system of decorum could accommodate such a usurpation of the center, but decorum is far from Empedocles' mind as he marvels — not without some apprehension, as we see from his upraised hand — at the unchained fancies of the imagination. And another discovery: the "centrist" reading in which he casts his view past the margin to the center, and the "marginalist" reading I have just given, are the same: the object of his vision is in both instances "the unchained fancies of the imagination." Through the simple act of looking at his ornament, Empedocles transfigures it, emancipating the grotesque and becoming his borders' border.

We can learn a good deal about the paradoxes of framing by studying this fresco. The entire composition lies outside the border of another, larger composition, and so frames it, as part of a complex border. But Empedocles' portion of the wall is bordered by a painting of a wooden frame which runs not only along the outside but also through the middle, cutting it into four pieces with a medallion in the middle. This medallion is also a porthole, a place to look both into and out from. We cannot overlook the four rectangles above and below this medallion (which appear to be two, divided by the frame running up the center), nor even those which frame the painter's initials in the upper corners. To say that something is "within" a frame is to imply that other things are unframed. This is logically impossible, however, since the frame frames both the inside and the outside, simple terms that suddenly become problematic. In Signorelli's design nothing is outside a frame; everything is a center from some point of view. And it is *grottesche* that fosters this realization.

What a paltry thing meaning is, that it can be created *ex nihilo* by a brush stroke, and then wiped out, or masked by another, similar brush stroke elsewhere. *Grottesche* foregrounds the mysteries of the processes of making and un-making meaning, for it represents the scene of transformation to and from the realm of the meaningful. Strikingly, the capacity to be both marginal and central also identifies the theme of Signorelli's frescoes. The vacuum of absolute meaninglessness created by the grotesqueries fathers forth the full presence that mankind enjoyed at the beginning and that will be regained at the end. At that time, it is prophesied, the two shall be one, the lion shall lie down with the lamb, the inside shall be the outside, and all binary distinctions shall be abolished. There could be no more apt image for the two-as-one than the matched panels on either side of Empedocles, nor for the abolition of distinctions than the metamorphic hybrids that surround him.

The study of ornamental art received a great stimulus in 1979 when E. H. Gombrich published *The Sense of Order*.[51] A companion volume to his earlier study of the process of representation, *Art and Illusion*, this book focuses on the art of the margin, on designs rather than signs. Gombrich argues that while figural art stimulates and gratifies our sense of meaning, ornamental art gratifies a more primitive demand for a sense of order. Analogies in biology and the logic of scientific discovery underlie this distinction. Even the simplest organisms appear to have innate "hypotheses" which they are continually testing against the world; Gombrich identifies such assumptions with the sense of order, and the testing process with the perception of meaning, or interpretation. In this way, ornamental art provides a frame by reassuring the viewer that what is bordered by it corresponds to our assumptions of orderliness and can be rationally tested. Decorative art, falling between the poles of absolute lucidity and absolute meaninglessness, has no ulterior motive and imparts no information. Most ornamental art tends toward the abstract and geometrical, exhibiting rhythmical or regular features that easily lock in with our tentative projections of order, thereby sinking below the threshold of attention, providing a background of reassurance.

When Gombrich's book is attacked, as it has been with unusual zeal, it is usually on the grounds that no design can be pure, that the perception of form cannot exist prior to the attribution of meaning. And, at many points of his discussion, Gombrich does seem almost sentimentally attached to the traditional Renaissance dichotomy. But if we look on the margins or in the interstices of his discourse, we can see that he is also sensitive to cases in which this dualism is compromised. Considering the frame of one Renaissance painting, he acknowledges "the effortless transition from representation to decoration" (161), commenting on the "oscillating interplay between representation, fiction and pure form" (162). Gombrich understands that the search for meaning can never be switched off entirely, but he is reluctant to discuss instances where the two impulses are simultaneously activated, where they do not complement each other, but seem to struggle for primacy.

The grotesque is such an instance, arousing without gratifying both the sense of order and the search for meaning, and collapsing the dualism on which the entire book is based. Gombrich's impatience with the uncertainties of grotesque art leads him into interesting contradictions, as in the following passage, in which he comments on Vitruvius' denunciation:

> ...the reaction of exasperated helplessness provoked by hybrid creatures, part plant, part human; part woman, part fish; part horse, part goat. There are no names in our language, no categories in our thought, to come to grips with this elusive dream-imagery in which "all things are mixed."... It outrages both our "sense of order" and our search for meaning.... "What is the point?" The point is that there is no point.... Not only do the limbs of these composite creatures defy our classifications, often we cannot even tell where they begin or end — they are not individuals.... Thus there is nothing to hold on to, nothing fixed, the *deformitas* is hard to "code" and harder still to remember, for everything is in flux. (256)

The voice of "exasperated helplessness" speaks clearly, too, in his descriptions of *grottesche* and its ancestors:

> In the prints by Cornelis Bos the monster is linked with the enigmatic, the mysterious, through allusions to Egyptian or Oriental divinities, all caught up in the strapwork which has replaced the scroll, making it hard to disentangle the decorative from the organic. Real legs protrude through the eyeholes of a mask. Acrobatic satyrs have clambered through the openings in the festooned strapwork. But what of the woman with the Egyptian headdress? How did she ever get into the fantastic structure which emphasizes her nakedness? We are not supposed to ask. (281. See Figure 13)

For one who has so eloquently reminded us of the futility of "trying to forget," Gombrich shows a surprising willingness to raise points and then tell us there is no point, to ask questions and then warn us not to ask.

In such warnings Gombrich joins Vitruvius, Bernard, the author of *Pictor in Carmine,* and the many critics of drollery, giving dramatic evidence of the seriousness of the challenge raised by the grotesque to our customary ways of thinking about the world, and particularly to our ways of describing it. Through Gombrich's descriptions we may see a lot more than we had, but we understand less — or, at least, our confusion is increased. The figures he describes require a detailed examination, but all the details are in revolt, provoking a writerly exasperation.

All grotesque art threatens the notion of a center by implying coherencies just out of reach, metaphors or analogies just beyond our grasp. The possibility that, if we strain hard enough, we can understand what the woman with the Egyptian headdress is doing in that fantastic assemblage does not merely stimulate us so that we can move on to other business, but, in its purposeful rearrangement of familiar elements, teases us with intimations of "deep" or "profound" meanings. Grotesqueries confront us as a corrupt or fragmented text in search of a master principle, which Ernst Kris likened to a "strong ego" to unify the parts. They hold our attention, especially if we are patient, imaginative, inquisitive, and impious. But although they are frustrating they are far from pointless, for with their help we can arrive at a better understanding of the methods of representation, of the relation between play and creation, and of the force of habit and convention in understanding. Looking at ourselves looking at the grotesque, we can observe our own projections, catching ourselves, as it were, in the act of perception.

Grottesche was contagious. For decades after the initial discoveries, the appearance of such ornament in a given place was often the first sign that the Renaissance had arrived. Florence and Rome exported a number of artists skilled at the new style to decorate the great houses and palaces of Europe (El Escorial, Fontainebleau, the Doge's Palace), and the style gradually merged with local ornamental traditions. For three centuries it was conventional, dispersing into the "minor arts," such as ceramics,[52] tapestries, endpapers, inlays for musical instruments, and domestic upholstery before finally settling back into the dust, becoming art history a second time.[53]

Grotesque and Grottesche

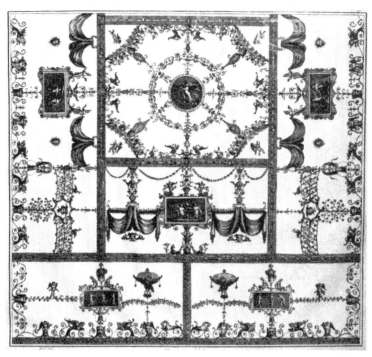

3. Nicolas Ponce, engraving from Domus Aurea designs, in *Descriptions des bains de Titus*, 1786.

4. Nicolas Ponce, engraving from Domus Aurea designs, in *Descriptions des bains de Titus*, 1786.

Figure 5. Vatican Loggia, decorated by Raphael and Giovanni da Udine.

6. Marcello Ferraro, detail engraving of pilaster in Vatican Loggia in *Les ornaments de Raphael*, 1860.

7. From *The Luttrell Psalter*.

Grotesque and Grottesche

8. Initial from Incunabula, Paris-Lyons, 1485-1489.

9. Initials by Lucas Kilian, from *Newes ABC Büchlein*, 1627.

10. Luca Signorelli, detail from the chapel of the Madonna of St. Britius, Orvieto Cathedral.

11. Agostino Veneziano, ornamental engraving, before 1520.

12. Marco Dente, ornamental engraving, 1525.

13. Cornelius Bos, ornamental engraving, 1546.

14. Peter Flötner, ornamental metal etching, 1546.

15. Lucas van Leyden, ornamental engraving, 1546.

16. Cornelius Floris, ornamental engraving, 1556.

17. Christopher Jamnitzer, ornamental engraving, 1610.

18. Nicasius Rouseel, ornamental engraving, 1623.

19. Jean-Marie Delattre, ornamental engraving, last quarter of eighteenth century.

Grotesque and Grottesche

20. Raphael, *The Transfiguration*, Vatican Museum.

The spread of *grottesche* coincided with, and was largely indebted to, the rise of printing and the medium of engraving.[54] Beginning in the late fifteenth century, books of ornamental prints were produced and distributed throughout Europe, advertising and developing the new style, offering a vocabulary of ornament for workers in all materials: in the words of one of these books, "*cette oeuvre...pourra servir aux orfèvres, peintres, tailleurs de pierres, menuisiers et autres artisans, pour esueiller leurs esprits, et appliquer chacun en son art, ce qu'il y trouvera propre....*"[55] These books of "*Grötisch für alle Kunstler*"[56] not only insured the perpetuation of the style *all' antica:* they opened it up to innovation, and to local variants. Thus we can trace in them the initial popularity of the Loggia designs (in the *Petits Grotesques* of Jacques Androuet Ducerceau, 1550)[57] and then, gradually, the incorporation of scrollwork, moresque ornament, terms (a human torso on a base; after Terminus, the god of boundaries), architectural elements, and a wealth of other features.

The history of these books would make a large book all by itself, a book which will one day be written.[58] Such a book would note in particular how *grottesche* was modified by each medium that borrowed it, and by each country in which it took root. The strongest roots were sunk in Germany and in the Netherlands, under the influence of such ornamental geniuses as Lucas van Leyden, Cornelius Floris, Lucas Kilian, Cornelius Bos, and Cristoph Jamnitzer.[59] Except for Jamnitzer's *Neuw Grottesken Buch* (Nürnberg, 1610), which was recently published in Germany,[60] these works have not been reprinted, but many individual prints were collected in the nineteenth century by A.P.F. Robert-Dumesnil and Goidefroid Ume,[61] and in the 1920s by Peter Jessen and by Rudolf Berliner, whose *Ornamentale Vorlageblätter des 15. bis 18. Jahrhunderts*[62] is an invaluable and astonishing collection of hundreds of designs, almost all of which derive from *grottesche*. These range from the elegant whimsy of Agostino Veneziano to the grossness or sheer lunacy of the German or Netherlandish designers, and from the faithful reproduction of the antique style to the transfiguration of that style into baroque at the end of the seventeenth century by Jean Bérain.[63] I have tried to give some impression of the scope of invention of these artists in Figures 11-19, but no sample is adequate. Taken all together, the print-books testify to the incredible fertility of Fabullus' designs, which, through the medium of Raphael, Giovanni, and other Renaissance artists, were still inspiring and attractive in the late eighteenth century, when Robert Adam went to Rome and copied the designs on the Loggias, returning to England to produce his own book of designs; which in turn inspired Michelangelo Pergolesi, who produced his own book.[64] After three — actually, after seventeen-centuries, *grottesche* still represented the latest advances in taste.

3. *Transfigurations*

Grottesche is gone; and we are left with grotesque. In every instance of the latter, the issues of the former are raised. In the welter of grotesque forms, these issues are the only constant, the only clear signal. The essence of *grottesche,* as I have said repeatedly, is that there can be no clear signals. Far from being confined to a particular time, place, and aesthetic mode, this message, in endlessly diluting forms, can be found anywhere, so that the grotesque, once a property of a handful of artifacts, is now almost unlimited in its possible applications.

As an example of how the issues of *grottesche* can be detected in unlikely places, I want to return to Raphael, for whom the Loggias were a partial solution to a problem he had been struggling for years to formulate. We can see this problem from one angle by looking at the Stanza della Segnatura, completed at the Vatican in 1511. This massive work consists of a series of frescoes (with *grottesche* between panels and medallions) depicting the "School of Athens," Adam and Eve, the judgment of Solomon, and Apollo and Marsyas. Nicole Dacos has linked this scheme to that of the Loggias, where Christian elements mingle with pagan ornament;[65] others have contended that the design expresses a synthetic vision in which knowledge and virtue are seen as aspects of the divine.[66] Regardless of which view we take, synthesis itself, the reconciling of apparently incompatible elements, is the key principle. Even more indicative of the difficulties and potentialities of synthesis is the altarpiece of *The Transfiguration* (Figure 20), now in the Vatican Museum. The theme of the transfiguration of Christ occupies the top half of the composition; the lower half illustrates the Biblical text that follows it (Mark 9; Matthew 17), the story of the healing of the possessed youth. The two incidents have no obvious narrative connection; they stand in both gospels mysteriously contiguous, almost as if a transition had been left out. Raphael saw something — perhaps how the boy could be said to be "transfigured" or Christ "healed" — as the creative mind will always "see something" in two things juxtaposed. Still, it is a strained composition and an odd theme. We might wonder why he did not do a more orthodox Transfiguration, without the possessed youth; or an Assumption of the Virgin: Titian's masterpiece in the Church of the Frari in Venice is similar to Raphael's painting in many ways but is comfortingly (even annoyingly) conventional. The originality of Raphael's conception lies in the coupling of antagonistic elements into an unexpected unity, and the challenge must have attracted him.

Some of the execution (most notably the figure of the youth) was performed by assistants.[67] But no competent apprentice could have conceived such a design, for it is exactly the kind of thing apprentices are taught to avoid. Not only is the relation between top and bottom unclear, but the styles necessarily used to depict the two scenes almost repel each other. Below, the contrasts are sharp, the figures strained, excited; above a mediating region of darkness, Christ is transfigured in the old iconographic mode in an even light, a disciplined geometry of conventional form and a purity of abstraction that counterpoints, and contradicts, the lower half. It is an artistic *coincidentia oppositorum,* with implications of the unity of creation, and creative acts divine and human, God's and the artist's; of the transfiguration of dust by spirit, humanity by Christ's sacrifice-one hesitates to be more specific, for the idea strains the capacities of pigment to signify.

The test is whether Raphael's matchless facility could hold in suspension radical dissimilarities, whether technique and conviction could discover some principle, some metaphor, that would fuse them into a unity. In *The Transfiguration* opposites are brought near but not actually merged. The dividing line is the blackness in the middle, which has no distinctive features, but a number of analogues. It is a spatial equivalent of "paradigm confusion"; or of the "conceptual leap" of metaphor, in which unlike elements are yoked by violence together; or of the "river" of death we cross at the margin of time and eternity. Or, finally, of the mental crisis, the interval of the grotesque, that we must suffer through on the way to the discovery of a radical new insight.

Some, less radical than Raphael, have been unwilling to follow the direction of the strong, urgent hands pointing into the blackness.

"What Raphael has conceived in the *Transfiguration,*" J. E. Freedburg writes, "no longer works as a genuinely synthetic image but as one in which disparates have been forced to coexist...."[68] The kind of schismatic unity that makes sense in a representation of The Last Judgment, with the Lord and heavenly host presiding over the chaos of a world in agonies of dissolution does not, Freedburg implies, make sense here, for the key to the code exists not in Scripture, nor in convention, but only in Raphael's mind. Raphael may have been thinking of sublimity but he has not communicated it, at least to this critic, who, aware of the possibility of a grotesque (with the unifying principle sensed but occluded and imperfectly perceived), has saved the artist from a scandal and decided that it makes no sense at all. Such an analysis treats the blackness as though it were empty of meaning. It seems more likely, however, that it is intended to be spiritually and intellectually as well as spatially the center, the region of the highest meaning.

The act of comparing a bit of ornamental whimsy to one of the world's greatest paintings is itself instructive: only the concept of the grotesque could bring them together. And together, they teach us that the grotesque is embodied in an act of transition, of metonymy becoming metaphor, of the margin swapping places with the center. It is embodied in a transformation of duality into unity, of the meaningless into the meaningful. And all these discoveries were available right at the start: they were the very first things revealed about the grotesque, and they remain its primary features.

CHAPTER THREE

Grotesque and Grotto-esque

The art that is frankly decorative is the art to live with. It is, of all visible arts, the one art that creates in us both mood and temperament.... In the mere loveliness of the materials employed there are latent elements of culture.... By its deliberate rejection of Nature as the ideal of beauty, as well as of the imitative method of the ordinary painter, decorative art ... develops in the soul that sense of form which is the basis of creative no less than of critical achievement.
—Oscar Wilde, *The Artist as Critic*

The less civilized a people is, the more prodigal it will be with ornament and decoration. The Red Indian covers every object, every boat, every oar, every arrow over and over with ornament. To regard decoration as an advantage is tantamount to remaining on the level of a Red Indian.... The urge to ornament ... is the babbling of painting.
—Adolph Loos

1. *Ornament and Atavism*

Does mankind aspire to ornament as a mark of advanced culture, or does it struggle out of it, retaining it only as a vestige? Is decorative art a sign of "aestheticism"; or is it a primitive impulse common to degenerates — and "Red Indians"? These questions, arising at the turn of the century in the midst of an energetic debate about decorative art, fortunately no longer seem to demand an unequivocal answer; we can entertain both possibilities. Actually, this option was possible as early as 1908, when Wilhelm Worringer, writing on decorative art in *Abstraction and Empathy,* said that the nostalgic identification with natural forces was generally a late product of civilization, a sign of cultural confidence that nature had been subdued and could now serve as a balm to the spirit weary of artifice. If we follow Worringer's argument, we can see how ornament can be both the supreme artifice and an invocation of the "natural." Sometimes, in fact, these qualities can inhere in a single artifact: Gombrich and others routinely discuss even highly sophisticated decorative art in terms of "apotropaic magic," "animation," regressive impulses, and so on.

Of all forms of ornament, the grotesque most fully embodies this tension between the archaic and the advanced. As the various uses of Vitruvius' diatribe sketched in the previous chapter attest, the charge of being "against nature" can apply equally to the Gothic and to the Baroque — curiously, to the two poles of development where the influence of "nature" is most likely to be felt. If we want to specify what "nature" means in this regard, how it influences a work of art, and how it relates to the grotesque, we must begin by discarding the concept of the "natural," for this term means nothing in terms of artistic form.

"The primitive" is another matter, for it has an ideology and an artistic style that can be readily identified. Moreover, its images still speak to us. Iris Murdoch's *The Unicorn* (1963)[1] dramatizes such a recognition. It begins with the arrival of a well-educated young woman on the southern coast of Ireland. She has answered a notice for a tutor and has come to take up her position. Her first moments are unsettling: there is no station, nobody to meet her. Eventually, help arrives, and as she is riding in the cart she notices one of the features of that part of Ireland — a Neolithic dolmen. Everything else had been "unexpected," or had made her feel "helpless and almost frightened," but for this dolmen she has other words:

> Two immense upright stones supported a vast capstone which protruded a long way on either side. It was a weird lopsided structure, seemingly pointless yet dreadfully significant.... Marian was suddenly overcome by an appalling crippling panic. She was very frightened at the idea of arriving. But it was more than that. She feared the rocks and the cliffs and the grotesque dolmen and the ancient secret things. (14–15)

The dolmen is only the first of many manifestations of Ireland's mythical past. Marian soon learns that the gardener is seriously thought to be descended from "the faeries," and, gradually, she finds herself snagged in an entire system of ancestral curses, taboos, castle-bound princesses, and other leftovers of legend and myth. Reality has fractured, and she is stranded, with a modern Oxbridge sensibility placed within a still-potent mythological system. The word *grotesque* is her response to the alien intimacy of this shadowy world which, though distant in time, yet radiantly continues to occupy its ancient, and her modern, space. The dolmen is not mere scenery (or "ornament"), as it might be to a tourist, but a real emblem, a factor in the present. Much later, Marian will reflect that "It was not exactly that she was 'broken,' but she seemed different, as if by some great loop or shift she had joined some other phase of her being" (214). For the reader, as for Marian, the great problem is one of genre: What sort of story is this? For much of the novel, the question is unanswerable. The only way to put the matter is to say that, as the heroine is participating in multiple, discontinuous stories, she is exploring the liminal areas of reality, the range of the grotesque.

This range is implied by *grottesche,* whose historical origins illuminate the lamination of time structures that marks the grotesque. The Renaissance knew that the designs on the Domus Aurea walls harbored mythological or "Pythagorean" enigmas; some of the figures derived from Ovid, whom Nero had read assiduously, and others from Greek and Egyptian sources. The leafy ornamental pattern itself comes from Arabic sources, especially those designs called by Westerners arabesques. Ludwig Curtius has traced the "second Pompeian style," including the arabesque, to Asia Minor[2]; but even this net is not wide enough, for mingled forms resembling these occur in Indian, Balinese, and pre-Columbian art. South American tribal art can be described as arabesque, and so can some of the forms found in Paleolithic caves in southern Europe.[3] Moreover, nearly all primitive art uses metamorphic forms to depict both deities and demons. The distinctive elements of *grottesche,* then, would seem to have originated in primitive or mythological cultures that had no concept of meaningless design. If *grottesche* is pure play, its antecedents were pure magic.

By the time it imported this style Rome was very far from being a truly mythological culture. Even in its early days Rome had borrowed its myths from Greece and elsewhere, and by Augustus' time it was a clearly historical society, with the sense of alienation, contingency, and destiny implied by a severance from the mythic past. What myths there were had been impressed into the service of history, grounding the present in "nature."⁴ Ovid begins his *Metamorphoses,* for example, with the creation of the world; then, moving through the myths that constituted the common inheritance, he concludes with the deification of Caesar. By Vitruvius' time, and certainly by Nero's, Romans were far more concerned about the "end of Rome" than about any "myth of origins," and in the face of such an apprehension over the future, the appropriation of an ancient decorative style appears as part of a large-scale effort to reestablish a lost contact with a primordial past. Conceiving one's house as a palace for a sun-king is a step in that direction, an attempt to make of one's life a solar myth. How fitting, then, that Fabullus should work in this adopted mode, which could be considered as mythology wrenched from its context, drained of its meaning, and shaped into an aesthetically pleasing design. Nero's enterprise was no different.

From the moment of its appearance in Western culture, *grottesche* represented an invocation of "some other phase of being," of a mythological culture that was permanently lost. In the previous chapter I spoke of the way in which grotesque ornament confused the opposed systems of the center and the margin; in this chapter I would like to restate this opposition as the split between mythological and historical ways of thinking. The hypothesis before us is simple: the grotesque consists of the manifest, visible, or unmediated presence of mythic or primitive elements *in* a nonmythic or modern context. It is a formula capable of nearly infinite variation, and one which, rightly understood, illuminates the entire vast field of grotesquerie.

2. *Myth, Metaphor, and Mediation*

That the formula may be rightly understood requires some discussion of the mythological consciousness as modern scholars have come to understand it.⁵ What is a "primitive element"? What kind of "world" does it invoke? And how does it appear in a "modern context"? We can begin by returning to Meyer Schapiro's description of the drolleries in the margins of Gothic texts. Speaking of the tiny human figures cavorting with hares, mice, cats, snails, and birds, Schapiro comments that we see the human being "in these strange re-embodiments as a being among the others in nature, and sharing in his movements and passions the instinctive mobility of the animal world.... It is a process of desublimation through which the distance between the natural and the civilized is abolished."[6] Interestingly, this "process of desublimation" also illuminates Signorelli's *grottesche,* of which Nicole Dacos says that it reflects a world in perpetual metamorphosis.[7] Signorelli's creatures manifest an easy transference of human, animal, and vegetable forms, a willingness to shuffle the pieces to produce an image of nature as mysteriously mingled and blended, a world in which the individual form is engulfed in a commonality that unites all orders of being. Perpetual metamorphosis is the central premise of mythic thought, which operates on the principle of the cosmic continuum. According to this principle, no realm of being, visible or invisible, past or present, is absolutely discontinuous with any other, but all equally accessible and mutually interdependent.

Lucien Lévy-Bruhl called this sense of unity the "law of participation," or identity between objects neither physically contiguous nor causally related; mythic thought in general, he said, was based on a "participation mystique." For the Bororo tribesmen of northern Brazil, for example, to regard themselves as a species of red parrot is no absurdity, nor even a metaphor, but a recognition and assertion of positive identity. Lévy-Bruhl characterized the mind that could sustain such thoughts "pre-logical," which was unfortunate and ill-informed, as Claude Lévi-Strauss later demonstrated by pointing out that certain tribes, including the Bororo, employed as many as several thousand botanical terms.[8]

But the "law of participation" is one of those resilient ideas which, having been superseded or discredited in its own field — even its author turned against it[9] — continues to be valuable in others. Reconceived as the "law of infinite metaphor," by which everything is potentially identical with everything else, it illuminates all of mythic thought, and thus the sources of our response to the grotesque. Aristotelian logic proceeds according to classifications that seek in the object itself its essential nature: each tomato realizes the idea of Tomato, and no other idea. Such an approach is directly opposed to mythic thought, which begins with an intuitive perception of metaphor, not in the sense that myth uses figures of speech, but in the root sense of the word — "carrying across" established boundaries, perceiving a unity of essence where Aristotle would perceive typological multiplicity. Aristotle begins the *Physics* with a refutation of the old (mythic) notion that Being is one. And although he is, in other writings, more sympathetic to metaphor, the very notion of metaphorical speech as being "nonliteral" is alien to myth, which knows only reality. When Dylan Thomas says that "The force that through the green fuse drives the flower/ Drives my green age," he is speaking metaphorically from an Aristotelian point of view, but literally from a mythic one.

One of the purposes of the extraordinary classificatory systems of which many tribes are capable must be to establish boundaries in order to break them down again. Lévi-Strauss compares systems of "totemic classification" to a "kaleidoscope, an instrument which…contains bits and pieces by means of which structural patterns are realized."[10] The primitive mind ceaselessly orders and re-orders the world, discovering in and through myth an all-embracing network of relations binding all things. When, in Iris Murdoch's novel, we find Marian saying such things as "Gerald is Peter now," or "Yes, you are becoming Hannah, now," or experiencing the sensation that Denis and Peter "merged strangely in her mind," we recognize that she has entered the world of dolmens and faeries, and is thinking according to the laws of mythological thought. We sometimes attribute these laws of myth to nature as the *prior,* for, according to an old saying, nature loves mixtures: *"la nature aime les entrecroisements."* But in fact, nature loves everything: purity, impurity, tenderness, cruelty, ugliness, beauty, rest, energy: all. The point is that, by the logic of "common sense," Gerald cannot be Peter, though we can assert kinship by saying "Gerald is Peter" as long as we recognize that we are not speaking literally. In a mythic narrative, however, the metaphoric is the literal, and nothing inhibits Actaeon from becoming a stag, Philomela a bird, Hyacinthus a flower, or Gerald Peter. Traversing categories, myth also ploughs the human into the natural: animals marry, stars form families, and water speaks. At the margin of figurative metaphor and literal myth lies the grotesque, both and neither, a mingling and a unity.

Our kind of logic is built on an avoidance of contradiction. Myth does not merely tolerate contradiction, but seeks it out and mediates it through narrative. According to Lévi-Strauss, the Oedipus myth mediates between the proposition that human beings are born from the union of man and woman, and the older "autochthonous" position, in which the human male is inessential for conception. Born from one or born from two? In this analysis, the myth reconciles these beliefs by subtly compelling assent to both propositions: "The purpose of myth is to provide a logical model capable of overcoming a contradiction."[1] Edmund Leach, who has learned much from Lévi-Strauss, says that the characteristic feature of myth is the mediation of oppositions: "In every myth system we will find a persistent sequence of binary discriminations as between human/superhuman, mortal/immortal, male/female, legitimate/illegitimate, good/bad…followed by a 'mediation' of the paired categories thus distinguished."[12] Sometimes a great many categories are efficiently mediated by a single figure, such as the "trickster," a worldwide type who, in the words of Jung, is

> God, man and animal at once. He is both sub-human and superhuman, a bestial and divine being, whose chief and most alarming characteristic is his unconsciousness…. He is so unconscious of himself that his body is not a unity, and his two hands fight each other. He takes his anus off and entrusts it with a special task. Even his sex is optional despite its phallic qualities: he can turn himself into a woman and bear children. From his penis he makes all kinds of useful plants. This is a reference to his original nature as a Creator, for the world is made from the body of a god.[13]

One of the ways we normally avoid contradiction is by assigning hierarchies of meaning. We do this in a multitude of ways, depending upon the situation: the most meaningful can be "the nearest," "that which is apparent to the senses," "that which we cannot see," or "that which corresponds to the teachings of _____" In virtually all instances, modern adult thought settles potential disputes by deciding that some things are more meaningful than others. Mythic thought, on the other hand, protests "against the idea that anything can be meaningless."[14] This analysis is by Lévi-Strauss, who is so fascinated by mythic thought that, in trying to apply its lessons, he contradicts its most fundamental point — that, whatever the relative placement of things, meaning and value are evenly distributed over the entire cosmos. "True reality," he says in *Tristes Tropiques,* "is never the most obvious…to reach reality one has first to reject experience."[15]

The mythic mind rejects nothing, especially "experience." Far more than the Greek or Roman myths, primitive or "totemic" myths are marked by an immersion in the physical stuff of the world, its liquids, solids, and gases. What distinguishes the primitive narrative is a tendency to treat everything — even the gods, even the dead — as a palpable and living presence. Long before the "dissociation of sensibility," consciousness clung tightly to physical properties, operating according to a "logic of the senses," and basing its speculations on such immediate and primary sensations as raw and cooked, fresh and rotten. The world revealed by this mode of thought is perforce a unity. For substance has no contrary, or, as even Aristotle notes, "The most distinctive mark of substance appears to be that, while remaining numerically one and the same, it is capable of admitting contrary qualities."[16] This remark is made in the course of the essay "Categories," the very title of which removes us from the immediate and physical to the abstract level of propositions, a level on which truth contradicts falsehood and meaning is confined to the immaterial.

Myth is the infancy of narrative, and inhabits more advanced ways of knowing as our own infancies inhabit us. Speaking of the *illud tempus,* or the sacred time of the Beginnings, before history and profane time, it offers even to many people today a release from the tensions and alienations of abstraction, healing the self divorced from the raw material of life and providing a tonic affirmation of the wholeness of existence[17] Karl Kerényi says that myth "provides a foundation" by enabling the teller of an oral narrative to "find his way back to primordial times." The mythic narrative is "a beginning ... fusing in itself all the contradictions of his nature and life to be."[18] To be "grounded" in this way is to approach the *mysterium coniunctionus,* the *coincidentia oppositorum,* that condition of psychic unity that is the goal of psychoanalysis, or at least of Jung's version.[19] It is one of the large paradoxes of wholeness that it cannot be imagined or figured except as a violation of natural laws, in monstrous or distorted form. The unnaturalness of wholeness helps explain Jung's protracted dedication to the study of alchemy, *opus contra naturam,* through which he sought to discover the secret of liberating divine potency from the humblest and grossest of physical substances.[20] In its extreme bodily orientation, its unblinking attention to the physical world, especially those parts that participate directly in the organic cycle of life, myth performs the same alchemical function, grounding the world in origins.

3. *Dirt, Disorder, and Divinity*

One origin we can learn about from the study of myth is the source of our powerful and contradictory feelings concerning things that are both high and low, both transcendental and descendental. This conjunction, explicit in all grotesques, reflects an archaic conception of divinity as being both sacred and "unclean." As part of its compromise with paganism, Christianity still invokes this conception—witness the popular reverence for and fascination with the bloodied body of Christ, or the *Transfiguration.* Outside the authority imparted by the institution and the tradition, however, such compromises still strike us as grotesque. Recall Dr. Johnson's complaints about *Lycidas:*

> This poem has yet a grosser fault. With these trifling fictions [of Jove and Phoebus, Neptune and Aeolus, etc.] are mingled the most awful and sacred truths, such as ought never to be polluted with such irreverent combinations.... Such equivocations are always unskillful; but here they are indecent, and at least approach to impiety, of which, however, I believe the writer not to have been conscious.[21]

The Christian divinity may be mutilated and crucified, but the Word is clean, free from the irreverent pollution of myth and its trifling fictions.

Dr. Johnson was attacking what he saw as a point of technical incompetence that approached impiety. But what we know about archaic religions enables us to see a double pollution. Not only are sacred and awful truths mingled with fictions, but in the world of myth, truth itself is polluted. What scholars call the "ambivalence" or "ambiguity" of the sacred reflects the beliefs that an object can be sacred and yet actual and palpable or, more important, that the holy is identical with the unclean. In a passage quoted a few pages earlier, Edmund Leach says that myth mediates oppositions by introducing a "third category which is 'abnormal' or 'anomalous'... This middle ground is typically the focus of all taboo and ritual observance."[22] The radical form of the ambiguity of the sacred is the notion of "sacred uncleanness," a concept that occurs throughout the form of alienated, fragmented, and decomposed myth we call grotesque.

The modern mind finds it especially difficult to see what qualifies filth to be sacred because we have lost the sense of participation in a living cosmos that renews itself in an organic pattern. But to the primitive mind, fertility is the expression of the life force itself, and issues as naturally from corruption as spring follows winter's death and shoots sprout from fructifying dung. Many primitive societies make no distinction between the holy and the defiled; everything that comes out of the body, for example, can, with proper ritualization, be made creative.[23] All the body's outcast substances are heavy with creation, and so the simplest bodily acts can be a medium of communication with the divine.[24]

In *Purity and Danger*,[25] Mary Douglas discusses the logic of primitive "composting religions" in which "That which is rejected is ploughed back for a renewal of life."[26] Frazer insisted that such religions betray the heathen childishness, but Douglas argues that they proceed according to a coherent idea of divinity, a strict orderliness, and a bold willingness to test the limits of one's grasp on reality. Dirt is the "byproduct of a systematic ordering and classification of matter, in so far as ordering involves rejecting inappropriate elements."[27] We could call an exquisite garden "immaculate," for example, though there is dirt in it; but the same garden randomly distributed throughout the kitchen would be dirty indeed, compelling the conclusion that "dirt" has no necessary connection with humus, but is essentially "disorder." Dirt aligns with the sacred in that both transcend categories, cross boundaries and defy conventions, running against our mental habits. Like the sun, God and dirt are impossible to focus on.

One tribe noted for its classificatory sophistication, the Lele, have discovered a perfect incarnation of ambivalence — the pangolin. Other animals may be hard to classify, such as the blue-rumped baboon, the cassowary, the anteater, the Tasmanian devil, the bat, but none of these *entrecroisements* approaches the comprehensive weirdness of the pangolin, which, in Douglas's words,

> contradicts all the most obvious animal categories. It is scaly like a fish, but it climbs trees. It is more like an egg-laying

lizard than a mammal, yet it suckles its young. And most significant of all, unlike other small mammals its young are born singly.²⁸

The significance of the single birth is that it enables the Lele to regard the pangolin as a mediator not only of various animal species, but also between the human and animal realms. Animality itself, the pangolin connects all classes and demonstrates through its very being a current of identity running through species. The Lele deal with the pangolin through an "inner cult"; "Instead of being abhorred and utterly anomalous, the pangolin is eaten in solemn ceremony by its initiates who are thereby enabled to minister fertility to their kind."²⁹

Such is the special logic of sacred uncleanness. Douglas says that it suggests "a meditation on the inadequacy of the categories of human thought," a meditation encouraged by many cults "which invite their initiates to turn round and confront the categories on which their whole surrounding culture has been built up and to recognize them for the fictive, manmade arbitrary creations that they are."³⁰ But this diagnosis might make the Lele too modern, too theoretical, as if the pangolin constituted a reflection on thought itself. The goal of the Lele's systematic deconstruction of categories is not simply insight into the fictive nature of human thought, but insight into the essential unity of particulate creation, a unity that grounds human culture in the rhythms of nature, from which all fertility derives.

The sense of continuity embodied in the pangolin contrasts starkly with modern ideas, which, especially in our soap-and-deodorant culture, are closer to the Hebrew than to the mythological idea of holiness. The abominations of Leviticus, for example, are meant to enforce rigid codes of order and purity of type. The phrase so often repeated, "It is perversion," is, according to Douglas, a mistranslation of the rare Hebrew word *tebhel,* a mixing or confusion. Holiness, by contrast, means "keeping distinct the categories of creation. It therefore involves correct definition, discrimination and order."³¹ The specificity of Leviticus with regard to animals that part the hoof and chew the cud is an attempt to segregate, or make taboo (which for us only means "hands off") those species which are unclean, i.e., those which "are imperfect members of their class, or whose class itself confounds the general scheme of the world."³²

To a modern mind, the most "grotesque" aspect of the ambiguity of the sacred is based on the harmless-looking belief that the powers that give life also take it away. This recognition, exfoliated, produces a system of practices and beliefs that scholars have called the "fatality/fertility complex," in which are gathered most of the attributes of the mythological consciousness. We are familiar with this complex through its modern version, the romantic theme of the union of love and death Janus faces of a single force that annihilates individual identity, absorbing it into the flux. But its roots are mythic. Rabelais' *Pantagruel* begins with the legend that after Cain slew Abel the earth was extremely fertile for one year, a sequence common to the mythic sense that death furrows and fertilizes Mother Earth. In the legend, as in many primitive myths, life feeds on death: blood inseminates the soil and the crops rise. In the same way, the pangolin is eaten that women may conceive, or the bloody testes of the castrated Uranos are flung into the sea, and Aphrodite germinates in the foam. In one version of Osiris' story, the god is hacked to pieces and buried, in a magical analogy of seeding the earth with grain. In the words of Erich Neumann, Osiris is both "the dismembered god" and "the procreative mummy with the long member."[33]

4. *The Art of the Grotto*

We have arrived at the point of origin, the grotesque: the mysteries of the fatality/fertility complex, and of virtually every other aspect of primitive religion, were celebrated through rituals practiced in that most sacred of all spaces — the cave, or grotto.

It may seem that the cave afforded Paleolithic man a measure of protection from a hostile environment. But the paintings, carvings, and remains discovered in southern France and northern Spain at such sites as Altamira, Peche-Merle, Font-de-Gaume, and Niaux tell a different story. Many of the caves in which artifacts have been found are too cold, wet, and remote ever to have afforded human habitation; even in those which were inhabited, the paintings can be reached only with great difficulty and risk, and some must have been painted with long rods.[34] Most cave artifacts and remains are found in just those areas where the danger of attack from the cave-lion and bear would have been greatest; relatively few are found near the safer entrance, the scene of domestic life. The obvious ritual significance of the placing of the burial sites, for example, enables us to understand the ideology of primitive man. And this ideology illuminates *grottesche,* its ancestors, heirs, and analogues.

From such evidence as the arrangement of skulls and the configuration of footprints, scholars have inferred that both burial and initiation ceremonies were conducted in the caves. There is no incongruity in such a coupling, for both rituals expressed a recycling ideology in which death in one mode was followed by rebirth in another. Cave burials frequently involved the practice of brain-eating, a custom that extended in some areas for over a quarter of a million years. The brain of the dead man was extracted, generally through the nose (see Herodotus II.86), and consumed so the living could acquire the merits and even the identity of the dead.[35] Mircea Eliade and others have argued that initiation rituals followed the same pattern of death and rebirth, in the form of a return to and emergence from the "Great Mother": the hero or initiate "dies" to one state of being by undertaking a "perilous descent" to a primal condition, figured as the belly of the whale, the womb of the Mother, or, later, the jaws of hell. As the mouth or uterus of Mother Earth, the cave is imagined as (in Eliade's phrase) a *vagina dentata*—a concept bristling with threat for us, but one that corresponds perfectly with the ambivalence of the return. After a dangerous ordeal in a cave which was often ritually transformed into a labyrinth, the hero, born afresh, issued forth to bestow boons on his fellows.[36] (Passing a test in the cave, with a sexual reward, is a durable pattern, acknowledged, as the "myth-critics" of twenty years ago liked to point out, even by Tom Sawyer when he takes Becky Thatcher into the cave of Injun Joe.) In light of the cult of the Great Mother, whose rituals were enacted in the grotto, Freud's association of "cave" with "woman" in dream-symbolism is, like so many of his revolutionary ideas, simply a long-forgotten commonplace.

When we turn to the paintings and engravings that constitute the richest legacy of Paleolithic man we confront, in addition to a mass of lines or markings whose meaning is uncertain, images of large beasts, hybrid human-animal forms, pregnancy, and death — an inventory of the concerns of their creators. Unlike the wall paintings of the Domus Aurea "grottoes," these designs did not meet with immediate, sympathetic understanding. At the time the caves were first explored, about a hundred years ago, scholars who had just accustomed themselves to the idea that early man may have been related to the ape assumed that the paintings found in them were frauds. After the dating was established beyond question, and skepticism as to their authenticity crumbled, the debate as to their meaning began. Many felt that the designs represented merely a rude pleasure in manufacturing images, in art for art's sake. The establishment of a theory of their meaning awaited a thorough cataloguing and chronology.

For this immense labor most of the credit goes to the Abbé H. Breuil, who brought half a century of intensive research to a culmination with the publication, in 1952, of *Four Hundred Centuries of Cave Art*.[37] On the basis of a thorough chronology, Breuil argues for two cycles of development, both evolving from simple to complex uses of perspective, color and line technique, with most of the famous polychrome art belonging to the climax of the second cycle, the "Later Magdalenian" period (c. 13,000–10,000 B.C.). Noting the many images of hunters, spears, and "wounded" animals in Later Magdalenian art, Breuil speculated that the caves were sacred enclosures, scenes of sympathetic magic where artists "killed" their game. According to Breuil, the placement of the images was random; what really mattered was the image itself, for its simple existence effected its purpose.

The hunting-magic theory of cave art dominated the field until 1965, when André Leroi-Gourhan published *Treasures of Prehistoric Art*,[38] a work that marks the evolution of cave-art theory from the simple to the complex. The rise of structural anthropology underlies Leroi-Gourhan's massive reevaluation, in which for the first time the spatial organization of the cave is considered crucial to its meaning. In Leroi-Gourhan's new system, which also involves a new chronology, the organization of forms reflects the cosmology of Paleolithic man. The system of thought articulated in the caves is based on the opposition of masculine and feminine principles, with feminine signs occupying central positions and masculine signs the marginal or end positions. This "sexualization" of non-human and even non-representational forms has always provoked criticism, for it is largely hypothetical,[39] but none of Leroi-Gourhan's opponents has denied the compelling brilliance of the interpretations that follow from it.

For Leroi-Gourhan, the horse is the chief masculine sign and the bison is the chief feminine sign: thus, "women/bison" figures at Peche-

Merle are evidence of a symbolic linking of the two components. Many "feminine" animals have markings on them that can be taken as spear wounds. While Breuil and his followers interpreted these as manifestations of a desire to "kill," Leroi-Gourhan argued that "making" was involved as well. The spear marks, he said, indicate a link between the killing of the beast and the act of intercourse: "it is highly probable that Paleolithic men were expressing something like 'spear is to penis' as 'wound is to vulva.'"[40] This fateful syllogism once established, other images reveal themselves: "Taken as symbols of sexual union and death, the spear and the wound would then be integrated into a cycle of life's renewal, the actors in which would form two parallel and complementary series: man/horse/spear, and woman/bison/wound."[41] These associations are even implied in other forms of cave art, including the well-known "Venus" figurines. One of these, "Venus of Laussel," appears obese and probably pregnant; she holds up an incised bull's horn, a symbol of lethal yet potent penetration. An engraved design at Les Trois Frères in southern France represents a hybrid figure with a bull's head and human legs approaching, in a state of ithyphallic excitation, a reindeer and a startled figure sometimes described as a "deer/bison."[42] Although we find many animals represented in cave art, including the stag, fox, weasel, vulture, reindeer, boar, hawk, lion, bear, and horse, it is the cross-breed figures such as the bull-man that carry the most information: he joins a series of mythic figures culminating in the Minotaur, waiting in the labyrinth to trample or "marry" captive maidens. Even today the horn is a symbol of agricultural abundance (the "horn of plenty"), physical danger, and sexual attraction.

The numerous hybrid images found in the caves have attracted the broadest spectrum of interpretation, including a kind of commentary that prefers not to interpret at all, but to see them as (in the words of one critic of Leroi-Gourhan) "a sort of ridiculous contradiction of all that characterizes the animal drawing, being ill-drawn, anatomically incorrect and sketchy."[43] And indeed, many "anthropomorphic figures," "têtes humaines grotesques,"[44] "ghosts," and the like do seem poorly executed compared to the overpowering renderings of animals at Altamira, Lascaux, or Les Trois Frères. But however skeptical we might be of the possibility of saying anything definite about the motives of Paleolithic man, it is surely not enough simply to pronounce these figures ridiculous and to move on. We must ask why, although we frequently find human "elements," we rarely find a complete human being; we must ask about the drives and inhibitions that generated such a number of hybrid or semi-animal forms; and why such forms "have a tendency to avoid defining the human form, leaving it in an indeterminate state, and, above all, trying to hide or to transform the face."[45]

Surveying a series of masculine figures characterized by "bestial" stylization of the face, Leroi-Gourhan concluded that earlier theories according to which such figures represented masked dancers were incorrect. Such stylization, he argued, may have accorded with the Paleolithic "canon of masculine beauty": "That some similarity to the faces of beasts may have been intended is not out of the question."[46] But some figures would seem to adhere to no possible canon of beauty. The "sorcerer" at Les Trois Frères, for example (Figure 21), is rendered as a male figure leaning forward, "his eyes big and round like those of a night bird (or a lion, or a 'ghost'), cervid antlers on his head, and the ears and shoulders of a reindeer or a stag. The lower part of the back is provided with a horse's tail, below which the sexual parts are seen, rather human in shape, but located where a feline's would be."[47] This figure, whom the Abbé Breuil described as the "god of Les Trois Frères," is the best known of the numerous hybrids, of which Siegfried Giedion has said, "Hybrid figures, taken in general, are antennae reaching out from earthly matter: recipients of invisible forces. They partake of the shaman." Their essential factor, he argues, is indetermination, which constitutes "their rightful being, their rightful nature."[48] Such figures are like those species described by Lévi-Strauss as selected not because they are "good to eat," but because they are "good to think."

The very anatomical indeterminacy of these figures is a prod to theory. In one of the most influential early studies of the caves, *The Gate of Horn,* G. Rachel Levy said that they possibly represented a "sacred marriage" on behalf of the animals, which primitive man regarded as divine.[49] Perhaps we can be more specific. As Giedion has pointed out, in many cases of composite figures there can be no question of masked dancers because "the hybrid continually changes its animal and human form from part to part and limb to limb."[50] It seems far more likely that they represent human beings with metamorphic powers. Lévi-Strauss records the narrative of an American Indian who says, "We know what the animals do, what are the needs of the beaver, the bear, the salmon, and other creatures, because long ago men married them and acquired this knowledge from their animal wives."[51] Women-bison, anthropomorphic figures, bull-men, sorcerers, and other metamorphic figures converge on the implication of human-animal intercourse, either "long ago" or in ritual re-enactment. This is, in fact, bluntly indicated in one engraved cave image of a pregnant woman lying beneath a reindeer. In other words, evidence indicates that whatever "marriages" were performed, either symbolically or literally, were not on behalf of the beasts as much as with them. The sorcerer figures may be the issue of human-animal marriages, or they may represent a ritual attempt to effect the rebirth of totemic ancestors. It has even been suggested that the sacred caves were the sites of ritual marriages involving either a bull or a bull-masked priest,[52] a ceremony in which humanity appropriated the powers of the animals, paid homage to the ancestral dead, and anchored itself in the natural world. This is a large burden for a few images to carry, which is why the most significant images are the most indeterminate. As one student of cave art has pointed out, "Ambiguity allows a great deal of potential information to be stored in very few symbols."[53]

As the original place of worship the cave has left its imprint on its successors, the shrines, altars, labyrinths, tombs, temples, ziggurats, and pyramids which, in the words of G. Rachel Levy, built upon the "foundation of ideas"[54] provided by the cave. Although her study concludes in ancient Greece, we could easily imagine the shape of further chapters. The Christian church, for example, is a sacred enclosure in which marriages and funerals are solemnized, and though it has reversed all the polarities of the cave, it has retained the basic pattern of associations. Instead of Woman guaranteeing fertility and contact with the primordial past by "marrying" a bull in the grotto, Man guarantees salvation in the heavenly, eternal future by "marrying" God on the cross. One of Baudelaire's more daring ideas was that Woman was to be aligned with raw nature, and the beasts. He wondered how a woman could enter a church — what would she have to say to God? Baudelaire had a strong mythopoeic sense (as in "Les Correspondences") and it is not hard to see that this is actually a mythic recognition taken from its context. For Woman is the center of "natural" or archaic religion, and we may well consider that her silence in the presence of the Christian god is amply compensated for by the feebleness, subordination, or co-optation by other species practiced on the human male in the grotto.

Figure 21. The "Sorcerer" of Les Trois Frères; watercolor and ink redesigning of cave painting by Abbé H. Breuil.

For Baudelaire, as for many discursive moderns, one attraction of primitive art is its brevity: where we would qualify, clarify and dilute, primitive man would compress a multitude of ideas into a single ambivalent form. Unavailable in reality, this compression of forms could occur only in art. Levy, who believes the masked-dancers theory, notes that the living force of the animal was "present in even greater potency within its manufactured symbol...." It is surprising, she says, "that art should hold so integral a position in this unity between animals and humans, as to render the image or emblem more sacred than the actual entity...."[55] How much more surprising is it when we consider that for many of the most important images there was no "actual entity," for they depicted things that neither are, nor have been, nor could be. Levy is speaking here of the "shamanistic" power of art to create a realm which is ambivalently real and unreal, dependent on and independent of "actual entities"— which we now see to be the first discovery, the first use of art. Thousands of years elapsed before Renaissance artists, by then long schooled in *mimesis,* reunited representation with *fantasia,* again under the aegis of the grotto. But this moment, too, passed; and it awaited a recent celebrant of the grotesque, Flaubert,[56] both a realist and an ornamentalist, to cultivate a "religion of art" that has found devotees even in this secular century, enabling us to recapture a sense of the potential for sacrality within the aesthetic form.

Recognizing the staggering burden of meaning of cave art, we could never accuse it of representing art for art's sake. And of course this form of grotto-painting is as foreign to Raphael's elegant decorations as one fresco can be to another: one reflects an exceptionally individualistic culture which can conceive of pure design and meaningless form; the other reflects an ideology in which even species flow into each other and in which everything is equally meaningful. Yet though the comparison may seem grotesque, maybe we can "see something" in the juxtaposition and try to illuminate the black gulf between them. To begin with, we cannot separate them on the basis that one is "natural" and the other "aesthetic." Many of the cave paintings are not only magnificent as works of art, but just as alienated as *grottesche.* And like *grottesche,* the cave paintings invoke, and thereby make ambivalently present and distant, an ancient code: they signify and embody antiquity, the origin. Cave art, despite its naturalizing theology, represents a first step in the articulation of the human personality, the human species. It reflects theology, and the rituals performed in the caves included inter-species intercourse, cannibalism, necrophagy, and sacrifice — all of which were intended to emphasize affinities with the natural world, and none of which is found in nature. If *grottesche* seemed to the Renaissance wholly aesthetic and divorced from nature, cave art is no less so: it is the natural condition even of primitive art to be unnatural.

There are further affinities that make "grotto-esque" seem more an etymology and less a pun for *"grottesche."* Although both cave art and pilaster art are manifestly fanciful, they are highly obedient to formal constraints. Ornament has only leftover space to fill; and much cave art, even at Altamira, consists largely of stressing perceived tendencies or implications in the rock masses. Moreover, the hybrid or indeterminate figures in cave art compel, like *grottesche,* a piecemeal description that enables us to see many forms in a single representation without enabling us to settle on a univocal meaning. Vasari's paradox — that *grottesche* presents imaginary beings "all as real as reality"— is a cave-echo of the ritual position of the sorcerer-figures, depicted, as Giedion says, in a state of "indetermination between the real and the imaginary."[57]

Together, grotto-esque and *grottesche* provide us with a binocular view of *grotesque*. In fact, if we wanted to construct a system of classification for all grotesqueries, we could do no better than to begin with an elementary distinction between those like cave art, in which, forms are compressed into meaningful ambivalence; and those in which, as with *grottesche,* forms are proliferated into meaningless ambivalence. Countless subcategories could be formulated, but this basic division accomplishes the most important task, of explaining why some grotesqueries seem to mean everything, even to signify the sacred, and others seem to corrupt meaning, to signify nothing: some, which we might, following Gombrich, call the "Gothic" variety, seem to face back to the cave, while others (the "Baroque") appear to face away from it. It is part of the permanent indetermination of the grotesque that these two forms do not divide the field cleanly between themselves, but inhabit each other like an ulterior motive, a silent negative.

Grottesche may epitomize superficiality, but the power of the cave is that of all things "beneath." It embodies a principle of formlessness, an adequate symbol for both the beginnings and the ends of things.

The cave, like myth itself, speaks of the oneness of creation, a condition of undifferentiation out of which we emerge, or into which we collapse.⁵⁸ Such a notion might seem to offer sweet succor to an overpsychologized and alienated culture, and some, whether through exuberance or fatigue, have embraced myth on that account, as though it were an option we could freely choose. That it is not should go without saying, but even if it were, we should look more closely at our "natural" responses to *la pensée sauvage*. Throughout his discussion of the influence of the Bible on western culture, Herbert Schneidau reports the response of the Jews to the "unclean" customs of "the nations"— a disgust, revulsion, and moral condemnation so strong that Hebrew culture, whose links to modern culture are manifest, could be said to be formed as the negation of the mythological cultures that surrounded it.⁵⁹ Though myth is often invoked in the name of lost innocence, full "presence," natural ecology, nostalgia for origins, or primitive communism, this is because we have romanticized it, losing sight of its real character, its actual practices. These we still stigmatize, calling them grotto-esque.

5. *Myth out of the Grotto*

Stigmatized though it may be, the mythological consciousness resists extirpation, and can be considered a permanent potentiality of the mind. The only possible, or necessary justification for considering the grotesque in the remote and exotic light of the grotto is that the field of "myth," which I have treated very selectively, offers a precise map of a certain region of consciousness, mostly suppressed, denied, or compromised, but always vital. Even without the keys to understanding, visitors to Lascaux have reported being impressed by an uncanny sense of psychological affinity with the creators of those vivid ideograms. Not only do the old myths die hard, but as Roland Barthes asserts,⁶⁰ we generate new ones daily, however short-lived and etiolated these may be. Lévi-Strauss says that his subject is not the thinking of primitives but "mind in its untamed state as distinct from mind cultivated or domesticated for the purpose of yielding a return."⁶¹

Although we no longer believe that savages are childlike, we have come to recognize that children are in many ways very like savages: children are intensely interested in the sensory, and especially intent on the alimentary and reproductive systems; they are indifferent to such concepts as tragedy, nobility, and sanitation; and they see the world in terms of such primitive notions as animism, metamorphosis, and anthropocentrism. Jungians are predictably attracted to the mythical and "archetypal" character of the child's cosmos, but many others, prominently including Jean Piaget, have used terms such as "participation," "spontaneous animism," and "consciousness attributed to things" to describe *la pensée enfantile*.[62]

Myth reflects the concerns of that part of the mind loosely defined as the unconscious, a fact seen early by Freud, who even planned at one point to revise his first major work, *The Interpretation of Dreams*, in order to take myth more fully into account.[63] Although he devoted his attention to the workings of the individual psyche, Freud acknowledged the recurrence of ancient patterns, and even based two of his most important general theories on mythic types, Narcissus and Oedipus. The latter assumes enormous importance for Freud as he gradually realizes that all adult development plays out the consequences of the child's handling of the Oedipal crisis. Discussions such as that of "The Return of Totemism in Childhood" in *Totem and Taboo*[64] have encouraged Eliade and others to suggest that the psychic world of the Freudian child is similar to that of primitive man. Eliade has, in fact, claimed that Freud's accomplishment was to historicize and personalize the *illud tempus*, locating it in earliest childhood rather than in the primordial past.[65]

Surprising as it may be in some quarters, this claim, I believe, is beyond serious dispute. Like the mythological consciousness, the Freudian unconscious is ruled by the powers of fertility and fatality, twinned opposites whose interaction produces the whole range of psychic behavior. In *Beyond the Pleasure Principle*,[66] Freud argues that "Eros" establishes ever greater unities and more cohesive wholes, and "Thanatos" constantly unravels them, striving for abolition and death. Most strikingly, the attributes of the id match up perfectly with the attributes of myth. The primitive mind protests against the idea that anything can be meaningless; there is nothing in the id (Freud says) "that could be compared with negation." Myth refers to a time out of time; "There is nothing in the id that corresponds to the idea of time; there is no recognition of the passage of time...." The savage mind does not seek to avoid contradiction; while in the id, "The logical laws do not apply ... and this is true above all of the law of contradiction. Contrary impulses exist side by side, without canceling each other out or diminishing each other...."[67] Mythical thought is always characterized by ambivalence; the id obeys "the inexorable psychological law of ambivalence."[68] Myth constantly reclassifies and rearranges the world; through "condensation," the unconscious brings together images that conscious common sense would keep separate.

To the ego, the id appears as "a chaos, a cauldron full of seething excitations,"[69] and when it "pierces into" the conscious mind we experience a distinct feeling of "*repulsion.*" Many of Freud's ideas continue to be unsettling where they are not unconvincing, but the diagram of the ego and the id is remarkably easy to live with; it has never encountered the violent resistance to which so many of his theories have been subjected. One reason for this assimilability might be that the howling demons of the id are homologous with those of Spenser, Milton, Dickens, and others who write of the monsters of Hell, London, or the dripping sea-caves of the mind. Freud's is the last of the great nineteenth-century dualisms, the capstone of a tradition that includes Blake's Reason and Energy, Schopenhauer's Will and Idea, Marx's bourgeoisie and proletariat (and their descendants, H. G. Wells' Eloi and Morlock), and Nietzsche's Apollo and Dionysus, to mention only the most prominent. This tradition has been continued in our time not only by mythographers who speak of the "lost world," but also by neurophysiologists investigating the right and left hemispheres of the brain. There is even evidence, as Gregory Bateson has pointed out, that not only dreams but animal behavior exhibit "lost world" characteristics: "They both deal in opposites, and they both have no tenses, and they both have no 'not,' and they both work by metaphor...."[70] On one side in all these constructs there is clarity, abstract logical order, stability, and linear time; on the other, formlessness, contradiction, ambivalence, instability, and cyclic or tenseless time. Once this elementary grammar is fixed in the mind we begin to see it everywhere, projecting it onto the Mason-Dixon line, the Mexican border, cellars and attics, city and country, and such Manichean categories as "white" and "colored."[71] Whenever it imagines an alternate world, a separate reality (Lewis Carroll's Looking-Glass world, J. J. Grandville's *L'autre Monde,* Alfred Kubin's *Die Andere Seite),* the mind turns naturally, if that word can still be used, to elements stored in the species memory, the infantile mind, the unconscious, the right lobe.

These dualisms define the margin of ambivalence inhabited by the grotesque. The ease with which we can formulate more and more versions of the same basic structure helps account for the enormous variety of grotesqueries we encounter, as well as the difficulty in defining, once and for all, what the grotesque is. One of these versions, tragedy and comedy, yields a compromise word that is frequently linked to the grotesque, tragicomedy. It is a word that Freud, an inveterate seeker after contradictions and double meanings, would have liked. The philologist Karl Abel had discovered that some words in ancient Egyptian imply their own negation; and Freud drew on Abel's work in his 1910 essay "The Antithetical Meaning of Primal Words" in support of his theory that words or signs in a dream can mean their own opposites,[72] I will discuss this notion at greater length in Chapter Seven in relation to Conrad, but it bears on the grotesque generally. Freud was attracted to Abel's findings because he saw in them confirmation of his own findings that gestures always and necessarily contradicted the impulses that generated them. Social behavior was always, for Freud, a masking. We should not be led into the easy and common mistake of thinking that the positive gesture masks the negative impulse, or vice versa. It is rather that the univocal gesture masks the ambivalent impulse. "Grotesque" always designates an unsuccessful masking, a dis-covery or revelation. Christianity may be greatly indebted to myth, but the unmediated co-presence of the two systems in *Lycidas* struck Dr. Johnson as grotesque, a mingling of awful truth with trifling fiction, his word for myth. And again the double pollution: univocal truth is mingled with fiction, and fiction is synonymous with mingling, as it can speak with any voice. Finally, "grotesque" demonstrates the Abel-Freud hypothesis in a curiously literal way. As it names no object, it is a noun and yet the antithesis of a noun; and as it modifies no noun, it is an adjective and yet the antithesis of an adjective.

In the first chapter I said that the incongruities of the grotesque object may be unified by some barely glimpsed concept. In the larger context of this chapter we cay say that the grotesque phenomenon eludes all its synonyms by impressing us with a remote sense that in some other system than the one in which we normally operate, some system that is primal, prior, or "lower," the incongruous elements may be normative, meaningful, even sacred. Grotesques disturb us with the prospect that the trifling fictions which we feel should not be there at all may in fact be another kind of Word, a tolerant kind in terms of which our Word is but one among many. To see that "myth" is everywhere (and everywhere in chains) is to recognize the omnipresence of this other system, and the constant potential for the grotesque.

6. *Dissonance, "Reality," and the Tradition*

The "other system" goes by many names. In describing its mythic face I have sought not merely to develop a new theory of the grotesque, but also to continue a tradition of discussion about the subject. In the nineteenth century, Sir Walter Scott, Ruskin, J. A. Symonds, Baudelaire, and others made the connection between myth and the grotesque.[73] The difficulty lies in the fact that nineteenth-century mythography was in such a rude and primitive state that those who regarded it as the clue to the grotesque were thinking mainly of the gnomes, sylphs, kelpies, centaurs, ogres, and fabulous beasts of folktales, legends, and myths. In our own century, on the other hand, when the conceptual tools are available for solid analysis, the connection with myth has gone unrecognized. The result is that both nineteenth- and twentieth-century discussions are all just out of focus, verging on the truth. This is not to say that they are without insight, for they are full of that. It is, rather, to say that for all the diversity and disagreements we encounter in discussions of the grotesque, the best of them converge on a single point that none of them quite glimpses.

Of all nineteenth-century theorists, Baudelaire had the keenest vision regarding the relation between modern man and his archaic past. For Baudelaire, laughter follows the Fall; the "essence of laughter" is not divine but diabolical or satanic. Human laughter recognizes a fracture, a contradiction, and betokens "an infinite grandeur and an infinite misery-the latter in relation to the absolute Being of whom man has an inkling, the former in relation to the beasts. It is from the perpetual collision of these two infinites that laughter is struck." This collision is clearest in the laughter occasioned by human conduct: a man slips on a banana peel, and we swell with satanic pride at the fact that he is ridiculous and helpless while we remain invincible and standing. This type of comedy is easy to understand, as its element is "visibly double — art and the moral idea." We see the image and understand its meaning. Baudelaire calls it the "significative comic."

The grotesque is quite different. It is an "absolute comic," for it "has about it something profound, primitive and axiomatic, which is much closer to the innocent life and to absolute joy than is the laughter caused by the comic in men's behavior." Baudelaire says that the primitive, especially those aspects of it which seem most ludicrous to us, does not occasion laughter if properly understood: "those prodigious phalluses on which the white daughters of Romulus innocently ride astride, those monstrous engines of generation, equipped with wings and bells — I believe that these things are all full of deep seriousness." Linked to the primordial, the grotesque is a *"unity* which calls for the intuition to grasp it." In this, it approaches Joy, for Joy is a unity; children, though they are budding satans, laugh joyful laughter. As dual, adult beings, we respond to the grotesque, this fragment of our primordial or infantile past, not with ordinary laughter but with an instantaneous, violent convulsion, "an insane and excessive mirth, which expresses itself in interminable paroxysms and swoons."[74]

In "Some Foreign Caricaturists," Baudelaire repeatedly speaks of the fabulous energy, the spontaneity, freedom, and inexhaustible abundance of the grotesque in Hogarth, Cruickshank, Goya, and Bruegel. It may seem inconsistent that Baudelaire recognizes Satanism and prodigious humor, the Fall and regeneration, in the same forms. But if we consider the way Christianity appropriated the figures of myth and converted them into the crowd of demons, so that Persephone and the Minotaur, those potent embodiments of fertility and fatality, came to reign in Dante's Hell, we can see the logic behind the apparent contradiction. If Hell contains myth, then damnation must always be tinctured with regeneration, and all poets are of the devil's party whether they know it or not. Homage to the devil as a creative source, whether by Milton, Blake, or Baudelaire, is a form of acknowledgment of the imaginative resources of myth. The tradition of T. S. Eliot has said so much about Baudelaire as an "inverted Christian" that it may be time to suggest that in some ways he is also an "inverted pagan."

Exposure to the grotesque is a kind of litmus-paper test of our sympathies with the lower world. Those less mythic-minded than Baudelaire betray themselves by their "distinct feeling of *repulsion*";

those more so, by their open-armed enthusiasm. Wolfgang Kayser, whose study *The Grotesque in Art and Literature* inaugurated the current line of grotesque-studies, epitomizes the first response. Like Baudelaire, he sees another "world" invoked by the grotesque, but understands only its demonic powers, and none of its regenerative capacities. He rightly describes this world as "totally different from the familiar one — a world in which the realm of inanimate things is no longer separated from those of plants, animals, and humans."[75] But his recurrent adjectives for this world — sinister, nocturnal, abysmal, ominous — indicate his bias and his limitations. That estranged world we can easily identify as the mythic world; and Kayser's agonies are a gauge of his investment in "the familiar world," his inability to step outside it.

One unaccustomed to ambivalence might be given pause by the juxtaposition of Kayser's study and Mikhail Bakhtin's *Rabelais and His World*. In this rich and learned book, Bakhtin, fully realizing the second response, bluntly contradicts Kayser at every possible point. Kayser's Rabelais "savagely [piles] epithet upon epithet to an ultimate effect of terror," dragging the reader "into the nocturnal and inhuman sphere,"[76] whereas Bakhtin's Rabelais not only knows nothing of terror, but also nothing of the private soul that experiences it. According to Bakhtin, Rabelais drew his inspiration directly from the joyous, festive, democratic, popular culture of the middle ages. This culture was organized around festivals, frequently held in conjunction with "official" celebrations, whose roots extended far back into the past, to the Roman Saturnalia and probably beyond. The Feast of Fools, the Feast of Beans, the Feast of the Ass, Carnival, all had their comic rites, cults, clowns, fools, giants, dwarfs, and jugglers, and frequently included among their activities elaborate and unrestrained parodies of the ecclesiastical or feudal authorities. Again and again Bakhtin stresses the gay courting of death and corruption, the bone-deep embrace of the metaphor of cosmos as body. Death for the medieval peasant was certainly as dismal a prospect as it is for us, but in his festivals he assuaged his fear by conceiving individual death as an organic element in communal regeneration: "Moments of death and revival, of change and renewal, always led to a festive perception of the world."[77] This festive world is wholly material, wholly alive, and universal. By the logic of the cosmos-as-body metaphor, popular culture relentlessly "degraded" the authorities, demonstrating not only that they had feet of clay, but that they stood in dung. In the riot of reversals, uncrownings, and parodies, everything abstract, ceremonial, official, and "clean" was transformed or translated into the "material bodily lower stratum," the zone in which excretion and conception occur, there to be regenerated. Systematic parodies and degradations produce what Bakhtin calls "grotesque realism," the "bodily participation in the potentiality of another world."[78] Bakhtin's "other world" is the unified, primordial world that the Romans conceived as the reign of kindly Saturn, the golden age of perfect democracy.

Reading Bakhtin, we may be encouraged to feel that by embracing the grotesque we can regain fullness of meaning, purity of being, and natural innocence, lying breast to breast with the cosmos and with our fellow creatures. In short, this is another case of using the grotesque as the tip of the wedge of liberation or breakthrough. But here the grotesque is actually the small end of alienation, a sign that though dualism may be temporarily abolished, it has invaded the structure of thought itself. The apprehension of the grotesque stands like a flaming sword barring any return to Paradise; the late medieval world is on the point of requiring the concept — a need Rabelais himself recognized, and, according to Bakhtin, filled. Bakhtin would have us believe that unity was still attainable by sixteenth-century folk culture through the universal laughter of Carnival, but he has missed Baudelaire's point about the satanic origin of all laughter. If "myth" is never stated but fully implied in Bakhtin's discourse, "grotesque" is the opposite — ever present, but foreign to his subject. And in this shuffle of words we can see the fate of myth, at about the time the Domus Aurea was discovered, on the brink of becoming "grotesque," metamorphosing into an alienated form, a ritualized interval of "participation" in a lost world. Underestimating the force of alienation in the grotesque, Bakhtin lays himself open to the charge Derrida makes against Lévi Strauss, of imposing on his subject a "sad, *negative,* nostalgic, guilty Rousseau-ist" sense of loss deriving from an unspoken "ethic of presence ... of nostalgia for origins."[79] Such a charge is easy to make, hard to avoid: even the Romans, with their fond recollections of Saturn, are guilty Rousseau-ists.

Bakhtin's use of the term "grotesque realism" implies that reality is all on the side of Carnival and scatological democracy, a fiction we believe only with disastrous psychological and social consequences. But even if we could purge ourselves of this "nostalgia for origins," we would find the grotesque twining around reality in other ways. This, at least, is one lesson of Erich Auerbach's *Mimesis; The Representation of Reality in Western Literature*,[80] the last work I am going to discuss here. Auerbach argues that western realism grew out of a reaction to the classical doctrine of the "separation of styles," according to which different types of subjects were represented through different levels of styles: "the sublime and elevated style was called *sermo gravis* or *sublimis;* the low style was *sermo remissus* or *humilis;* the two had to be kept strictly separate."[81] All that contributed to the stability and greatness of the state, all that revealed man in a tragic or noble condition was portrayed in the high style, which was grandiloquent, stylized, and highly rhetorical-in a word, fictitious. Beneath this sphere of moral significance and official equipoise was the world of what Auerbach calls reality—earthy, routine, and common, the unfiltered sensory life of the everyday. In its domestic aspect, this reality was simply beneath the high style and was reserved for light, pleasant, and colorful entertainment, as in Petronius. But reality had a darker side, connected with the vulgar and possibly orgiastic growth processes in the depths; toward this side the high style maintained an aristocratic disdain or contempt.

As the classical world and its decorums began to crack up under the volcanic pressures of reality (unruly mobs in the cities, barbarians at the gates), the separation of styles, which had depended upon order and class distinctions, began to fracture too, so that the grotesque, which had been confined to low comedy, began to appear in descriptions of the aristocracy, in the form of a "whole gallery of gruesomely grotesque and extremely sensory-graphic portraits...." As depicted by a fourth-century historian, Ammianus Marcellus, even the rulers were "grotesque and sadistic, spectral and superstitious"; and the entire world is full of blood frenzy, exhaustion, and "grim and magically rigid gestures." The rebellion of the low convulses both state and style: the mighty shiver on their thrones while diction becomes overburdened and harsh and "constructions begin, as it were, to writhe and twist."[82]

The situation Auerbach describes can serve as a model for the relation between decorum and the grotesque. All systems of decorum, whether political, cultural, or artistic, are designed to keep the low and the marginal in their places. But they are afflicted with built-in obsolescence. Beginning with the assumption that value and meaning are not randomly or equally distributed throughout the cosmos (the mythic assumption), they systematize methods of discriminating the meaningful from the meaningless. These methods naturally develop into customs and traditions, which naturally decay into clichés and formulae that are, naturally, themselves meaningless. As this condition is perceived, meaning, which must go somewhere, migrates to the low or marginal. Revolutions seek to reverse the meaningful/meaningless opposition, moving the bottom to the top in the name of greater fidelity to "reality." Grotesque is a word for that dynamic state of low-ascending and high-descending. Those like Bakhtin who espouse the cause of the low speak of "grotesque realism"; those like Kayser who stand with the status quo speak of grotesque nightmares. But this crisis in the sense of reality is created by the systems of decorum we devise precisely in order to avoid such experiences. Trying to think in logical types and strict categories, we make ourselves prey for the imps of the indeterminate. Trying to escape ambivalence, Oedipus-like we run right to it.

One way to escape this dilemma is to develop a system of decorum with indeterminacy or ambivalence as the norm. For Auerbach, Christianity is such a system, entering the crumbling classical world with a new principle that horrified educated pagans, of the "mingling of styles." Through the Incarnation and the Passion Christ had shown that the highest sublimity was compatible with the humblest and most ignominious forms of sensory life, and this transfiguring discovery shattered the old world along fault-lines that made class distinctions irrelevant. The elevation of Dante's style, for example, consists "precisely in integrating what is characteristically individual and at times horrible, ugly, grotesque, and vulgar with the dignity of God's judgment — a dignity which transcends the ultimate limits of our earthly conception of the sublime." Auerbach discovers a number of mutations of the "mingling of styles": in Rabelais' "promiscuous intermingling of the categories of event, experience, and knowledge" which demonstrates the "vitalistic-dynamic triumph of the physical body and its functions";[83] in miracle plays in which the Passion and crude farce are directly juxtaposed; in the life of St. Francis; in Montaigne's fusion of the concrete-sensory with the moral-intellectual.

Auerbach's chapter on Montaigne, the central one of his book, is one of the subtlest tributes ever paid to the author of the *Essays*. Auerbach has an acute perception of the relation between Montaigne's "centrality" and his vivid receptivity to the marginal. Montaigne occupied a mental world of the most amazing variety, even describing his essays as "grotesques and monstrous bodies, pieced together of divers members, without definite shape, having no order, sequence or proportion other than accidental."[84] Always absorbed by the wayward, the deformed, the eccentric, and the freakish, his attention is yet constantly detached, kindly, pure, and alive, escaping the psychological probing it seems to invite. The conclusion to the *Essays* is monumentally equable: "The most beautiful lives, to my mind, are those that conform to the common human pattern, with order, but without miracle and without eccentricity."[85] The mental poise capable of such a sentence does not counterbalance the grotesque but accepts it, regarding it without pity, undue fascination, or revulsion simply, as part of the human condition. The aberrant and anomalous, because they too are human, can instruct us as profitably on the subject of reality as can more decorous masters.

The subject of Montaigne's final essay is humility. Although many grotesqueries seem exceptionally aggressive, many others are informed by a modest acceptance of a fallen or impure state. The anonymous craftsmen of the misericords, liberated from ecclesiastical constraints, expressed their piety as well as their impishness by producing marvelous little monsters with the same humor and understanding they devoted to the portrayal of domestic life—watermills, milkmaids, sporting events, animals. Such flexibility in the sense of reality may seem paradoxical, but anybody who thinks on "the human condition" is led to paradox. Thomas Browne described Man as a "great and true Amphibium whose nature is disposed to live, not only like other creatures in divers elements, but in divided and distinguished worlds"; Addison said that though Man is "associated with angels and archangels, and may look upon a being of Infinite Perfection as his Father, and the highest order of Spirits as his brethren, may, in another respect, say to Corruption, Thou art my Father, and to the Worm, Thou art my Sister."

Insofar as the human condition is paradoxical, the marginal is the typical precisely because it is marginal. Monsters are for Montaigne quintessentially human because they defy understanding. Speaking "Of a monstrous child" with a parasitic twin protruding from its breast (a true Amphibium), he says,

> What we call monsters are not so to God, who sees in the immensity of his work the infinity of forms that he has comprised in it; and it is for us to believe that this figure that astonishes us is related and linked to some other figure of the same kind unknown to man. From his infinite wisdom there proceeds nothing but that is good and ordinary and regular; but we do not see its arrangement and relationship.[86]

Montaigne's sympathy to pied beauty does not compromise the center, but strengthens it, for it admits everything as a possible center, and admits that the true center is beyond our grasp. Faith in "God" is a faith in the hidden order of apparently disorderly things, the hidden meaning of the apparently meaningless. For Montaigne, there was no true grotesque, because no absolute incongruity. And this is the final paradox: really to understand the grotesque is to cease to regard it as grotesque. Or, as Coleridge says in the final line of "This Lime-Tree Bower My Prison": "No sound is dissonant which tells of Life."

PART TWO

Wherever the human mind is healthy and vigorous in all its proportions, great in imagination and emotions no less than in intellect...there the grotesque will exist in full energy.

—Ruskin

CHAPTER FOUR

Walking on Silernce: The Lamination of Narratives in *Wuthering Heights*

Many the wonders but nothing walks stranger than man.
—Sophocles, *Antigone*

1.

The classic, Frank Kermode has said, "is a book that is read a long time after it was written" by competent readers without institutional constraint. The classic is an appropriate subject for a T. S. Eliot Memorial Lecture, where Kermode made his remarks, but his conclusions about why generations of readers return to a certain few texts would hardly have met with the approval of Eliot, who himself held severe notions on classics and classicism. We read classics, Kermode argues, partly because of their susceptibility to a wide variety of reader response, a susceptibility that enables the text to escape from its original period-culture and to speak to us from a privileged moment, timeless yet contemporaneous with ours, whenever ours happens to be. The classic text is distinguished by its high level of significant indeterminacy; the repair of indeterminacy gives rise to the generation of meaning.[1] Generations of readers die off, liberating the text from their necessarily culture-bound interpretations, and permitting later generations to explore and to repair other, newly discovered lesions, or gaps of indeterminacy in the surface of meaning. As Kermode says, "it is surely evident that the possibilities of interpretation increase as time goes on. The constraints of a period culture dissolve, generic presumptions which concealed gaps disappear, and we now see that the book, as James thought novels should, truly 'glories in a gap,' a hermeneutic gap in which the reader's imagination must operate, so that he speaks continuously in the text." [2]

The chapters that follow concern four classics, at least in the primary sense that they continue to be read and offer conspicuously rich opportunities for the generation of meaning. Interpreters of such texts have problems as well as opportunities: the very openness of the invitation defeats, or at least renders partial and provisional, all interpretive responses. Faced with this dilemma, as they always are, even with non-classic texts, readers must themselves find a way to "glory in a gap," to profit, rather than suffer, from indeterminacy and ambivalence. Nothing better prepares a reader for such a challenge than a study of the grotesque. I have chosen the subjects of the next four chapters not so much because they are pure nuggets of grotesquerie as because the issues these texts raise are common literary and aesthetic problems, and because a study of the grotesque can help us understand these problems better. To consider the classic from the point of view of the grotesque may seem an impudent enterprise, but if Kermode's view of the classic is correct, as opposed to, say, Eliot's, then we can begin under the authority of an immediate affinity: the grotesque shares with the classic an independence from time, place, and culture achieved in part by a surplus of significance, a pronounced hospitality to interpretation.

As it happens, one of Kermode's classics is also my first one, *Wuthering Heights*. Kermode begins his contribution to the tradition of interpretations with the following sentence: "When Lockwood first visits Wuthering Heights he notices, among otherwise irrelevant decorations carved above the door, the date 1500 and the name *Hareton Earnshaw*."[3] Grotesque-study pays off instantly: as any properly sensitized or competent reader can see, Kermode has missed the crucial detail. The sentence to which he refers reads: "Before passing the threshold, I paused to admire a quantity of grotesque carving lavished over the front, and especially about the principal door, above which, among a wilderness of crumbling griffins and shameless little boys, I detected the date '1500,' and the name 'Hareton Earnshaw'" (14).[4] A sentence pregnant with meanings to be born later in the text; the author in fact aborts no part of it, least of all the carvings above the threshold. As will be my general practice in these chapters, I will precede an analysis of the text with a discussion of the aspect of the grotesque that most illuminates it, an area defined in this case by that wilderness of crumbling griffins and shameless little boys. Seen through the lens of the grotesque, *Wuthering Heights* appears as an exploration of the mysteries and potentialities of the threshold, a decontraction of the carvings above it.

2.

These carvings are probably no more than conventional late Gothic ornament. At worst, such ornamentation might be obscene; in this instance, it is merely tasteless, for it straddles a threshold in decorative art without deciding between the two styles which it holds in suspension. The older style represented by the crumbling griffins is especially interesting. In Chapter Two I discussed the ornamental functions of gargoyles and chimeras briefly, but told only half the story, neglecting the doctrine mingled with decoration. About this doctrine there has been considerable debate; Bernard of Clairvaux's complaint about the distraction (and the costliness) of Romanesque ornamental monsters was not an isolated event, but part of a continuing controversy. Eight hundred and fifty years after Bernard, we still do not know. Otto Springer has contended that gargoyles are sanctioned by the Bible, in Psalm 22:21 and certain images in Isaiah. Others have located dubious "origins" in the remains of prehistoric Silurian beasts dug up during the Middle Ages. The Abbé Auber, whose massive *Histoire et theorie du symbolisme religieux* (1871) articulated a system for interpreting nearly every brick in the cathedral, held that they represented the devils conquered by the Church and made to do the menial labor of sewers (all gargoyles are functional waterspouts).

A cannier, or at least less frustrating, way of interpreting monsters and hybrids is implied by Otto von Simson in his discussion of the ideas of Dionysius the Pseudo-Areopagite, who taught that all created things are manifestations of God. How can this be, considering the manifest imperfection of so many of His creatures?

> The Pseudo-Areopagite answered this question by pointing to the frailty of our intellect, which is incapable of perceiving God face to face. Therefore, God interposes images between Him and us. Holy Writ as well as nature are such "screens"; they present us with images of God, designed to be imperfect, distorted, even contradictory. This imperfection and mutual

contradiction, apparent even to our minds, is to kindle in us the desire to ascend from a world of mere shadows and images to the contemplation of the Divine Light itself. Thus it is, paradoxically enough, by evading us that God becomes gradually manifest; He conceals Himself before us in order to be revealed.⁵

Gargoyles could be considered images of the "screen," figures for the world we perceive with earthly eyes. Compounded of multiple natures, they body forth the multiplicity of the world, and remind us that unity lies beyond our grasp. Their meaning is that they do not mean; we understand them by failing to understand.

Whether they are intentionally incomprehensible or not, these creatures frustrate the modern researcher because there are no contemporary documents to explain their function or significance. They were executed without ecclesiastical supervision by stonemasons who, working sometimes at great heights, had considerable freedom to gratify their own fancies. Liberated from the tyranny of representation and proportion, their fancies ran to play, to marginally representational forms that teased the viewer and drew attention to the process of creation itself. We can try to imagine the sense of freedom felt by a stone carver who, instructed only to make a waterspout, or to punctuate the rhythm of the architecture with some kind of ornament, could luxuriate not only in unfettered stonecraft but in a tradition that stretched as far back as stone carving itself. "The slang of architecture,"⁶ as one writer calls it, grotesque ornament was probably created in a spirit of indifference to symbolic meaning by artists who were simply accustomed to them, or by apprentices who learned them from portfolios of carver's designs handed down from their masters. But no matter how meaningless these forms of ornament may have been to their creators, most students of the subject agree that, like drollery, with its process of desublimation, and like *grottesche,* with its invocation of antiquity, Gothic ornament reaches back to a pre-Christian mythology much older and essentially at odds with the theology of the cathedral, to a code once meaningful but now an ornamental cliché.

In its early days the Church advanced not by subjugation of the popular mythologies, a strategy that would most likely have resulted in Christians' becoming an outcast nomadic tribe of fanatics, but by accommodation and subtle appeasement. The old temples were converted into shrines for Christian worship, and sacrifices were accepted not in honor of the local deities but of the patron saint of the church.[7] Whatever their initial misgivings, the early Christians soon recognized that local popular mythologies, with their veneration of animals and the dead, and their belief in demons, dragons, fabulous beasts, spirits, and witches, were wonderfully suited to their purposes: by converting these figures into images of sin, vice, or the devil, the Church could educate the populace in dramatic fashion through the use of familiar images whose fearsomeness was well understood.

Theology collaborated in this appropriation of myth, encouraging a re-interpretation of its monsters and metamorphic forms. Early in the sixth century, Boethius established the principles of such interpretation:

> ...anything which turns away from goodness ceases to exist, and thus...the wicked cease to be what they once were. That they used to be human is shown by the human appearance of their body which still remains. So it was by falling to wickedness that they also lost their human nature. Now, since only goodness can raise a man above the level of human kind, it follows that it is proper that wickedness thrusts down to a level below mankind those whom it has dethroned from the condition of being human.
>
> The result is that you cannot think of anyone as human whom you see transformed by wickedness.... So what happens is that when a man abandons goodness and ceases to be human, being unable to rise to a divine condition, he sinks to the level of being an animal.[8]

This view of metamorphosis as the expression of moral degradation had immediate effect on Christian art, especially the arts of the margin. Hybrid forms may represent unresolved conflicts, or contamination by evil. D. W. Robertson has written of the medieval assumption that "a man corrupted in some way by sensuality might exhibit animal characteristics, or even plantlike features."[9] This interpretive tradition gives us fresh eyes with which to view the gargoyles and the illuminations: however playful and innocent the stone carvers may have been, the Church provided an official view of their grotesqueries, one that recognized that the search for meaning could never be entirely switched off. As Robertson describes it, this official view was that every form, no matter how ludicrous, had a clear moral application:

> ...a lion in a manuscript decoration may be based on an earlier artistic tradition rather than on observation of actual lions, and this animal may be stretched into a long vertical to fit the column of an initial, graced with an ornamental fishtail to make a flourish, and even given rudimentary wings; but this lion may nevertheless suggest a demon, a vice, a vicious person. To reinforce the suggestion that a lion may have "human application" he may be made parallel in some fashion with a human form or given "human" characteristics.[10]

Through arguments such as these, the Church rationalized the incorporation of its antagonist into itself, preserving a Neolithic paganism of which we have almost no other traces, so that myth lives in the Church and nowhere else.

Whether because it makes the Church appear fallible, "human," or merely confused, this line of argument has enjoyed a perennial popularity. Its latest and most radical incarnation is in Anne Ross's 1974 study, *Grotesques and Gargoyles: Paganism in the Medieval Church*,[11] in which the author attempts to trace a clear and direct connection between the strange figures of the medieval church — the foliate heads, biting heads, devouring heads, bicorporate figures of indeterminate species, hermaphrodites, dragons, centaurs, and "Nobodies"— and specific figures in local mythologies. Most scholars would be wary of interpreting an image of the Antichrist as the Green Man, a folk figure with a long and vital tradition in Northern Europe, and who, like the devil, is a horn-bearing creature with hoofs and tail. But caricature always speaks some truth, and the very possibility of such a split reference opens up a multitude of possibilities for complex interpretation of medieval Christian ornament. Any representation, for example, of the Last Judgment, or of Hell, immediately becomes suspect as a masked repository for the banished images of an ancient and familiar paganism, part of a complex and unofficial system of double meanings and ironic references.

Such a counter-interpretation would have been far more likely in the tenth century than in the fifteenth, for the element of myth, having served its purpose, was gradually phased out, and the search for meaning in decorative designs became if not entirely switched off at least subordinated to the sense of order; increasingly, what meaning was discovered was consonant with Church doctrine and purpose. In fact, Emile Mâle, the great pioneer and popularizer of the study of Christian paganism, insists that even in the eleventh century most decorative art was copied from sources whose iconographic significance was almost entirely obscure: "Decorative art of the Middle Ages began with imitation, and these so-called symbols were often carved from the design of some Persian fabric or Arabian carpet."[12] Mâle cites other possible sources, including certain Anglo-Saxon manuscripts, to make the point that

> The English monks of the sixth century who half in a dream created this strange decorative art, were Christians with something of the old vague paganism of the Germanic tribes still clinging to them. These ancient monsters lurked in the depths of their consciousness, and under their brushes there came back to life fabulous serpents who dwelt in marshes, and winged dragons who guarded treasure in the forest and defended it against the heroes. A whole unconscious mythology reappears in their manuscripts.[13]

Interestingly, Mâle denies any possibility of lingering resonances, any chance of meaning: "The Romanesque sculptors, who so frequently adapted the illuminator's work, copied these living arabesques, attracted simply by their intricacy of line, for these vague dreams of another race and another world could for them have had no meaning."[14] If Ross's sculptor is sly and insidious, knowing better than his masters what he was up to, Mâle's is a *tabula rasa,* an innocent, a blankminded child delighting in "gay invention or good-humored raillery," exulting in the exhibition of craft. "If ever works of art were innocent of ulterior motive," he says, "surely these are... All attempts at explanation must be foredoomed to failure."[15]

The poverty of both positions is apparent. Interpretation always falls between the poles of absolute certainty and absolute indeterminacy, but there is no cause for praise or for censure, as interpretation accompanies every act of perception whether we want it to or not. Bernard's complaints about the decorative excesses of the Cluniac churches indicate not that the monsters we have been studying had no meaning at all, but that, if they were permitted to occupy the capitals, the friezes, the tympanum in a conspicuous way, their meaning, their evocation of a vanished pagan world, might be recognized. Bernard was no opponent of monsters, for the great Bible of Clairvaux, executed under his direction, has many drolleries in the margins; he simply wished them confined to their proper sphere.

Accordingly, the Gothic churches of succeeding centuries banish hybrids and monstrosities to the roof, the choir stalls, and the exterior; Gothic capitals are all foliate. Gone is the atmosphere of magic that pervades Leon, Toulouse, Burgundy, Durham, and Provence; Gothic, as exhibited at Chartres, Paris, Rheims, and Amiens, is more accessible to the intellect, altogether more "spiritual"; what drolleries there are have become objects of ridicule. These changes reflect a decreasing intimacy with ancient myth. As Hans Weigert has said, "romanesque Madonnas were archetypal mothers, descendants of the *Magna Mater,* the mysterious goddess of fertility, whose worship has merged into the cult of the Virgin. The Gothic Madonna is a real-life mother, though of a greater beauty; she has become natural."[16] By the Renaissance, the process of purification is more advanced — it can never be complete — with the result that gargoyles and other stone creatures virtually disappear from the church. The Royal Chapel at Granada, built around 1520 by Ferdinand and Isabella, is one of the first major ecclesiastical structures to be wholly free of Gothic influence. Among other losses, the chapel is free of gargoyles, but their ornamental function and perhaps some of their dim symbolism has been taken over — by *grottesche,* which proliferates on the retable between panels with such conventional centers as St. John the Baptist, the Crucifixion, the Pieta, St. Jerome. By the mid-sixteenth century in much of Europe, *grottesche,* sometimes diluted by the local ornamental mode, had largely replaced the old stonework, substituting designs that were inventive, playful, "artistic," and nearly guaranteed to be meaningless. Art had conquered mythology, it seemed, and after over a millennium of church-building, paganism, the ancient foe, had finally been tamed into loveliness, and disgrace had become merely graceful.

But no matter how attenuated, the force of the grotesque always resists being confined to its "proper sphere." Ernst Kris provides a coda to the story:

> Although the grinning gargoyles on Gothic cathedrals are intended to turn away evil, they look terrifying enough perched high up among the gables and gutters. Their development is interesting. In the thirteenth century these figures of an apotropaic magic are still terrifying. In the fourteenth, they tend to become mere comic masks; by the fifteenth century the process is complete and, instead of threatening, they are only intended to amuse.... The mechanism which determines this functional change of the object is a general one.... Jekels (1926) attempted to explain the secret of comedy as a displacement of the tragic guilt from son to father, and we may add the aphorism: When we laugh at the fool, we never forget that in his comic fancy dress, with bladder and cap, he still carries crown and scepter, symbols of kingship.... The intermediate position of the comic between pleasure and the warding off of emotion, especially fear, even finds expression in our speech. The French word *drôle* has undergone a transformation in meaning from the uncanny to the comic. The word *komisch* in German, as well as the French word *drôle* can be used even today to denote anger or surprise...; and the English word "funny" can be used in a similar way.[17]

3.

We can turn now to *Wuthering Heights,* beginning by noting a striking resemblance between Heathcliff's career and the history of gargoyles. One of the early reviewers, in fact, commented that the book seemed to have been written by Quilp, whom Dickens specifically likens to a gargoyle.[18] Like the gargoyles, Heathcliff represents an older system gradually phased out, but still retaining, even in its most enfeebled state, vestiges of its ancient power. We can see Heathcliff's phases clearly, as they are marked by disappearances and returns. He begins a nasty little horror, a goblin child who seems "possessed of something diabolical" (61), though he earns the trust of old Earnshaw, who brings him into the family to sleep with the children. Upon exposure to the Lintons, the "spiritual" side of Christianity, which is antagonistic to the "lost world," the concept of Earnshaw fractures: Heathcliff is ejected from the childhood bed, Cathy begins her rise, and Hindley, his descent into Heathcliff's power. After a three-year absence, Heathcliff returns looking more intelligent than before, and retaining "no marks of his former degradation"; though a "half-civilized ferocity lurked yet in the depressed brows and eyes full of black fire," his manner is "quite divested of roughness, though too stern for grace" (84). This is an era equivalent to the Romanesque, with Edgar in the role of Bernard, who, contemplating Isabella's marriage to Heathcliff, dreads "the degradation of an alliance to a nameless man"; Edgar knows that "though Heathcliff's exterior was altered, his mind was unchangeable, and unchanged" (88). In their climactic confrontation, Edgar tells Heathcliff that his presence "is a moral poison that would contaminate the most virtuous" (99) and denies him admission into the house. With the death of Catherine, Heathcliff's "better half" (152), Edgar's ban is effected, and the nameless man is consigned to the outside, though his power there is great. By the end Heathcliff is a superannuated tyrant, and if his presence is neither ludicrous nor decorative, it is increasingly irrelevant; Catherine and Hareton scheme behind his back, and Nelly Dean addresses him with the quizzical fearlessness with which one might approach a glaring stone drollery: "'Tell me why you are so queer, Mr. Heathcliff. Where were you last night?'" (259). Heathcliff is so queer because he is an extreme case of the crushing of the successive into the simultaneous: his existence compresses a history that took centuries to enact. Nor is it concluded. At the end, Heathcliff, though buried "beneath," still walks the moors with Cathy in a shadowy existence comparable to the secondary meanings of *"drôle," "komisch,"* and "funny."

The question raised by the gargoyle — Is this compatible with God's majesty? — is translated in the novel into a question about Heathcliff: Is this, too, human? Heathcliff is called a "hellish villain," a "fiend," a "devil" (many times), a "cuckoo," and a "goblin." Nelly feels on one occasion when he is gnashing his teeth and foaming like a dog that she is not "in the company of a creature of my own species" (134). It is asserted that he has "kin beneath," that he is a "ghoul, or a vampire," and that he is "only half a man-not so much." These doubts gather into Isabella's sincere and precisely phrased inquiry concerning her new husband: "'Is Mr. Heathcliff a man? If so, is he mad? And if not, is he a devil?'" (115)

Such questions are put so often and with such urgency that they are no longer completely figurative, but acquire a quasi-literalness that takes them out of the category of verbal abuse. They signal real doubts as to Heathcliff's nature. The reader can no more dismiss these doubts than can Nelly Dean or Isabella, with the result that a single question has dominated the criticism of *Wuthering Heights* from its appearance until the present: What kind of book is this? Is this, too, a "novel"? One of the very first reviews to appear concluded, after a catalogue of the author's confusions, that "we must leave it to our readers to decide what sort of book it is."[19] They have not yet decided. E. M. Forster classed it as prophecy, a mode whose "theme is the universe" and whose "face is to unity."[20] Even though there are only four truly prophetic writers —the other three are Melville, D. H. Lawrence, and Dostoevsky — Emily Brontë, he admits, is anomalous even in such select company. In the 1960s Q. D. Leavis was still untangling the tale's "incompatible fragments and disjointed intentions at different levels of seriousness," deciding, with a firmness worthy of St. Bernard, that Yorkshire realism, as exemplified in Nelly Dean, Joseph, and Zillah, was the center, and Heathcliff was peripheral, receiving "very perfunctory attention."[21] These and many others either implicitly or explicitly support the notion that the novel is, in the word of V. S. Pritchett, "unique."[22] But this assertion of singularity has recently been contradicted by James Kincaid, who, segregating four distinct genres in the narrative, has held it up as an example of an "incoherent text,"[23] a class into which all narratives fall. Heathcliff, an anomalous human character but an exemplary grotesque, is the source of this confusion; his being filters through the world of the text in a manner described by Cathy, "like wine through water" (72). If the question, Is Mr. Heathcliff a man? is not exactly the same question as, Is this text a novel? at least they may have the same answer.

One of the characteristics that makes this text rest uneasily in the company of other novels is the pre-Jamesian use of multiple narrators, all of whom play a part in the story they tell, and all of whom must therefore be distrusted. At least this is the assumption of post-Jamesian critics: "the reader," writes one, "must maintain a constant skepticism about the alterations Nelly must have made in the remembered speeches of her characters and also about the alterations Lockwood may have made in his transmission of Nelly's report and in his own remembrances of conversations he himself heard."[24] To maintain this "constant skepticism" is like applying transistor technology to repairing a barn door, a charge easily enough demonstrated by pointing to the negligible, even negative, interpretive results of such skepticism. If we assume that all accounts swerve from the truth, then we must be able to construct a "true" *Wuthering Heights* by eliminating such excesses and omissions and distortions as can be inferred from a character analysis of the various narrators. We cannot: skepticism in this regard is a dead end.

The major obstacle to such a reconstructed truth has never been noted: the fact that all narrators, as long as they are telling the story, speak in the same voice. Although each is distinguishable when not narrating the events that constitute the story of Heathcliff, all such differences are elided once the narrator slips into that story. Nelly loses her aphorisms and regionalisms, Isabella drops her dashes and her impetuous whining. Even Zillah takes a polish:

> That was a great advance for the lad. She didn't thank him; still, he felt gratified that she had accepted his assistance, and ventured to stand behind as she examined them, and even to stoop and point out what struck his fancy in certain old pictures which they contained; nor was he daunted by the saucy style in which she jerked the page from his finger.... (234-35)

Cathy, in her childhood diary, surrenders her customary violence of expression and moves toward a neutral literary middle:

> I reached this book, and a pot of ink from a shelf, and pushed the house door ajar to give me light, and I have got the time on with writing for twenty minutes; but my companion is impatient and proposes that we should appropriate the dairy woman's cloak, and have a scamper on the moors, under its shelter. A pleasant suggestion-and then, if the surly old man come in, he may believe his prophecy verified.... (27)

Even the boy Heathcliff, narrating Cathy's capture at the Lintons, adopts a "literary" ungainliness: "'What prey, Robert?' hallooed Linton from the entrance" (48). It is possible to piece Heathcliff's story together by omitting the personal intrusions and the bits that serve as transitions to and from this story. Though there are many tellers, this tale is remarkably univocal.

The speech of the narration, with its overall plainness, its occasional self-consciousness and forced phrasings, and its lengthy sentences, is characteristic of the speech of no one of the characters when they are speaking naturally. This takeover of the narrator by the narrative is particularly obvious at the junctures where a character slips out of the narrative, such as the end of Chapter XIV and the beginning of Chapter XV. Nelly concludes her account: "Notwithstanding, my journey homeward was sadder than my journey thither; and many misgivings I had, ere I could prevail on myself to put the missive into Mrs. Linton's hand." In the next sentence she becomes herself: "But here is Kenneth; I'll go down, and tell him how much better you are. My history is *dree* as we say, and will serve to wile away another morning" (130). The chapter ends; Lockwood is left musing by himself, a condition we discover him in again a week later when the next chapter begins. He has been listening to Nelly all week, and now wishes to tell us what he has heard. His own prettified style is clearly unacceptable for the tale, a problem he solves ingeniously: "Another week over-and I am so many days nearer health, and spring! I have now heard all my neighbour's history, at different sittings.... I'll continue it in her own words, only a little condensed. She is, on the whole, a very fair narrator and I don't think I could improve her style" (130). The next sentence begins the story, which continues, in slightly condensed form, for fifteen chapters. This is his most prodigious feat of memory, but not his only one. Earlier, he had recalled the exact words of Cathy's diary, despite the tempests of the night.

What I am suggesting is that, in a wholly un-Jamesian way, the narrators themselves are effaced, and not the "truth." They do not narrate, but are narrated by, the narrative. Lockwood comes to Wuthering Heights, and dreams not his dream but Heathcliff's, the dream of the window. His speaking fifteen chapters (chapters?) of another's words is only one example of the narrative's detachment from, rather than distortion by, its tellers: it gets itself told virtually without their mediation, even against their will. In a post-Jamesian narrative the effect of Chinese-box narration might be to displace the creative presence or to put the narrated events into question. In "Menelaiad," in *Lost in the Funhouse,* for example, John Barth plays with narrators within narrators to an absurd extent that stresses the technical aspect of narration — and therefore the alienation of the narrative from the mythic material that is its subject. But in *Wuthering Heights* there is no such alienation and the effect is the opposite: we are aware that everything is sifted through strata of personality, and also aware that this counts for nothing. We are drawn away from technique, away from characters, away even from author, and toward the story. Now all stories have to get told, and convention permits a certain improbability in the telling. But in this case such a convention is conspicuous, so we can see what it looks like.

What it looks like is myth, which spreads like a stain not only through narrators but through entire cultures, disregarding even language barriers. Myth effects its totalizing and unifying functions through a perfect transmissibility achieved in part by an indifference to language: myth loses nothing in translation; it is intended to be translated. According to Lévi-Strauss, even the plot can be deformed without damage to the myth, which consists ultimately only of structures. All versions of a myth are equally the myth, even Freud's "version" of Oedipus or Sylvester Stallone's of Cinderella, for the myth is independent of language, character, point of view, and narrative sequence.[25] As Lévi-Strauss says, in words that apply equally to *Wuthering Heights,* myth "has no author"; it "speaks itself."

Another casualty of the effacement of the narrative personality is the time scheme of the narrative, which, again, sets it apart from other novels. Prose narratives are generally highly attentive to causality, to the relationship between past, present, and future. In *Wuthering Heights,* both the immemorial past and the eternal future are ploughed into the present. The past seems massively alive, but featureless and vast; it is wholly realized in the repetition of family names, the continuation of family pursuits, family habitations. The future is more complicated. It is constantly invoked in the form of heaven and hell, but invoked in such a curious way that Forster could say that "no great book is more cut off from the universals of Heaven and Hell."[26] Forster may be thinking of Cathy's dream, where she enters heaven with her heart breaking for her beloved Wuthering Heights, and is thrown out by the angels. But he is also reflecting the fact that, especially for Cathy and Heathcliff, the afterlife entails a translation but not a relocation: it happens *here*. If he lost Cathy, Heathcliff says, "Two words would comprehend my future — *death* and *hell*"; and then adds, "existence after losing her would be hell" (125–26). But hell can be in anticipation, too, for when he returns after his three-years' absence he tells Nelly to carry a message to Cathy, adding, "I'm in hell till you do" (82). At the point of death, Cathy scolds her lover, tormenting him with the prospect of her imminent escape into "that glorious world" (134): "You have killed me," she says, paradoxically but with no sense of incongruity; "I only wish us never to be parted — and should a word of mine distress you hereafter, think I feel the same distress underground, and for my own sake, forgive me!" (133) Emotion is independent of life; one can feel "the same distress" underground as above. No story has a terminus, only a slight change of scene. For Heathcliff, in fact, the real story does not begin until death, when, liberated from the hell of chronological bodily life, his essence — no disembodied spirit but a physical quality of his corpse — can creep through the clay to mingle and fuse with Cathy. The energies of this subterranean story, which is out of time and therefore no "story" at all, drive the novelistic story, which is not "superficial" but only "on the surface," deforming it according to its own pattern, making it strange.

For Heathcliff and Cathy there is no sense of a future in any way resembling the present. There is only the anguish of individuation above, and the peace of fusion below. Bounded by the infinities of past and future, present time, the time of novels, is an interruption, an atypical gap tormented by memories and anticipation of bliss, which is to say, the absence of stories. Above-ground time in *Wuthering Heights* is precisely demarcated: events are calculated sometimes even to the hour, and bound together by a before and after causality that required C. P. Sanger to employ a lawyer's knowledge of wills and intestacies in unraveling the plot's intricacies.[27] These intricacies are the plot, the means by which Heathcliff acquires property through the manipulation of legal documents. The success of this manipulation depends not upon the grandeur of his wrath, nor upon his titanic love for Cathy, nor yet upon his harnessing the wind or unleashing the thunder; it depends upon split-second timing. If Lawyer Green reaches Edgar Linton's bedside in time, the will can be altered, putting Thrushcross Grange in the hands of trustees so that Heathcliff cannot get it. (He does not, having been bought off by Heathcliff.) Heathcliff finally obtains the property because Catherine marries Linton in the nick of time, just before Linton dies. Sanger traces all these events in his article, which has achieved considerable fame because it reveals an unexpected but wholly consistent and undeniably "real" plot that accounts for so much that mere passion seems inconsequential, an ornament to a story that might have been called *The Man of Property*. But from another point of view, all the events Sanger discusses seem equally inconsequential, for the narrative presents the resolution of a pattern so primordial and ancient that it seems carved in granite, like the date 1500 above the threshold to Wuthering Heights. Compared to Sanger's dates, that date constitutes a different species of time, with units so large that hours and minutes, days and weeks, dissolve into unreality as bits too infinitesimal to measure. As a series of events, the narrative is both excruciatingly exact and wholly indifferent to sequence and precise calculation, a tension even Sanger acknowledges in reducing the plot, which his analysis has shown to be filled with suspense, to a diagram of relationship so balanced, so neat, that he comments, "In actual life I have never come across a pedigree of such absolute symmetry.... It is a remarkable piece of symmetry in a tempestuous book."[28]

Sanger is not the only critic to attempt to explain the novel by means of spatial structures such as charts, diagrams, or tables.[29] The receptivity of the text to this kind of explication indicates its affinity to classificatory systems rather than to the linear system of time we normally associated with narrative. This affinity is more evidence of the text's unusually direct and unmediated indebtedness to myth. All novels have a spatial dimension which we acknowledge whenever we talk of "form," "pattern," "structure," "point of view," "surface meaning," etc., but this spatiality is generally not the theme of the novel, but a side effect of "craft": its working-out produces a sense of "fitness" or "resolution." If *Wuthering Heights* caricatures the novel's attention to linear time, causality and the irreversible event on the one hand, it also caricatures the novel's attention to structure on the other. While the plot is going forward through irreversible events in time, it is also standing still, presenting replicated acts in space. Replication, by which I mean something stronger than mere parallelism, is everywhere. Lockwood fears that Cathy may turn out to be a "second edition" of her mother, and this fear is not idle. Hareton is a second edition of Heathcliff, rising from ignorance and degradation to ownership of the property. The simple repetition of names within the Earnshaw line engenders a repetition of event: Edgar will lie dead with Catherine beside him; shortly after, another Linton will die, with the same Catherine seated beside him. This is Linton Heathcliff; and in recalling his death we may recall Heathcliff's dream of himself lying side by side in the grave with Cathy, their cheeks frozen together. The third Linton, Isabella, is connected to Catherine through their sullen imprisonment at Wuthering Heights under Heathcliff. And all the crossings between Grange and Heights, beginning with Heathcliff's and Cathy's ramble on the moors, have analogues in the others. Such patterns of replication give rise to spatial analysis partly because their origins are clearly the family structures and the bipolarity of Grange and Heights, which is to say the space of the novel.

This space is so huge and hugely potent as to compel and define human character itself. Before Cathy's incarceration at the Grange, there seems to have been little or no intercourse between the two houses; there is no indication that Lintons and Earnshaws had ever intermarried. Each house produces the kind of person appropriate to its setting. Hindley's marriage is presumably typical: an Earnshaw goes out and retrieves a cipher whose presence is necessary for the generation of more place-defined Earnshaws. The impression given is as close as a novel can come to the mythic principle of autochthony, according to which fertility is attributed to place rather than to biological generation.

Emily Brontë is even stranger than she seems. Within a primitive kinship system, identity is shared, regardless of status. According to her compromise between myth and biology, people can mysteriously inhabit one another, occasionally peering out from the other's eyes. According to Isabella, when Cathy dies, she migrates to her brother: "Now that she's dead," she tells Heathcliff, "I see her in Hindley; Hindley has exactly her eyes, if you had not tried to gouge them out and make them black and red...." (150). Nelly's words are no mere figures of speech; they account for Heathcliff's attack on Hindley's eyes more convincingly than any other explanation. Heathcliff's yearning for a quasi-physical fusion with Cathy expresses this confusion of myth and biology; we are "one" with our mates in a figurative sense, but he knows nothing of metaphors, nothing of "as if." This is why he is so tortured by resemblances: they are to him identities which, as a biological outsider, he cannot attain. Near the end, Heathcliff ponders the problem of Hareton: "when I look for his father in his face, I find *her* every day more! How the devil is he so like? I can hardly bear to see him" (240). Catherine is not only a second edition of her mother, but a version or retelling of Hareton. As Nelly informs Lockwood, "Perhaps you have never remarked that their eyes are precisely similar, and they are those of Catherine Earnshaw" (254). Approaching death, and total fusion, Heathcliff's metaphorical faculty begins to go berserk:

> what is not connected with her to me? and what does not recall her? I cannot look down to this floor, but her features are shaped on the flags! In every cloud, in every tree — filling the air at night, and caught by glimpses in every object by day, I am surrounded with her image! The most ordinary faces of men and women —my own features — mock me with a resemblance. The entire world is a dreadful collection of memoranda that she did exist, and that I have lost her! (255)

If Heathcliff flows through Cathy like wine through water, Cathy is also in Heathcliff: "'I *cannot* live without my life!" he cries; "'I *cannot* live without my soul!" (139) After she dies, he prays constantly for her "'to return to me — her spirit" (229).

Heathcliff is both the most physical and the most spiritual character imaginable. But this is only one among so many contradictions that we could fairly say that ambivalence itself is the key, the governing principle of his character. In the queer frozen world of the novel, Heathcliff is utterly without precedent, an anomaly. And yet he is a perfect image of that world and can be seen as a highly efficient figure, a condensed version of it. And, in gathering into himself the contradictions of a half-mythic, half-historical world, he also embodies the torsions of the text itself.

The Grange-Heights world takes the form of a tiny, furiously active indoors organized along family lines; and a huge, inchoate, nearly sentient but alien outdoors, the moors themselves.[30] With no traceable biological origins, Heathcliff has strong connections with this outside, and is cast in the role of the Other. The name he is given reinforces his connection to the outside. But the name actually refers to a border: the Nab, where Heathcliff and Cathy are seen "walking" at the end of the novel, is literally a cliff of heath, marking the margin of Wuthering Heights property. And so it is fitting that "Heathcliff" also reinforces a connection to the inside, as it was the name of an Earnshaw son who had died in childhood. A remarkable phoneme, mediating and modulating between biological and autochthonic generation. As his only name, it gathers antimonies into itself, making two into one.

He is entirely a creature of doorways, windows, and other boundaries. Where a margin is, there will Heathcliff be, permitting transit, destabilizing, unlocking combinatory possibilities. As an autochthonous being, he sponsors the moorlands, which Cathy discovers through him, conceiving in the process a love that "resembles the eternal rocks beneath" (74). Heathcliff speaks for what Lévi-Strauss calls the mythic sense of sacred space: "It could even be said that being in their place is what makes [objects] sacred for if they were taken out of their place, even in thought, the entire order of the universe would be destroyed."[31] But, in a characteristic paradox, he both inculcates a sense of the sacredness of space and destroys that sacredness as well. His expedition to the Grange with Cathy upsets the ancient order of things, shattering the grip of autochthony, and inaugurating the long series of trips back and forth, all with the single aim of biological generation. A ramble on the moors means exposure to the Grange, an alternative, significant human culture. Cathy has a choice; space is now seen not only as a place in its own right, but as a form of existence *between* houses. The world has cracked open, and human personality, hitherto a function of Grange or Heights, flourishes in the gap.

A certain poignancy attends Heathcliff. As embodied ambivalence, he can open entrances others could not have opened for themselves, or he can bar them, but he cannot fully occupy any place. By the same evolutionary logic that attracts her to Heathcliff as a principle of advancement, Cathy must reject him, once she is exposed to Edgar, as a principle of regression. Catherine is a transitional figure, too, the first pioneer to make the crossing. She acts on behalf of future generations, in which Heathcliff can have no part, as he has no human origins.[32] But the depth of her alliance with Heathcliff is vividly indicated in the famous passage where she tells Nelly, "I *am* Heathcliff — he's always, always in my mind — not as a pleasure, any more than I am always a pleasure to myself — but as my own being — so, don't talk of our separation again — it is impracticable…" (74). She is a martyr to biology, giving up her home "out there" as an act of evolutionary self-sacrifice. Kermode says of Heathcliff that he is "neither wholly master nor wholly servant, the husband who is no husband, the brother who is no brother, the father who abuses his changeling child, the cousin without kin." Similar phrases could be applied to Cathy — the sister who is no sister, the daughter who is no daughter, the mother who is no mother, the lover who is no lover, the wife who is no wife. If Heathcliff is no human "character," but simply embodied ambivalence, Cathy is all too human; which is to say, she lives in multiple and mutually exclusive worlds.

In *The Raw and the Cooked*,[33] Lévi-Strauss advanced the theory that myth always explores and mediates the binary distinction between nature and culture, or "raw" and "cooked." The fact that this distinction can be so directly applied to Grange and Heights, with Heathcliff in the position of mediator, indicates the depth to which myth is woven into the novel: everything that makes the text unusual, everything that raises the question of genre or category, can be traced to the vivid presence of such mythic attitudes and concerns. Can we be more specific? As it happens, Lévi-Strauss provides the means by which we can.

In his famous essay on *Oedipus Rex,* Lévi-Strauss discusses the "Theban" myths as mediations of a felt contradiction in human nature, a confusion surrounding the origin and place of humanity:

> The myth has to do with the inability, for a culture which holds the belief that mankind is autochthonous…to find a satisfactory transition between this theory and the knowledge that human beings are actually born from the union of man and woman.[34]

Like Emily Brontë's novel, the myth stands at the crisis point in the evolution of the concept of "the human," mediating between the old and new positions through a "fugal" structure that balances images implying the "overrating of blood relationships" on the one hand with images implying the "underrating of blood relationships" on the other.

Born from one, or born from two? This is the question beneath the riddling question, What sort of creature walks on four legs in the morning, two legs at noon, and three legs in the evening? Oedipus' answer is "Man." Catherine's is scrawled on the ledge of a window at Wuthering Heights: "a name repeated in all kinds of characters, large and small — *Catherine Earnshaw,* here and there varied to *Catherine Heathcliff,* and then again to *Catherine Linton"* (25).

Is humanity within nature (four-legged, like the animals), outside of nature (bipeds without feathers), or half in, half out? As lion/eagle/human, the sphinx, like Heathcliff, poses this question by his very existence, for it is human, animal, and grotesque, or mingled. Oedipus's answer indicates that the solution to the riddle of "Man" is "Sphinx," for it implies an acceptance of all three possibilities. Yet hidden in this acceptance lies a crucial concession to the new and a rejection of the old. There is a logical progression, an arc of increasing alienation, from four legs to three to two. The sphinx permits a retention of the old principle while fostering a recognition of the new. Heathcliff works in this way for Cathy. Through him she tacitly surrenders the view of the nonessential or insignificant mate, and passes over to a new, biological view, represented by Edgar Linton.

4.

The riddle is posed again in the second generation, with Catherine actually assuming all three names. By the end of the novel, an Earnshaw has become a Linton, and a Linton an Earnshaw, walking to the Grange with her husband; and Heathcliff, who created these marriages but who himself walks impossibly on three legs, is through. Like the griffins above the threshold, he crumbles while the little boys, figures of biology, continue to disport. After Cathy's death, Heathcliff metamorphoses, appearing now as an older principle in monstrous form, the chaos against and out of which creation must struggle. He appears as Evil. Edmund Leach and others have compared the Oedipus myth and the Adamic myth on the basis that they both explore the logical basis of incest categories;[35] Heathcliff's conversion from sphinx to serpent enables us to see other connections between the myths, just as the myths enable us to see worlds within worlds in the novel.

What does the serpent mean; and how does it help us understand Heathcliff? Responding to the first question, J. Coppens has built a formidable case for the serpent in Christian art as a symbol of ancient gods of vegetation. A "chthonic" animal from beneath the surface of the earth, the serpent does not represent sexuality itself but rather the "temptation to place sexual life under the influence of the licentious pagan cults and so to surrender it to dissolution."[36] It may also represent autochthony itself, with the Garden as sacred, fertile space: Eve does not become pregnant by Adam until after she has left it. According to Paul Ricoeur, the serpent is the "only monster who survived from the theogonic myths," the only one which has conspicuously *"not* been demythologized. The Yahwist only says — and it is a capital point — that he also is a creature."[37] The serpent is "chthonic" paganism that is left unreconstructed, but made into evil.

Ricoeur's study of *The Symbolism of Evil* is the most systematic attempt to understand the dynamics of such conversions, and many of his conclusions apply with surprising directness to Heathcliff. One side of our world, Ricoeur says, confronts us only as chaos, and is symbolized by the chthonic animal. The serpent is thus a part of ourselves we do not recognize: it represents "this passive aspect of temptation, hovering on the border between the outer and the inner; the Decalogue calls it 'covetousness' (Tenth Commandment)."[38] This inner affinity, receptivity, or responsiveness to temptation could account for the fact that, as Leach says, Christian artists have always given "the monster a somewhat hermaphrodite appearance while still indicating some kind of identification between the Serpent and Eve herself." Hugo Van der Goes, Leach adds, "puts Eve and the Serpent in the same posture; Michelangelo makes Adam and Eve both gaze with loving adoration on the Serpent, but the Serpent has Eve's face."[39] William Blake is even more daring: in "Satan Exulting Over Eve" and "Elohim Creating Adam," the serpent appears first *entwined* around Eve, and then *as part of* Adam himself. As Ricoeur says, the serpent symbolizes "something of man *and* something of the world...the chaos *in* me, *among* us, and *outside."*[40] With deep roots in mythic "participation," evil is the "consecration of multiplicity in ourselves,"[41] undermining our pretenses to a discrete, individual, and pure identity.

There are temptations and temptations. The connection between the repellent serpent and the fantasies of sexual extravaganzas, personal heroism, and consumer paradise with which our communications media bombard us may not be immediately apparent. But Isabella Linton could explain the connection, for she married a manifest demon, picturing in him "a hero of romance" (126). In the Adamic myth, temptation attacks "woman," a figure for the point of weakness through which evil enters the human being. Ricoeur argues that, as all humans have this point of weakness, evil is never truly external: except as humans let it, it does not live. This inside-outside quality also describes Heathcliff. We are so accustomed to seeing him as a creature of fabulous sexual dynamism and intellectual power, of raw force and all-conquering will, that we overlook the fact that he never once initiates a significant action. For all his visibility, his direct influence is practically nil. Moreover, what force he does exert is almost wholly benevolent.

The demonstration of this point requires a careful attention to details of plot. Let us begin with Heathcliff's very first action, which is typical of all the rest. Old Earnshaw has given ponies to both Heathcliff and Hindley, but Heathcliff's has fallen lame and he wants to exchange ponies. As always, his approach is direct: "You must exchange horses with me; I don't like mine, and if you won't I shall tell your father of the three thrashings you've given me this week, and show him my arm, which is black to the shoulder" (41). In response, Hindley beats him, and Heathcliff replies that if Hindley throws the iron weight he has seized, old Earnshaw will be informed of Hindley's threat to turn Heathcliff out of doors as soon as the old man died. Hindley throws it anyway, striking Heathcliff in the chest. Nelly, who has observed everything, intervenes, with the narrative comment that Heathcliff could at that moment have gone to the master and "got full revenge by letting his condition plead for him ..." (41). Hindley gives him the colt, and Heathcliff says nothing to Earnshaw.

Now who has forced the exchange? Not Heathcliff, who has merely suggested it. In a much more direct way, Earnshaw has forced it: the threat of punishment persuades Hindley that his interests are best served by the trade. In fact, Hindley himself has compelled agreement to Heathcliff's suggestion by abusing him so cruelly. Old Earnshaw favors Heathcliff solely on merit, for Hindley is reckless and irresponsible, and Cathy is "too mischievous and wayward for a favourite" (40). Heathcliff is patient, forbearing, selfless, sober, and honest, saying "precious little," as Nelly admits, "and generally the truth" (40).

Hindley is also to blame for Heathcliff's acquisition of Wuthering Heights. It is he who invites Heathcliff in when he returns after his three-years' absence, he who desires Heathcliff to join a game of cards, he who loses money, he who requests that Heathcliff return the following evening. And when the property has been gambled away, it is Hindley who turns vindictive, attempting to murder Heathcliff when he returns to the house after his graveyard vigil over Cathy. On this occasion, Heathcliff, after disarming Hindley and gaining entry, does indeed beat Hindley; but then, in Isabella's words, he exerted "preterhuman self-denial in abstaining from finishing him completely," finally dragging Hindley to the settle and binding his wounds (147). Later, as the doctor Kenneth attests, Hindley purposely drinks himself to death. Throughout, Hindley is the sole agent.

And yet somehow Heathcliff's presence is crucial and poisonous. He is nowhere more influential than in the incident in Chapter XXVII where he apparently compels the marriage of Catherine and Linton. But here as elsewhere he is highly visible but largely redundant.

The attachment was formed before Heathcliff had ever seen the boy, when Linton was brought to the Grange after his mother's death. Linton is almost immediately, and legally, removed to the Heights, and Catherine, against advice from Nelly and the specific commands of her father, goes to great pains to seek him out. Heathcliff is blunt with Nelly concerning his plans: "My design is as honest as possible. I'll inform you of its whole scope...that the two cousins may fall in love, and get married" (174). But this design is not his at all, for it is proceeding independent of him. All Heathcliff does is to place Linton in Catherine's way, where he would have put himself anyway, and enjoin him to be "cheerful" (214). Later, when she is prevented from writing, Catherine visits Linton secretly, and when she finds herself trapped in Wuthering Heights by Heathcliff's demand that she should marry Linton before leaving it, she must take full responsibility. The event is so constructed as to exonerate Heathcliff entirely. Nelly, Catherine, Linton, and Heathcliff meet on the open road. Linton is ill and wishes to return to the Heights. Heathcliff's wish, which Linton expresses, is that Catherine take him back. When she demurs, Heathcliff instantly offers to take Linton back himself rather than violate Catherine's "filial scruples" (214). But for some reason, Catherine suddenly insists on joining Linton, who has clung to her, and taking him back herself. As

Heathcliff tells her later, "You cannot deny that you entered my house of your own accord, in contempt of [your father's] injunctions to the contrary" (218). She does not even try to deny it.

Once in, Catherine agrees to marry Linton even before Heathcliff demands it of her: "I promise to marry Linton — papa would like me to, and I love him — and why should you wish to force me to do what I'll willingly do of myself?" (218) In fact, he does not force her. He does not even detain her, Linton does: he tells Nelly that he can get the key any time he chooses (223). Heathcliff has scarcely a villainy to call his own. Even Nelly steals sin from the devil, meditating during her incarceration that "all the misfortunes of all my employers" sprang from her own "derelictions of duty." She even concludes that "Heathcliff himself [was] less guilty than I" (220). Heathcliff is not guilty at all, for in all his acts, he is, as Isabella says regarding his ferocious beating of Hindley, "not the aggressor" (148).

Heathcliff is, rather, a black hole into which others fall if they are not securely anchored; or a principle of chaos that enters if the doors and windows are not fastened. Isabella is a perfect example. A charming young lady of eighteen, she evinces a "sudden and irresistible attraction," a dramatic Heathcliff-event that leaves her powerless to avoid him (88). The prospect of such a marriage revolts Edgar, who counsels her; it appalls Cathy, who scolds her. And on the night of their elopement, Heathcliff hangs her dog so she can be certain of his character before marrying him. She is certain; and she marries him. It is an utterly anomalous and inexplicable event, which is yet replicated everywhere — especially in Catherine's curious attraction to Linton, who has some of the Heathcliff magic despite his sugar-sucking effeminacy.

Linton is a true Heathcliff creation. The father looks in vain for any trace of himself in the son, for Linton seems simply a more whining and contemptible version of Isabella: "'Where is *my* share in thee, puling chicken?' " (169). His share is precisely nothing. Biology is a function of family and place; biologically, Heathcliff counts for nothing. Linton is a product of Isabella and nothing.

Heathcliff's other creation, Hareton, demonstrates another facet of negativity. So degraded under his foster father's tutelage that Catherine could weep outright "at the bare notion of relationship with such a clown" (160), Hareton is described again and again as a brute, an animal, an exquisite artistry of debasement, forever sunk, as Heathcliff says with some pride, in "his bathos of coarseness and ignorance" (178). How does one come to such a condition? In Hareton's case, the answer is simply neglect. But one side of neglect is freedom. As Hareton says, when still a boy, "he [Heathcliff] says I mun do as I will" (95). Heathcliff is never accused of mistreating Hareton; indeed, somehow the lad has gotten to be a competent farmhand. Heathcliff has merely allowed — as he always allows — nature to take its course. Hareton is in this sense "nature's" foster child and inmate, Man. The worst that can be said about him is Nelly's estimate that "he was never taught to read or write; never rebuked for any bad habit which did not annoy his keeper; never led a single step towards virtue, or guarded by a single precept against vice" (161). In other words, he is illiterate and talks like a Yorkshireman. He has no vices; he loves his parent; he is comfortable with himself. Many children, raised under parents more like Hindley than Heathcliff, may envy such an upbringing.

To conceive Heathcliff as a negative force is not at all incompatible with earlier descriptions of him as a mediating force, or even as an expression of mythic potency. The early history of the Church reveals not only how myth became evil but also how evil became nothing, a gap in creation, an absence of being, a privation. This tradition goes back as far as the Pseudo-Dionysius — who himself had developed an older theory held by the Neo-Platonists. We can trace it through Augustine, Boethius, and Aquinas, all of whom derive their ideas in part from Old Testament attacks on mythic deities. "All the gods of the nations are nothing," the Psalmist says (96:5); and Yahweh addresses the false gods: "You are nothing and your works are nought; to choose you is abominable" (II Isaiah 41:24). Augustine expresses the concept through the common metaphor of disease:

> In the bodies of animals, disease and wounds mean nothing but the absence of health; for when a cure is effected, that does not mean that the evils which were present — namely, the diseases and wounds — go away from the body and dwell elsewhere: they altogether cease to exist; for the wound or disease is not a substance, but a defect in the fleshly substance.... Just in the same way, what are called vices in the soul are nothing but privations of natural good. And when they are not transferred

elsewhere: when they cease to exist in the healthy soul, they cannot exist anywhere else.[42]

Those who would seek Heathcliff as a positive force commit, in terms of interpretation, the Manichean heresy, to whose seductive comforts Augustine himself was so vulnerable. According to this doctrine, espoused by a teacher named Faustus, "it is not we who sin but some other nature that sins within us."[43] Edgar Linton is something of a Manichean, for he is fascinated, almost hypnotized, by the figure of Heathcliff: "he dreaded that mind; it revolted him; he shrank forebodingly from the idea of committing Isabella to its keeping" (88). In his final confrontation with Heathcliff, Edgar tells him, "Your presence is a moral poison that would contaminate the most virtuous..." (99). Augustine could gloss this curious pronouncement according to the beliefs of the Manicheans, who held that evil was a substance, "a shapeless, hideous mass, which might be solid, in which case the Manichees called it earth, or fine and rarefied like air. This they imagine as a kind of evil mind filtering through the substance they call earth."[44] Edgar's reaction to Heathcliff may be irrational, but Heathcliff must count among his enemies reason itself. In his logic, *p* and *not-p* — himself and Cathy — can occupy the same space at the same time: contemplating his imminent death, burial, and brain-eating orgy, he tells Nelly that "by the time Linton gets to us, he'll not know which is which!" (228–29). To think of such a prospect is anguish to the reasonable mind. As Ricoeur says of "Defilement," "What resists reflection is the idea of a quasi-material something that infects as a sort of filth, that harms by invisible properties, that nevertheless works in the manner of a force in the field of our undividedly psychic and corporeal existence."[45]

The idea of nothing does not lodge easily in the mind; the natural impulse is to fill a gap, even if only with "a quasi-material something," and for this reason a form of Manicheism is hard to avoid. In words Edgar Linton would comprehend, Ricoeur comments that "Dread of the impure and rites of purification are in the background of all our feeling and all our behavior relating to fault."[46]

Laws are intended to establish the definition of order and thereby discourage disorder, or impurity, which is punished by incarceration. But, through infection, laws are sometimes agents of the very contamination they combat. This infection enables us to understand a final riddle of Heathcliff-the source of his power. It is the law. Whatever gains he makes, the law has secured them. In his words, he keeps "strictly within the limits of the law" (227), so strictly that, from a certain point of view, it could be said that everything that happens would have happened without his intervention. He has permitted and attended, but he has not compelled. The law has done that. The flinty testament he makes to the lawyer Green at the end of his life —"'I've done no injustice, and I repent of nothing'" (262) — is no display of unregenerate wickedness, but simple truth.

5.

The nearest thing to Heathcliff in narrative is not another character, but the court of Chancery in Dickens's *Bleak House*. The tangled cluster of laws by which both Heathcliff and Chancery operate conceal a sucking void into which the weak — Hindley, Richard Carstone — fall to their ruin. Heathcliff works like a poison, Chancery like a vast fog; they both pollute and defile, and they both require expiation. In both novels the law is so intertwined with evil that the authority and legitimacy of law itself are brought into question, with the result that both novels are obsessed with questions of bastardy, legitimacy, and confusion over origins. The otherwise puzzling disfigurement of Esther Summerson's face can be interpreted as part of an obscured ritual of purification, a ritual enacted in *Wuthering Heights* by the third generation.

The act that finally breaks Heathcliff's hold is Catherine's teaching Hareton to read. It is a beginning as decisive as "Call me Ishmael," and for the same reasons. For what Hareton learns to read is his own name, and this constitutes an act of alienation, a recognition that such a self exists, and that it can participate in a symbolic system of which writing is the medium. He learns that he is somehow identical to the house, for his name is carved in its stone. And when, later, he is able to read the date next to the name he is initiated into the phenomenon of biological generation spawning creatures like himself in time. He has connected, in short, with time, place, home, mind, meaning, and self. A new era has begun for Hareton and Catherine, and the future, which now exists for the first time in his mind, is theirs. Griffins crumble while little boys caper, fugue yields to sequence, sacred space gives way to linear time, autochthony to biology, defilement to expiation, and myth to novel. Is the text a "novel"? And is Heathcliff a "man"? The answer to both is, It is *becoming* one.

Leo Bersani has written that, by using a two-tiered structure, Emily Brontë is "telling the same story twice, and eliminating its originality the second time."[47] It is more accurate to say that she eliminates its antiquity. For what is missing when Catherine and Hareton pattycake off to the Grange are the ancient taboos — pollution, temptation, the sphinx. From here on it will be all gentleman-farming, honest dealings, sincere piety, Christmas puddings, healthy male heirs, and three-decker novels. *Wuthering Heights* (originally published in two volumes) is itself a kind of three-decker novel, for beneath the novelistic situation at the end lies buried the system of thought from which the novel has just emerged, which I have compared to early Christian thought on sin and evil. And beneath this there is the drama whose sources are far older, and whose main features are gathered into the myth of Oedipus. Noting that beneath the Hebrew word *TeHom* (translated in Genesis 1 as "the deep") lurks the divine Babylonian monster *TIAMAT,* Geoffrey Hartman speculates that a similar stratification may characterize language in general: "Reading a poem is like walking on silence-on volcanic silence. We feel the historical ground; the buried life of words."[48] Volcanic silence may be more audible in *Wuthering Heights* than in other novels, but all narratives, no matter how third-generation they may seem, have generations buried beneath. And on rare occasion, these earlier generations may be seen to *walk* over the secularized and alienated spaces where novels now live.

If this text appears to be a bundle of discordant elements with no effective dominant principle, part of the responsibility lies with the historically accreted character of language, and part with the stratified nature of the human psyche. Nobody would want to apologize for bad writing, of which there is plenty in this novel, on that account, but we may at least recognize that any attempt to express the totalizing vision Emily Brontë was getting at is going to be disorderly. In this case that disorder has permitted, if it has not compelled, the range of interpretations by which the novel continues to live. That this disorder, characterized by the coexistence of primitive and modern elements, the lamination of mythic and novelistic narratives, illuminates and is illuminated by the grotesque, has been an implicit argument throughout. And as a single entity capable of sustaining multiple and mutually exclusive interpretations, or a single space into which are compressed the sequential activities of time, *Wuthering Heights* is an exemplary and exceptionally complex grotesque. But insofar as this narrative is typical rather than unique, the case broadens in its implications. To that extent, we can say that the most comprehensive image for the literary grotesque is narrative itself.

> The narrative is the most exemplary representation of the literary grotesque.

CHAPTER FIVE

Permeability and the Grotesque:
"The Masque of the Red Death"

Let us not look for our disease outside of ourselves; it is within us, it is planted in our entrails.
— Seneca

Fools! Did not he who made the outside make the inside too?
— Luke 11:40

Perhaps in reality we are dead.
— Plato

    Heathcliff's special allure is the sense he fosters that identities are not necessarily discontinuous, but could flow into each other. This sense of flowing-into is a consistent quality of the grotesque, in which not only identities, but codes, systems, and distinctions of any kind are thrown together with no dominant principle that would enable us to determine what the entity is by itself, what is properly the inside and what the invader outside. In grotesque forms the alien outside has merged decisively with its victim-mate-self to produce a condition of such exquisite disorder that it is impossible to distinguish host and parasite.[1]

    "Common sense" implies that boundaries are well defined, identities are clearly distinguished, and, as Bachelard says, the metaphor of inside and outside "has the sharpness of the dialectics of yes and no, which decides everything."[2] No law of logic is more fundamental than that p and *not-p* cannot occupy the same space simultaneously,[3] but Bachelard speaks for a larger point of view when he says that "Being does not see itself.... It does not stand out, it is not *bordered* by nothingness...."[4] From the longest view, all things are fragments of "Being," the world is one, and there is no absolute outside at all: all boundaries are but geometrical metaphors, convenient fictions.

We maintain these fictions with special stoutness when personal identity is in question, as it is in the following meditation on form by Nabokov's most endearing hero, Professor Timofey Pnin:

> I do not know if it has ever been noted before that one of the main characteristics of life is discreteness. Unless a film of flesh envelopes us, we die. Man exists only insofar as he is separated from his surroundings.... It may be wonderful to mix with the landscape, but to do so is the end of the tender ego.[5]

Discreteness is a psychological as well as a physical necessity, but in both senses survival requires a continual compromise of the principle of separateness. If that film of flesh did not have certain openings in it that permitted passage between inside and outside, there would not be much hope for the tender ego either. We live by inhaling the outside to the inside, and expelling the inside to the outside. Air, an empty fullness, a medium of exchange that is also the thing exchanged, is a figure for this paradox, that the essence of the inside is its mortal enemy, the outside; and that the discrete structure of a human being would perish and revert to common elements if it were not continually penetrated by the most common element of all.[6]

Having extracted the life from the air we breath, and diffusing it to the body (which binds us to the world of death and dying), we exhale dead air without capacity to quicken. And so death, the Outside, is a constant presence inside. Philippe Ariès says that this was the discovery of the macabre art of the fifteenth and sixteenth centuries, and quotes the lines of Pierre de Nesson (1383–1442) to the effect that the "worms which devour cadavers do not come from the earth but from within the body, from its natural 'liquors'":

> Chacun conduit [du corps]
> Puante matière produit
> Hors du corps continuellement.
> (Each conduit [of the body]
> Constantly produces putrid matter
> Out of the body.)[7]

According to Mikhail Bakhtin, Rabelais drew on a medieval conception of the body that grew out of paradoxes like Nesson's:

> ... [The grotesque body] is not a closed, completed unit; it is unfinished, outgrows itself, transgresses its own limits. The stress is laid on those parts of the body that are open to the outside world, that is, the parts through which the world enters the body or emerges from it, or through which the body itself goes out to meet the world. This means that the emphasis is on the apertures or the convexities, or on the various ramifications and offshoots: the open mouth, the genital organs, the breasts, the phallus, the potbelly, the nose.

This body is presented as a "phenomenon in transition, an as yet unfinished metamorphosis, of death and birth, growing and becoming"; it is "not separated from the world by clearly defined boundaries; it is blended with the world, with animals, with objects." The rampant belching and farting in Rabelais is accorded a spiritual value because of its connection with the mediating and unifying air. In Bakhtin's reading this blending signifies transcendent merriment, the pure joy of unimpeded process, the affirmation of a rich, dynamic, sensual, festive, cosmic Oneness. For Bakhtin, this Oneness is realized not only through flatulence but also through the carnival mask, which with its bulging eyes, open mouth, and outsized nose all "going out to meet the world" takes in the notions of "gay relativity" and "the merry negation of uniformity and similarity."[8] For Bakhtin the mask imparts a true, i.e., collective (as opposed to a trivial and private), identity to the wearer.

But the mask hides other mysteries. Charles Dickens recalled one of his first toys, a Christmas mask which, taken from its carnival context and ritual New Year's celebrations, evoked a radically different response:

> When did that dreadful Mask first look at me? Who put it on, and why was I so frightened that the sight of it is an era in my life? It is not a hideous visage in itself; it is even meant to be droll; why then were its stolid features so intolerable?...Was it the immovability of the Mask?...Perhaps that fixed and set change coming

over a real face, infused into my quickened heart some remote suggestion and dread of the universal change that is to come on every face, and make it still?...The mere recollection of that fixed face, the mere knowledge of its existence anywhere, was sufficient to awaken me in the night all perspiration and horror, with "O! I know it's coming! O! the Mask!"[9]

Between Bakhtin's and Dickens' masks there seems a great gulf fixed, but they are the same mask, and the message is, in both cases, Oneness. Dickens simply reminds us that this message, when considered individually rather than from the point of view of the species, is not necessarily "gay" or "merry."

Rilke has provided an account that demonstrates this ambivalence in action. The narrator of *The Notebook of Malte Laurids Brigge* recalls a childhood experiment in costumes and disguises enacted before a mirror in the attic: "Hardly had I donned one of these suits, when I had to admit that it had me in its power; that it prescribed my movements, the expression of my features, even, indeed, my ideas.... Still, the more varied my transformations the more assured was I of my own identity." He discovers a mask that, although it fits his own face closely, feels "singularly cavernous"; while turning before the mirror, he knocks over a porcelain figurine. He tries to remove his mask to inspect the damage, but finds that it will not come off; and now the mirror appears to assume control:

> While I strove with measurelessly increasing anguish to tear myself somehow out of my disguise, it forced me, by what means I know not, to lift my eyes, and imposed on me an image, nay, a reality, an alien, unbelievable monstrous reality, with which, against my will, I became permeated: for now it was the stronger, and it was I who was the mirror. I stared at this great, terrifying, unknown personage before me, and it seemed appalling to me that I should be alone with him. But at the very moment I thought thus, the worst befell: I lost all knowledge of myself, I simply ceased to exist. For one second I had an unutterable, sad, and futile longing for myself, then there was only he — there was nothing but he.[10]

The free play of the self among masks inaugurates a progression that ends with the annihilation of the self. The mask that had solidified the self, granting it provisional form, drains the self, absorbing its essence. If the literary text can be compared to the grotesque mask (which it can: both are mediums through which the world "enters" the self and the self "goes out to meet the world"), then we can regard Rilke's passage as an exemplary fable of the act of reading. In this Aesopian view, the passage warns us of the dangers of entering into a too-close "identification" with the text; or of giving in to the temptation to accord it the status of reality. On the other hand, we should be equally warned against regarding the text as wholly discontinuous with the self, as if the mask did not fit. The text is most profitably regarded in its grotesque sense as a permeable membrane, capable of both guaranteeing the self and extending it.

2.

Before approaching "The Masque of the Red Death," we should try to understand what Poe himself meant by the term "grotesque." This is a traditional subject for Poe critics, who have compiled enough discussion to warrant a bibliography on "Poe and the Grotesque."[11] The difficulty arises from the fact that though Poe used the word with obvious purpose, there is no telling exactly what that purpose was. One of the few relevant near-facts on which much argument is based is that Poe had probably read Scott's *Fortnightly Review* (July 1827) article on the fantastic in the tales of E.T.A. Hoffmann. Scott had argued that the fantastic issued from the embattled vapors of an overheated or sickly imagination, and that it was a jumble of parts whose only aesthetic justification was as "the temptation of a saint, or the torture of a sinner." "Vividly accessible to the influence of imagination," but little "under the dominion of sober reason," fantastic art was capable only of representing the "terrors of a guilty mind." The common inference is that Poe — overheated, sickly, tempted, tortured, and guilty — may have found in Scott's article both precedent and program, modeling his art on Hoffmann's.

Poe's utterances on the subject are elusive and vaporous. In his prefatory statement to the 1840 collection of *Tales of the Grotesque and Arabesque,* for example, he says simply that "The epithets grotesque and arabesque will indicate with sufficient precision the prevalent tenor of the tales herein published." Daniel Hoffman, applying these categories to other Poe stories not included in this collection, distinguishes crisply between them: "In art work, *grotesque* signifies the depiction of monsters in an elaborate, foliated setting; while *arabesque* refers to an intricate pattern, geometric design, which does not reproduce the human form."[12] He suggests a pairing principle, with, for example, the satiric "King Pest" serving as the grotesque to the nonhuman majesty of "The Masque of the Red Death." Another critic, Patricia C. Smith, refers to generally available contemporary discussions, suggesting that although the terms were often confounded they were usually distinguished on the basis that the arabesque was exclusively floral, following the Mohammedan injunction against representing human or bestial forms; the grotesque, also a fantastical mixture, included not only floral or vegetal forms but also of representations of men, beasts, genii, buildings, etc.[13] So while the charge of having no type in nature could be made against the grotesque, it could not be made against the arabesque, for in forms such as the snapdragon nature herself had given the type, hinting of intra-realm correspondences and affinities.

This distinction could well have been crucial for Poe. If the grotesque suggests unnatural partition and the arabesque organic recombination, they may have appeared to him as instances, perhaps as the very type, of a division that characterizes all of Poe's thought. It is conventional, for example, to speak of Poe's mind as embracing both the indefiniteness of music and the exactitude of mathematics. Allen Tate provided the most radical version of this formula, diagnosing Poe as suffering from an extreme case of Cartesian dualism, viewing man as "an angel inhabiting a machine and directing it by means of the pineal gland."[14] The artist's "catastrophic acceptance" of this metaphor led him, according to Tate, into contradiction and obscurantism. But Poe did not accept bifurcation; he rebelled against it, seeking always to discover the unifying principle which could reintegrate parts and retrieve a lost unity. In Poe's aesthetic theory the Many does not contradict the One; it awaits it.

The One comes most frequently in the guise of Taste or the "laws of gradation so visibly pervading all things in Earth and Heaven."[15] These laws order the hierarchy of separate mental faculties according to universal principles of proportion. "The *highest* genius," he says in number XXIII of "Fifty Suggestions," "is but the result of generally large mental power existing in a state of absolute proportion — so that no one faculty has undue prominence." Grotesque, by contrast, suggests an anarchy of parts, the absence of proportion. In "Four Beasts in One," a little-known sketch, Poe describes the ancient city of "Epidaphne," where the people worship a baboon as god and a "camelopard" with the head of a man as king. The entire city is a riot of degradation and filth: "Surely this is the most populous city of the East! What a wilderness of people! What a jumble of all ranks and ages! What a multiplicity of sects and nations! what a variety of costumes! what a Babel of languages! what a screaming of beasts! what a tinkling of instruments! what a parcel of philosophers!" This whole turn-out constitutes an extended definition, for the narrator has prefaced his description with a rhetorical question: "does not the appearance of Epidaphne justify me in calling it *grotesque?*" If any further justification for this name were needed, we could point to the manner in which this city epitomizes a condition which necessitates and anticipates the One: the camelopard, we are told in the first paragraph, had usurped the throne just "a hundred and seventy-one years before the coming of Christ."

Sometimes Poe could be sanguine about the capacity of the creative imagination to transcend the corruption of the flesh, the degrading affinities with animals, and the bondage to death. In a Coleridgean footnote to his review of Halleck and Drake, he says, "imagination is, possibly, in man a lesser degree of the creative power of God." The creative act establishes right order and through it we can perhaps arrest decay and blunt the gnawing tooth of time. Or, as he says in "The Poetic Principle,"

> Inspired by an ecstatic prescience of the glories beyond the grave, we struggle by multiform combinations among the things and thoughts of Time to attain a portion of that Loveliness whose very elements perhaps appertain to Eternity alone.

The consistently binary form of Poe's thought enables a certain freedom in substituting terms. Thus we can say that the arabesque, as pure form or non-referential ornament, summons up the kind of wholeness, unity, and loveliness that exists out of time. The grotesque, on the other hand, corresponds with "multiform combinations" of time, acts of creation straining toward unity and eternity but embedded in partition and decay. These large speculations may enable us to undo a small but difficult knot, a point in "The Masque of the Red Death" where the narrator, referring to the revelers, says, "Be sure they were grotesque," and, two sentences later, describes them as "arabesque figures with unsuited limbs and appointments."

3.

The antithesis structuring this tale again opposes changeless art and unstructured organic life. Human thought struggles against primal pointlessness; the masked ball with the Red Death; the conscious aestheticism within the abbey walls with the unnamable, unutterable force abroad, which has no form but dances invisibly in the air. Organic life is marked by its color: red: choler. From Biblical times red has been associated with the plague, especially the contagious viral cholera as opposed to the flea-carried bubonic plague known as the Black Death. In England through the time of Pepys, corpse-bearers were required to carry red wands, and infected houses had red crosses painted on the door.[16] The heart, the body's clock, is also red, though it may figuratively be said to be black, like the ebony clock that oversees Prospero's revels. Like many Poe stories, this is a tale of pursuit. Here, it is the serpentine ensnarement by red Life of the fugitive Idea.

To escape the plague Prospero and his thousand hale and hearty companions lock themselves within the abbey, welding the bolts behind them. Among the company were "all the appliances of pleasure. There were buffoons, there were improvisatori, there were ballet-dancers, there were musicians, there was beauty, there was wine. All these and security were within. Without was the 'Red Death.'" Art resides securely within, but it is defective in taste. The narrator describes the masked ball in terms that Kayser calls "perhaps the most comprehensive and authoritative definition of the grotesque ever given": "There were much of the beautiful, much of the wanton, much of the *bizarre,* something of the terrible, and not a little of that which might have excited disgust."[17]

In locking himself within, Prospero has made a statement about boundaries, implying that the Red Death can be thwarted by the interposition of walls, as if it belonged to the same order of being as a mad dog or a cannonball. This is one sense of "mask," the assumption that a surface, potent against invasion, can protect the inside. The failure of welded bolts in this regard is replicated in the failure of the masked ball, the failure of art, to immunize.

Let us look closely at Prospero's creation. He has appointed seven rooms, six of art and one of nature, a pattern greatly favored by creators.[18] Each of the first six rooms has a dominant color, one leading on to another not by a straight corridor but by an irregular passageway that prevents one from seeing more than one at a time, a limitation that accords with Poe's preference for poems and tales that can be perused at a single sitting.[19] Illumination is provided by braziers of fire standing in a "closed corridor which pursued the windings of the suite," projecting their rays through the tinted glass of "a tall and narrow Gothic window." Red, the color of the organic outside, has followed them inside the abbey, has "pursued" them down the corridor, observing them through the windows; disguised by being filtered through the various colored panes, it even reddens their revels: an undercover agent, obtaining employment in the duke's household, plotting his death. The windows themselves may have some emblematic significance as permeable membranes in which the domains of the organic and the mental interpenetrate; images, in other words, of fiction itself. In the seventh room (where ticks the ebony clock) the dominant color is black, but the panes are red; it is the room of death.[20] All the reds in the story converge in the figure of the Red Death, who passes through all the rooms, gathering their colors into himself, before turning to stand in the shadow of the clock. "Who dares insult us with this blasphemous mockery?" the prince demands hoarsely as "his brow reddened with rage." Prospero's masked ball is also a *danse macabre* not only because the revelers are larval corpses (as Nietzsche said, the living are but a species — a rare species — of the dead), but also because they are merely lifeless masks of the Red Death itself, which is "within."

The tale is constructed on a series of such buried puns. Perhaps the most complex is the following: when the clock strikes the hour, the musicians cease their playing, the waltzers stop dancing, and there is "a brief disconcert of the whole gay company." They are deprived of music: they are dis-concerted. They are also dis-concerted in being deprived of ease, for the giddiest grow pale and the aged sweat in confused revery. Third, they are dis-concerted in being deprived of the integrity of effect Prospero had intended in making each room separate and unique, for the toll sounds through them all, linking them in the same way as the infectious red.

The clock might seem to introduce time into a timeless realm, but in fact many kinds of time collide at these points. There is, for example, waltz-time, with its regulated intervals. This kind of time is momentarily overruled by "the Time that flies," which is beyond human regulation, though it can be demarcated, in "clear and loud and deep and exceedingly musical" tones. Like the clock and the waltz, mortality has a beat: in the seventh room ticks the clock; in the other six, in masked concert, "beat feverishly the heart of life."

Against this surplus of time-schemes operating without (in the clock), within (in the heart) and at the margin (in the waltz) may be measured the futility of fleeing from the time that flies in pursuit. The ball can mask time but cannot deny it, any more than the panes can deny entrance to the fatal red. And here we encounter another pun. Despite the fact that the revelers are described as "masquers," Prospero conducts no masque. The word is mentioned only in the title; the tale itself speaks only of a masked ball, held within the abbey, whose host is Prospero. This is what the revelers believe they are attending. What they do not realize is that, in every sense that counts, they are spectator-participants at a masque which has been conducted over the entire country, which recognizes no boundaries, whose host is the parasite, the Red Death. In precisely the moment when — in the very act by which — they seek to deny him, they join his ghastly revels.

Dwelling ironically "within" Poe's, Shakespeare's Prospero has a keener sense of the limitations of art. *The Tempest* ends with liberation and reconciliation rather than with hideous death because, though Prospero knows all too well the rankest faults of the world, he also understands that he inhabits that world himself. So although his masque ends in a vision of earthly bounty and a dance of reapers and nymphs in celebration of true love, it is an insubstantial pageant that vanishes instantly when Prospero recalls Caliban's real threat against his life. No dreamwork he can create will avail him against Caliban. As it is Prospero who creates them, it is Prospero who declares, "Our revels now are ended." When he says, comparing human life to the phantasm just fled, "We are such stuff as dreams are made on," he recognizes immediately a sign that he is vexed and troubled, and takes a walk to calm himself, to dismiss such idle metaphorizing, and to make plans. Poe's Prospero, however, believes the metaphor. He does not dream; he becomes a dream. At least the narrator says so: "To and fro...there stalked, in fact, a multitude of dreams. And these — these dreams — writhed in and about.... The dreams are stiff — frozen as they stand.... And now again the music swells, and the dreams live, and writhe to and fro...." For Poe's Prospero this is no mere fancy but a desperate strategy: dreams cannot contract cholera. This Prospero never says, "Our revels now are ended" simply because if he had his way they never would. But dreams and revels must end, and if Prospero does not end them, Caliban or the Red Death, both ambiguous mixtures of unregenerate, murderous Nature and the supernatural-demonic, will.

Shakespeare knew, too, that midnight was the hour. In *A Midsummer Night's Dream,* the masque that concludes the play is undertaken in full awareness that it is an "aery nothing" meant only to "ease the anguish of a torturing hour" (V.i.37). After the dance Theseus bids the company retire: "The iron tongue of midnight hath told twelve. / Lovers, to bed, 'tis almost fairy time" (V.i.363–64). What sort of fairies, we discover when Puck enters:

Now the hungry lion roars,
And the wolf behowls the moon;
Whilst the heavy ploughman snores,
All with weary task fordone.
Now the wasted brands do glow,
Whilst the screech-owl, screeching loud,
Puts the wretch that lies in woe
In remembrance of a shroud.
Now it is the time of night
That the graves, all gaping wide,
Everyone lets forth his sprite,
In the church-way paths to glide. (V.i.371–82)

Formidable fairies, whose world is not to be intruded upon, nor whose powers over the night questioned. A masque can ease the anguish of an hour as long as it is the proper hour. The dance was delightful but Puck rights the balance between its world and the world outside, a balance that, if not maintained by the revelers, will be by the lions.

Shakespeare's image for the Unnamable Ender of Masques is the lion. Another, in a context closer to Poe's, is the Lamb. The Red Death, we are told, "had come like a thief in the night." Six times in the Bible it is prophesied that Christ will come in this manner to unmask Himself at the Revelation, ending all earthly revels.[21] The last kind of time in this tale is the Day of the Lord.

Numbers themselves contribute to thematic closure. The duke makes seven rooms: three (the number of divine creation) plus four (the number of human creation). The waltz is in three-quarters time. The waltz ceases and the rooms become one at the hour of twelve, or three times four: by so much is human art "the lesser degree of the creative power of God." Ten is the perfect Christian number: three times three plus one, implying a Trinitarian unity. Prospero had presumed to raise this number to the third power by inviting a thousand companions, reserving the position of divine totality (ten times ten times ten plus one) for himself. The Red Death enters, spoiling the symmetry, to remind them that there is yet one greater who embraces all of them including Prospero; and his mark is death, which embraces them as securely as sixty minutes "embrace three thousand and six hundred seconds of the Time that flies."

When the Red Death stands in the shadow of the clock, temporality and atemporality, outside and inside, and mask and masque, merge. The point, of course, is that they have never been truly apart. The final sentence, "And Darkness and Decay and the Red Death held illimitable dominion over all," simply realizes the plainly stated implications of the first, that "The 'Red Death' had long devastated the country." The tale closes in relentlessly from "the country" to the seventh chamber.

We can observe this closure or encirclement in the conduct of the narrator, a man with a shrewd understanding of court politics. He had begun with declarations, such as: "No pestilence had ever been so fatal.... But the Prince Prospero was happy and dauntless and sagacious.... The wall had gates of iron.... The abbey was amply provisioned." The first two paragraphs are innocent; their tone is lofty and austere, it is Red Death narration. But when we enter the abbey we discover that the narrator has been, apparently, of the prince's persuasion all along, for his tone changes. Forgetting, like the others, about the Pest, he reveals himself as the implicated, tongue-lolling fellow traveler who addresses us thus intimately: "It was a voluptuous scene, that masquerade. But first let me tell you...." Reliable ground gives way, and everything begins to float. After describing the reactions to the clock — for which he summons his old tone — he gives an insolent toss of the head and assures us, "But in spite of these things, it was a gay and magnificent revel." In short, the narrator follows the established principle of counterintelligence, When in Rome. Having materialized in time for the party he hastens, at the appearance of the Red Death, to regain his dignity, impenetrability and invisibility, and become a bodiless voice. Watch him disappear:

> In an assembly of phantasms such as I have painted, it may well be supposed that no ordinary appearance could have excited such sensation. In truth the masquerade license of the night was nearly unlimited; but the figure in question had out-Heroded Herod, and gone beyond the bounds of even the prince's indefinite decorum. There are chords in the hearts of the most reckless which cannot be touched without emotion. Even with the utterly lost, to whom life and death are equally jests, there are matters of which no jest can be made.

And on down to "And Darkness and Decay and the Red Death...."

Earlier I suggested that the color red can be seen as a mask for the Red Death. The preceding paragraph describes the narrator in the same terms, as an undercover agent working for the plague. This bizarre connection is reinforced by another pun. This tale, like many Poe works, is concerned with the implications of narrative, of the process of rendering into artifact and the living death granted by this process. Pursuing this narrative we experience "read" deaths. Not only is the narrator "working for" the plague; narration is a plague, a kind of death, itself. The tale is the autobiography of a disease, beginning with a symptom and ending with death and silence. Emerging into articulate being in the first sentence, the tale stalks (narrates) its subject, penetrates it, becomes it (as revelers become dreams), and ceases to exist when they die. It even, in the first paragraph, prescribes its life term: half an hour.

Death conquers all at once. When the plague becomes Prospero, the subject (the narrator) becomes the object (the "subject" of his tale), and consequently expires. Life is synonymous with articulation and death with silence, with the condition of having "nothing left to say." Perfect health is similarly inarticulate. The French anatomist Marie Bichat wrote in 1800 that "Health is the silence of organs. Disease is their revolt." Tales narrate trouble, the mid-region between the silence of health and the silence of death. Disease, then, is akin to "difference," by which both words and bodily organs rise above the threshold of awareness, or communicate. In Prospero's last room, the only one in which "the color of the windows failed to correspond with the decorations," speaking red is imperfectly differentiated from silent black, a flaw which portends the advent of the Red Death, as well as imaging mortal life and narration, which infects its subject with design and fixity as a condition of existence.

4.

Among the revelers, the Red Death, and the narrative, a generous sharing of essence obtains. All three mediate between life and death, organic existence and aesthetic design. Such a sharing of essence among objects normally opposed accounts for the tale's grotesqueness, not the prince's addiction to the *bizarre*. Not merely confronted with the grotesque, the revelers become themselves grotesque, in two ways at once: through the proliferative anarchy of the masked ball, with its improvisatori, its buffoons, its bewildering sensory overload; and through the stunting, warping, or other bonsai effects imposed by the wearing of masks. Moreover, they experienced the sensation of the grotesque at those moments when they are reminded of the illegitimacy of their existence. This realization occurs once an hour at the tolling of the clock; it is preceded by revelry and succeeded by "a certain nameless awe." The moment itself is the time of "brief disconcert," and is fully realized at the tolling of twelve when the figure of the Red Death is recognized, and there arises "at length from the whole company a buzz, or murmur, expressive of disapprobation and surprise — then, finally, of terror, of horror, and of disgust." Having presumed that their masks were Bakhtinian, embodying a merry negation of uniformity and a celebration of regeneration, they are reminded that the point of any mask is the obliteration of personal identity; since they have segregated themselves from the culture on the outside, in which alone a common regeneration might be attained, this obliteration means for them, simply, death. In donning their masks for private ends, they mime their private ends. The grotesque does not merely characterize an element of the story; the story is about the grotesque; it is an allegory of the outside — becoming — inside, the human center becoming ornament; it is a melodrama of the margin.

Poe's imagination and art flourished only at that margin, for only there could he interpose a fiction between himself and a fate impossible to confront directly. In his work this fate generally goes by the name *death*, which helps explain why his fictions are so obsessed with premature burial, dismemberment, torture, plotted and investigated murders, and the experimentation with liminal states such as hypnotism and mesmeric revelation. In these acts or conditions, life and death flow into each other. This is Poe's art: between silent health and silent death comes disease or infection, which calls forth narrative.

The word as plague. Poe's influence on the French tradition is well known, but it is generally assumed that the tradition in question begins with Baudelaire and ends with Valéry. But there is evidence in the wonderful conclusion to Derrida's *Of Grammatology* that the French tradition was speaking Poe's language before he was born, and that it is speaking it still. Commenting on Rousseau's belief that writing is the "supplement" of spoken language, which is itself closer to the source, or wordless thought, Derrida suggests a moral, and a mortal progression, away from the origin and source of life, and toward alienation, death, and evil: "phonetic writing is not absolute evil. It is not the letter of death. Nevertheless, it announces death."[22] Prospero and his fellows move in this direction, breaking links with the spoken language of the people, isolating themselves and creating an alienated, and therefore evil and deathly, art. But, as Poe well knew, there was no choice. Outside, in the tale, death is universal. Life can be purchased inside, but only by means of the masque, in which the individual self is annihilated.[23] Nor could death be avoided by another form of art, for all language is alienated from the "origin," and therefore death-tending. In the following sentences, Derrida almost seems to have been reading Poe:

The sickness of the outside (which comes from the outside but also draws outside, thus equally, or inversely, the sickness of the homeland, a homesickness, so to speak) is in the heart of the living word, as its principle of effacement and its relationship to its own death.[24]

For Derrida, who maintains that "exteriority is constitutive of interiority,"[25] there is no writing at degree zero, no escape from substitution, no capture of the origin. Death is the essence of language, or, as he says elsewhere, the condition for a true act of language is to be able to say, "I am dead."[26] It is only one sign of Poe's surprising contemporaneity that we find this post-structuralist paradox "absolutely *bursting* from the tongue" of M. Valdemar at the conclusion of a fiction that explores in an especially vivid way the linguistic possibilities at the margin.[27]

Prospero's Word is also Derridean, or Valdemarian. In effacing himself as a mortal being and presenting himself as an artifact, he is trying to say "I am dead," a statement which, if believed, would exempt him from further death. Prospero and Poe were alive to the ambivalence of the word, its power to grant a conditional life even as it guaranteed death. In one of the dialogues so little known but so highly revealing, Poe discusses "The Power of Words" as akin to "vibrations" in the circumambient atmosphere. As an "impulse on the air," every creative act, every word, "must, *in the end,* impress every individual thing that exists *within the universe."* The air is thus, "the great medium of *creation,"* as it is, in "The Masque of the Red Death," the great medium of destruction. This may explain why Poe found it necessary and life-giving, for example, to interpose the fiction of "The Philosophy of Composition" between himself and the fact, the fate, of another fiction, "The Raven," masking inner compulsion as aesthetic law and biographical event. In a similar vein, his detective stories furnish metaphors of the ways one might ease the friction of necessity by inserting a fiction of "objectivity." But Poe knew how fictional objectivity was. The godlike M. Dupin is sometimes permitted to observe and conquer, but Prospero, a kind of reverse detective who also seeks to become objective (object-like), is shown to be subject to a higher power. The desire to forfeit the anguish of existence for the serenity of pure appearance and impersonality lies behind much of Poe's art.

On occasion we are permitted to regard this trade-off as successful. But on many others we are forced to perceive beauty itself as a mask for the Worm.

We can now make a final distinction between the grotesque and the arabesque. Prospero's goal was the transformation of men and women into arabesques — pure, whole, harmonious, and nonhuman design. The tolling of the clock reminds the revelers that they are living in time, and so mere grotesques, or *human* arabesques "with unsuited limbs and appointments." Their revelation parallels that of Poe's reader, for, at times, when the spell is broken, we are suddenly struck with the shabbiness of his cheapjack shaman's tricks, his meretricious taste (for all his preaching about Taste), and pomposity. But when spells are broken, bare, forked reality is revealed, and Poe's grotesqueries of style are, a generous heart might argue, always intended. He designed them, it could be said, to shatter his own illusion and to make us contemptuous of the devices that had so enchanted us. They are there to enable the reader to unmask his fictions, despite the dread certainty that he will find them "untenanted by any tangible form." For Poe was a Prospero who could not help but break his wand, exposing his art, the only means he had of attaining unity, for the ragbag parody of real creation that it was. In the tale I have been discussing, the creation of the suite of rooms parodies Genesis, the death of the thousand and one parodies Revelation. The masked ball itself is an image of all human activity in between — the aping of the Word, the making of fictions.

This was Poe's half-kept, half-revealed secret: that all his art was parody, that it was all grotesque. He had sought to escape this truth by devoting himself to short poems and brief tales, striving for unity of effect by eliminating or arresting transitions, the points of partition. But in narrative art transition is continual, an endless discord, a series of "devices" gathering force from the beginning until the climax, the point of revelation. The only escape from transition, or from devices, is to be sought, impossibly, either before the Word or after the End.

CHAPTER SIX

Metaphor, Marginality, and Parody in
Death in Venice

The inky sky over the Doldrums and the oppressive atmosphere are more than just an obvious sign of the nearness of the equator. They epitomize the moral climate in which two worlds have come face to face. This cheerless sea between them, and the calmness of the weather whose only purpose seems to be to allow evil forces to gather fresh strength, are the last mystical barrier between two regions so diametrically opposed to each other through their different conditions that the first people to become aware of the fact could not believe that they were both equally human.

— Claude Lévi-Strauss

1.

In the previous chapter I considered some ways in which the solid boundaries of the represented "realistic" world (the castle walls) could be compromised or exposed as fictitious by the infiltration or penetration of a subtler fiction, a purer art, figured in the unrepresentable air. This compromise of boundaries was as fatal to the sense of realism as to the revelers. In Poe's story the grotesque was achieved not by the clash between reality and fantasy, but by the subversion of one fictional principle by another more radically fictional. In this chapter I want to extend and adapt this argument by examining a work that explores its own generic identity, Thomas Mann's *Death in Venice*.

Most theoreticians of genre agree that no work is entirely true to its genre, and that prose narratives especially are mixed modes, with a number of subordinate genre-signals clustered around a single dominant principle. In this respect, the ways in which Mann's narrative constantly threatens to switch from a realistic to a non-realistic mode are interesting because they caricature the multi-generic signals of narratives in general. One way to categorize these signals has been suggested by Roman Jakobson, whose terms metonymy and metaphor have been widely adopted as improvements on the less precise terms realism and symbolism or romanticism.[1] For Jakobson, metonymy designates a relationship between objects characterized by random and possibly meaningless contiguity, such as that between pen and paper. Metaphor, on the other hand, designates a sharing of essence that cuts across immediate contexts, so that one object is seen as a version of another, such as pen and finger ("The moving finger writes, and having writ, moves on..."). Realistic novels are dominated by metonymy, according to which boundaries are firm and objects are solid and discrete, as they are in "the world"; non-representational forms such as symbolism, romanticism, dream-narrative, or myth (when considered as fantasy), are dominated by metaphor.[2] Because of the powerful psychological pressures on the reader to consider language either as referential or non-referential, it is difficult to see how a work could be dominated both by metonymy and by metaphor, for the mind would not rest on that knife-edge. But it is equally difficult to see how a work could be either wholly metonymic or wholly metaphoric, for the result would be on the one hand a naïve and ultimately incoherent identification of language with physical objects; and, on the other hand, an equally incoherent severance of language from those objects. All narratives, though dominated by one principle, must incorporate the other as a subordinate element. One of the primary tasks of interpretation, therefore, is to establish the "mix," the relative position of, and interaction between, the two principles.

This subordination pertains at the sentence level as well: every metonymy is capable of being converted into metaphor, and every metaphor is built on the ruins of a shattered metonymy. We distinguish between them not on the basis of syntactical features, but on the method of interpretation required. The statement "Hector is a man" can be verified by looking at Hector, but the statement "Hector is a lion" appeals only secondarily to the carnal eye, and primarily to what Kermode, in *The Genesis of Secrecy,* calls the "spiritual" eye. "Hector is a lion" can never be adequately paraphrased by any number of referential statements. "Hector is brave" plus "Hector is warlike" plus "Hector is fearsome" does not equal "Hector is a lion." Such statements not only arbitrarily exclude other possibilities (such as "Hector is hairy," "Hector lets the women do the work," and "Hector walks on all fours"), but they miss the crucial element of absurdity, the factor of referential impossibility, the confusion of the carnal eye. The metaphorical statement concretely affirms a condition so confused or preposterous that the mind, unable to establish congruence between the statement and any set of objects, escapes into an ambivalent domain of the literal/nonliteral.

Thus metonymic incongruity is transfigured into metaphorical congruence. To take another example: the relationship between me and the typewriter I am now using is metonymic; but if someone came to me and said, "You are a typewriter," I would first recognize a grotesque crushing-together of man and machine, self and other, and then, unable to match language with reality in a concrete or referential way, would consider an alternate possibility, that "typewriter" designated certain functions or qualities. In terms of these, it is possible that my typewriter and I might be said to have some common principle of identity. As this is an unfamiliar metaphor, it would require a good deal of imaginative work to discover the common ground that permitted the metaphorical interpretation. In more familiar metaphors, such as "the gnawing tooth of time," the referential is more easily and quickly transcended. In dead metaphors of clichés, such as "to come to a head" (I speak dermatologically, as the Reverend Mr. Chasuble might say), the referential is not considered at all. In all metaphors with a spark of life, the referential (usually called the literal) always confronts us. It is a prior phase, whose self-annihilating absurdity motivates us to the act of interpretation that completes the understanding of the metaphor. It is the phase of the grotesque, which, as I said in the first chapter, occurs primarily as a naïve experience, a function of the literal, in the context of referential art. Considered referentially, metaphors are grotesques; they parody themselves.

If we turn to the problem of representation in general, we find that we cannot free ourselves from parody. This is especially apparent in representations of the "spiritual" world. That quintessence of scholasticism, the debate over how many dancing angels could be accommodated on the head of a pin, for example, may be a foolish question about dancing and pinheads but it is a very serious one about language, and about representation as "embodiment." The issue is what sort of form angels have, and the reason this question seems imponderable is that "angel" confuses the distinction between concrete and abstract nouns: a concrete noun must occupy space; an abstract noun cannot "dance." All concrete nouns are trammeled in matter, for language does not have the equivalent of a mathematical point with position but no dimension (although we have words for such entities: quark, lepton, monad). Any number of mathematical angels could dance on a pin, but for linguistic angels space may be limited. The linguistic angel, contaminated by the flesh, is a degraded or parodic mathematical angel.

But parody is more pervasive than this unusual example would indicate. In a 1916 essay on language, Walter Benjamin asserted that all articulation was parodic, for every word was a parody of the Word, an "uncreative imitation" of God's "creative verb." The Fall is "the moment of birth of man's language," after which the word "must communicate *something* now, outside itself."

> This is really the original sin of the spirit of language. As it communicates outside of itself the word is something of a parody, by an explicitly mediate word, of the explicitly immediate word, of God's creative word; it is the Fall of a fortunate essence of language in Adam, who stands in the middle.³

We could add that if all words parody the Word, they also parody the Flesh, substituting signs for objects, impulses, and sensations that, unnamed and uncategorized, exist in a state of infinite potentiality. And we could sum up by saying that, if one is looking for flesh, the word "flesh" is a poor substitute; while, by comparison with the word "flesh," actual flesh is a poor substitute. Again, poor Adam, and his descendants, "stand in the middle."

As these examples indicate, and as Poe recognized, parody has a theological dimension. It is defined by the substitution of an object or a representation analogous to a perfect original in every way, but in all points inferior, low, or structurally simpler, so that the substitute stands in an inverse relation to the original. The theological dimension of parody is especially visible in those forms of religious devotion that stress intimate contact between the fallen replica and the "perfect original." The possessed youth in *The Transfiguration* is a parody of

Christ; in fact, we can see the progression from God to Christ to sinner as a parodic sequence, the redemptive power of which is activated by the kinship between categories, between a type and its (increasingly degraded) copy. Christ is a saving parody.

Hence in one characteristic passage in her *Revelations* Dame Julian of Norwich (c. 1343–1417) dwells with monumentally tender patience on a vision of the dead body of Christ: "His nostrils too shrivelled and dried before my eyes," she notes, "and his dear body became black and brown as it dried up in death." And "the dear skin and tender flesh, the hair and the blood, were hanging loose from the bone gouged by the thorns in many places. It seemed about to drop off, heavy and loose, still holding its natural moisture, sagging like a cloth."[4] Modern readers might feel they could have been spared such attention to detail, but the point is not merely precision of rendering. Rather, it is the demonstration of the absoluteness of Christ's redemptive capacity. Such a passage proves that, despite the human bondage to death and corruption that might seem to be an absolute and fundamental dissimilarity between humanity and divinity — which might seem to snap the chain of resemblances and thereby consign humanity to dust — there is a sense in which human death merely parodies Christ's. In short, the passage justifies the statement that mankind is made in the image and likeness of God. To the mystic, Christ functions like a metaphor, enabling one to speak of the unity of body and soul, death and eternal life, God and Man.

Mystic faith typically passes through the parodic to this metaphor, through the grotesque to the sublime. This principle could be illustrated by many events in the life of St. Francis, such as his famous Christmas mass at the stable in Grecchio, which he celebrated before ox, ass, and *praesipium*, bleating the word "Bethlehem" like a lamb. Or we could think of St. Catherine of Siena who, tending the wounded, found herself overcome with revulsion; and as a corrective to an imperfect piety, drank off a bowl of pus. Only a determined belief could leap from love of God to that bowl; only a powerfully synthetic imagination could forge the notion that "accepting" the one was not merely equivalent but identical to "accepting" the other, even though one was wholly unembodiable and the other was the most degraded form of body. The incident is an extreme example of what Auerbach called the Christian "mingling of styles." It is also an example of the operation of the metaphorical imagination, of the kind of mind that perceives similarity in dissimilar things, the kind of mind that sees the far and the near, the concrete and the abstract, the sacred and the unclean, on the same plane.

We should distinguish at this point between parody and an adjacent mode, caricature. The substitute of caricature, in Freud's formulation, "brings about degradation by emphasizing in the general impression given by the exalted object a single trait which is comic in itself but was bound to be overlooked so long as it was only perceivable in the general picture."[5] Caricature attempts to unlock the image's essential nature, to aid its self-interpretation. It represents, therefore, a tendency; or as Ernst Kris says, it attempts "to reveal the true man behind the mask of pretense and to show up his 'essential' littleness and ugliness."

The serious artist, according to academic tenets, creates beauty by liberating the perfect form that Nature sought to express in resistant matter. The caricaturist seeks for the perfect deformity, he shows how the soul of the man would express itself in his body if only matter were sufficiently pliable to Nature's intentions.[6]

As it follows a prior tendency, caricature is less aggressive than parody — though, for the same reason, its attack is more intimate and more devastating.

Like most caricature, most parody presents a double or split reference, in that while we apprehend the substitute we recall the original. These commonplace forms Baudelaire would call the ordinary or significant comic, which he said was "visibly double — art and the moral idea." But the grotesque forms of both characteristically appear as a unity, an impossibly single form that, as Baudelaire says, "calls for the intuition to grasp it." Caricature and parody become grotesque by uniting the "moral idea" (which I have been calling the perfect original) with the representation in such a way that the two are fused into one. With caricature this unification occurs through the original's resolving itself into a single trait, without proportion or balance. Hitlerism, for example, is a grotesque caricature of the Germanic admiration for order and national pride.

The parodic replica also achieves the grotesque by fusing with the original. The O.E.D. provides a perfect illustration of this kind of takeover, citing a reviewer's comment on an 1891 translation of *The Divine Comedy:* "This is to grotesque Dante, not to translate him." What the reviewer meant by this comment was that although the book in hand was clearly, recognizably, and unarguably Dante's, the poet was present only in a consistently debased and inferior version. Sometimes "the inferior" is simply "the prior." In this spirit, one editor of Genesis laments the "absurd and childish tradition" of the creation and flood found in ancient Babylonian texts, grudgingly conceding that they bear "a grotesque resemblance to the majestic account" of Moses. The editor of the Babylonian Genesis, on the other hand, asserts proudly that his documents "confirm, elucidate and supplement the Hebrew chronicles," abounding not in parodies but in "striking parallels" to the Old Testament.[7]

For a more complex example of such fusion we can turn to a passage from the memoirs of Fanny Burney's father, who recalls that, by the age of 39, Boswell had acquired the habit of assuming

> ...an odd mock solemnity of manner, that he had acquired imperceptibly from constant thinking of and imitating Dr. Johnson; whose own solemnity, nevertheless, far from mock, was the result of pensive rumination. There was, also, something slouching in the gait and dress of Mr. Boswell, that wore an air, ridiculously enough, of purporting to personify the same model. His clothes were always too large for him; his hair, or wig, was constantly in a state of negligence; and he never for a moment sat still or upright upon a chair. Every look and movement displayed either intentional or involuntary imitation...for his heart, almost even to idolatry, was in his reverence of Dr. Johnson.[8]

The complexity of this example lies in the ambiguity of the concept of the "original." For this figure is a simple parody of "Dr. Johnson"; but it is a grotesque parody — a degraded version inseparable from the original — of "James Boswell," a man whose heart, almost even to idolatry, was in his reverence of "Dr. Johnson."

Johnson-Boswell returns us to the concerns with which this chapter began. If the grotesque parody has the effect of contaminating the origin, we can see why such a notion would be useful in analyzing the midpoint between metonymy and metaphor. For metonymic language, the language of realism claims to have its origin in "the world." Metaphoric language, on the other hand, breaks the hold of the referential world, locating its origin in language, or the copying process, itself. If, as in grotesque parody, it becomes impossible to segregate origin from copy, then both metonymy and metaphor are subverted or contaminated by each other. For Thomas Mann, suspicious of the pretenses of art to represent reality, and equally suspicious of the pretensions of artists who would claim for art an autonomous existence, grotesque parody was a natural mode.

In a work Thomas Mann knew intimately, Goethe's God tells Faustus that he *"muss als Teufel schaffen,"* a phrase on which Northrop Frye has commented that it must mean rather more than that he must work like the devil. But how does the devil work? We can see Mann's answer in his own incarnation of Faustus: he works like an artist. Adrian Leverkühn's music is stolen from the devil (and from Schoenberg, who indignantly demanded it back), but its origin in Leverkühn's life is an inherited predilection towards parodic creation. In his youth the composer had witnessed experiments performed by Father Leverkühn which explored and tested the boundaries between the animate and the inanimate. Father Leverkühn, the narrator reports,

> had succeeded in making a most singular culture; I shall never forget the sight. The vessel of crystallization was three-quarters full of slightly muddy water...and from the sandy bottom there strove upwards a grotesque little landscape of variously coloured growths: a confused vegetation of blue, green, and brown shoots which reminded one of algae, mushrooms, attached polyps, also moss, then mussels, fruit pods, little trees or twigs from trees, here and there of limbs. It was the most remarkable sight I ever saw.... He showed us that these pathetic imitations of life were light-seeking, heliotropic, as science calls it. He exposed the aquarium to the sunlight, shading three sides against it, and behold, toward that one pane through which the light fell, thither straightway slanted the whole equivocal kith and kin: mushrooms, phallic polyp-stalks, little trees, algae, half-formed limbs. Indeed, they so yearned after

warmth and joy that they actually clung to the pane and stuck fast there.

'And even so they are dead,' said Jonathan, and tears came in his eyes, while Adrian, as of course I saw, was shaken with suppressed laughter.[9]

As these zoophytes attest, Mann shared Poe's conviction that human creation is parodic, a "travesty of innocence."[10]

In fact, Leverkühn makes many Poe-esque utterances, including a declaration of his abhorrence of transitions because they give the game of art away: "The work of art? It is a fraud. It is something the burgher wishes there still were. It is contrary to truth, contrary to serious art. Genuine and serious is only the very short, the highly consistent musical moment...." Is Mann saying here that the work of art is a parody of art? It is certain that, especially in his early years as an artist, he felt that the forms and language in which he was compelled to work were exhausted, and fit only for parody. Far from being an irregularity, a kink in the artistic process, parody was central to the enterprise. In this respect he would agree with the Russian formalist Viktor Shklovsky, who regarded *Tristram Shandy* as both "a parodying novel" and "the most typical novel of world literature."[12] It is a parodying novel because it foregrounds all the "devices" by which novels at that time created the illusion of reality; it is a typical novel because novels are nothing more than the sum of their devices. Mann's ironic narratives about artists beset by ironies reflect his belief that art consists of parody; and that his own art was a parody of parody, a pathetic imitation of a pathetic imitation of life, which, though heliotropic, was yet dead.

All Mann's opinions are colored by this paradoxical or dialectical understanding of his own condition. He praised Baudelaire, for example, as a man whose artistic gods were the unlikely pair of Poe and Wagner (who differ most strikingly on the subject of the appropriate length for a work of art). Wagner himself interested Mann for his reconciliation of nationalistic myth and Christianity.[13] After many doubts Mann finally declared himself in Freud's corner, commending him especially for having balanced the conscious mind with the unconscious; and, contrariety doubled, for having articulated the poles of the unconscious mind as Eros and Thanatos.[14] Freud's discussion of narcissism first appeared in his book on Leonardo in 1910, the year before Mann composed *Death in Venice,* and indicated a possible integration of myth and psychology. In the same year, Mann was writing on Fontane, describing the artist's conservative/corrosive impulses as simultaneous debts to myth and psychology: "these are opposites, and where they live together in one and the same mind, where the 'poetic' is joined together with the 'literary,' there will be contradictions."[15] Mann eventually became a passionate adherent of Jung, who explored this combination with an immeasurably greater zeal than Freud felt appropriate. In 1941 Mann wrote to his friend Karl Kerényi that the union of myth and psychology "represents no less than the world of the future, a human community that is blessed by a spirit from above and 'out of the depths that lie below.'"[16] Mann's continuing interest in and reference to Schopenhauer's *Will and Idea* and Nietzsche's *Apollo and Dionysus* indicate that, whatever the specific content, it was the form of contradiction or dialectic itself that fascinated him.

Much of Mann, including his pronounced tendency toward the grotesque, can be illuminated by this affinity for paradox. In 1924 he wrote of Conrad's *The Secret Agent* that it reflected the values of a world in which the categories of comedy and tragedy had broken down; the grotesque, he asserted, was a parodic sublime, "the only guise in which the sublime may appear" in such a world. G. Wilson Knight stated this idea precisely in his 1930 discussion *"King Lear* and the Comedy of the Grotesque" in *The Wheel of Fire:* "the comic and the tragic," Knight says, "rest both on the idea of incompatibilities, and are also, themselves, mutually exclusive: therefore to mingle them is to add to the meaning of each; the result is but a new sublime incongruity."[17] Equally pertinent to Mann's own grotesque is his 1918 attack on his brother Heinrich's exaggerated social satire, in *Meditations of a Nonpolitical Man.* Art, Mann says, must be compounded of passivity (the "humbly receptive and reproductive manner of Impressionism") and activity (the "sovereign, explosive, ruthlessly creative outpouring of the spirit"). Art falls between extremes of Impressionism and Expressionism, Tolstoi and Dostoevsky, Realism and Fantasy. The grotesque falls on the "active" side but has not wholly lost touch with the real:

> But if we allow that the expressionist artistic tendency has in it a more spiritual impetus towards the violation of life, we

must surely draw certain limits to the "freedom of art" which is at issue — it will have to draw them itself. The grotesque is properly something more than the truth *(das Überwahre)*, something real in the extreme *(das überaus Wirkliche)*, not something arbitrary, false, absurd, and contrary to reality. An artist who rejected all responsibility *vis-à-vis* life, and who went so far in his rejection of impressions as practically to cast off every obligation towards the forms of life as it is, and only allowed the imperious emanations of some absolute art-demon: such an artist would surely be the greatest of all radical fools.[18]

At the far end of Impressionism lies neutral record; at the far end of Expressionism lies presumptuous art uncorrected by reality, metaphor without brakes, pure dream. Art always pulls toward Expressionism in an attempt to throw off its chains of responsibility to reality. Its motivation for this "violation of life" is "spiritual," but the effect is moral degradation, for in renouncing impressions art rejects the quotidian, the honorable banalities that constitute a responsible life. The grotesque stands at that point of breakthrough, at the margin between a healthy imaginative vigor and a corrupt indulgence in the mind's unrealities. It is dangerously true, and its prevalence in Mann's work marks at once his estrangement from and fidelity to the bourgeois ideal.

3.

The grotesque stands as a warning sign of writing's dangers, which may be characterized as the tendency to constitute an autonomous system unconnected to the ground of being or the origin of meaning — unconnected to reality or nature. According to Mann, nature redeems language; in a context that both complements and contradicts Mann's, Derrida maintains that nature, or the illusion of a unified pre-linguistic ground, is the corruptor itself:

The natural, that which was inferior and anterior to language, acts within language *after the fact,* operates there after the origin, and provokes decadence or regression. It then becomes the posterior seizing the superior and dragging it toward the inferior. Such would be the strange time, the indescribable diagram of writing, the unrepresentable movement of its forces and its menaces.[19]

Derrida provides a context in which we might consider *Death in Venice* not only as the story of an artist in difficulty but also as an exploration of the difficulties of writing. Within such an exploration, human characters, actions, and passions have a part, but they are emblematic of "forces and menaces" intrinsic to all narrative. From this point of view, degeneration is not something that happens to a particular man, not an event, but a constant potentiality in writing.

Derrida makes his remarks in the course of a commentary on Rousseau's *Essay on the Origin of Languages,* a treatise with which Mann would have been very comfortable, for its terms are nearly his own. Rousseau speaks of the North-South opposition that characterizes both language and passion, and asserts that language naturally moves towards ever more exacting literalness and precision. In the process of becoming prolix, dull, and cold, language effaces (to use the Derridean term) its origin, with the consonantal northern pole asserting itself over the passional vocalic South. (We must think of Tadzio as the object of a long-suppressed and multi-faceted passion: one of his forms is as an incarnate vowel, "a long-drawn-out *u.*") Like other Mann protagonists, Aschenbach embodies a North-South tension: his father is a Northern official in the judicature; from his Bohemian mother he inherits "swifter, more perceptive blood," "foreign traits," an association with music, and "an ardent, obscure impulse" (8).[20] Mann's terms replicate Rousseau's; but it is more surprising to see them replicated in Derrida as well. For the image of the origin in the text is the primal swamp of the Ganges, the jungle toward which he ever tends; and this jungle is the corruptor, the origin of the plague. Extravagantly Northern at the beginning of the narrative, Aschenbach gravitates toward the South, Tadzio (one of a series of "absolute art-demons"), the Ganges, and the origin of language all at once. On this last point, Derrida is specific: "language is originally metaphorical. According to Rousseau it derives this from its mother, passion. Metaphor is the characteristic that relates language to its origin. Writing would then be the obliteration of this characteristic, the 'maternal characteristics.'"[21] And the subject of *Death in Venice* can be conceived as metaphor seizing metonymy and dragging it toward parody.

To understand metaphor as the maternal ground from which language has arisen and toward which it may degenerate is to begin to understand the extraordinary sense of "inevitability" imparted by the narrative. For although Aschenbach renounces "knowledge," "sympathy with the abyss," and "the flabby humanism of *tout comprendre, c'est tout pardonner*" as a means of "obliterating" the maternal metaphor, he is pulled back toward them, toward a sense of the connectedness of things, by the gravitational allure of the natural. Remarkably, the sense of inevitability accelerates as the events become increasingly unusual; it accelerates despite the interweaving of dream into the realistic narrative, the proliferation of mythic figures and references; it accelerates despite the increasingly exotic psychological condition of the protagonist. Inevitability seems inversely proportionate to probability; necessity, to rarity. And this can be only because Aschenbach, in his grotesqueness, rushes toward a "natural" condition.

It was this progression that provoked D. H. Lawrence to accuse Mann of "banality," of falling prey to the "rotten" Flaubertian doctrine of "Nothing outside the definite line of the book."[22] Lawrence's own method, and his morality, were precisely the opposite. The double novel *The Rainbow* and *Women in Love* begins with a vision of the generations of Brangwens living close to the immemorial rhythms of the earth, a celebration of the replicable, the shared, the familial, in which there are no individuals, only Brangwens, and "Brangwen" is a mode of being sanctified by the ages and the place. But the novel moves relentlessly out of the primordial swamp and into the drier air of dis-integrated individuality, ending with Birkin and Ursula, living in a world recognized as contemporary, struggling to achieve a condition for which there is no precedent. Lawrence points toward a new heaven and new earth, one of the most attractive features of which must have been that (as it says in *Revelation)* "there was no more sea." Mann's hero begins at that point of achieved individuality toward which Lawrence's grope, but then half-willingly abandons it. Aschenbach begins in a condition of metonymy: Aschenbach the solitary warrior of the soul, with neither family nor friends, with no interests other than his work — he is his honored self, illuminating but not illuminated by the world, attached to nothing, replicated nowhere. His personal condition is reinforced by the metonymic character of the narrative. We encounter him in the historical, specifiable world, walking down a "realistic" Prince Regent Street in Munich on a spring afternoon in "19—." The uncertainty in the date is the sole de-realizing element, the only opening for the sense of reality to leak out, and the figural or archetypal to enter in. Aschenbach seems, however, no creature of the fancy or imagination, but a dense figure, even one composed from verifiable facts drawn from the lives of Platen, Goethe, Winckelmann, Mahler, and even Mann himself, who attributed his own thinly disguised works to his protagonist, and who had himself vacationed in Venice. Mann went so far as to acknowledge these circumstances by saying that "Nothing is invented in Death in Venice."[23] In other words, up to a certain point, it seems that nothing at all is "within the line of the book," but all derived or adapted from "life," the category of the external. The tale so offended Lawrence because the hero surrenders rather than acquires his significant features, his differentiating marks. The tale ends in the sea; the hero is diluted, for he replicates and is replicated by all the figures he has encountered — even Venice, even death itself.

How does this happen? Where is the point of transformation, the origin of corruption where the solidity of metonymy begins to soften into the liquidity of metaphor, where the discrete first betrays evidence of becoming the replicable? If we can locate such a point, we will have discovered not only the point of the grotesque, but also the crux of the narrative, the still point on which the action turns. The problem, in thematic terms, is to find the spot where Aschenbach begins to dilute, or to "identify" with the various characters he encounters.

As this process of identification ends in death, we may rephrase the question to, When does he begin to die? The common-sense answer, of course, is that he, like the rest of us, has always been dying, but that this is beside the point in considering the dynamics of the text. I would argue, however, that it is precisely the point, for one of the striking features of the text is that the end, which appears to be a radical reversal of the beginning, is always already present. No matter how far back we go, we discover that the contamination that results in Aschenbach's death has already occurred. For example, we can see that the very traits that constitute his isolation actually bind him to the world. He is from the start bent on fame, on achieving for himself a unique position in the world; but this fame rests "on an inner harmony, yes, an affinity, between the personal destiny of its author and that of his contemporaries in general.... The real ground of their applause is inexplicable — it is sympathy" (10–11). This flow of sympathy is given form by a mutual commitment to "moral fibre": "And yet: this moral fibre, surviving the hampering and disintegrating effect of knowledge, does it not result in its turn in a dangerous simplification, in a tendency to equate the world and the human soul....?" (13) Sympathy is thus aligned with metaphor, the tendency to equate dissimilar things, and so Aschenbach is connected in a metaphorical manner not only to his readers who honor him but also to "the world," which he forces to bend beneath the sceptre of form, the form of his own soul. Connections extend even beyond the world, however; they spread out to infinity. Early in the narrative he ponders "the mysterious harmony that must come to subsist between the individual human being and the universal law, in order that human beauty may result..." (27–28). Temperament and accomplishment had set Aschenbach apart, a moral example. But they also draw him into the circle of humanity and out to the world, out to "universal laws." All these circles are vicious, resulting in dangerous and morally dubious simplifications. The points of sympathy provide lesions through which structure seeps from the poet-protagonist to the world, from the part to the whole. They help explain, in a nearly technical way, the process of entropic simplification that marks his career.

So the search for the crucial event, the momentous decision, is more problematic than it had at first appeared. We are now considering the possibility that any element or image from the scandalous conclusion may be traced back to an origin at the honorable beginning. Let us take as an example the monstrous dream near the end, an event that appears to mark the beginning of the final phase of Aschenbach's degradation, climaxing a rising line of action and preceding the denouement of his death. In it, his "senses reeled in the steam of panting bodies, the acrid stench from the goats, the odour as of stagnant waters — and another, too familiar smell — of wounds, uncleanness, and disease." The crucial point comes when he "joins" the figures of his dream: "But now the dreamer was in them and of them, the stranger god was his own. Yes, it was he who was flinging himself upon the animals, who bit and tore and swallowed smoking gobbets of flesh — while on the trampled moss there now began the rites in honour of the god, an orgy of promiscuous embraces — and in his soul he tasted the bestial degradation of his fall" (68). He wakes to find himself "shattered, unhinged, powerless in the demon's grip," his thoughts now characterized by "the fantastic logic that governs our dreams" (72). The rhetoric of the narration implies that at this point the absolute art-demon of the *Meditations* has finally seized him, and that his condition upon awaking is different in kind from any previous state. But this dream, in which he becomes the slave of Dionysus, the "stranger god," is implicit or latent in an earlier dream, decidedly one inspired by "his own god" twenty pages earlier. Already smitten by Tadzio, he awakens early one morning, goes to his window to await the coming day, and muses, his dazzles soul "new-risen from its sleep," drifting in and out of a dream peopled by Cleito, Eos, Cephalus, and Orion, and strewn with roses, baby cloudlets, putti, amoretti painting a rosyfingered dawn. This dream is the later dream's "proper-not," for it reverses all its significant characteristics. The constant technique of the story, however, is to reveal, through the inversion of background and foreground, such proper-nots as proper kin. Here this conversion is made possible by the later ascendance of what is, in the early dream, mere detail: amid the general profusion of pastel, the steed of the sungod mounts into the sky with "godlike violence," striking the poet with "forgotten feelings, precious pangs of youth" which "now returned so strangely metamorphosed — he recognized them with a puzzled, wondering smile" (49). Behind the cloudlets thunder the divinities, pleasure merges with pain, and the familiar metamorphoses into the alien. No wonder he is puzzled; for this dream is pure confusion, mediating not only between dreaming and waking, but also between the beginning and the end, stretching back to the childhood of the race and his own childhood, and forward to the final dream in which his corruption is completed.

To describe the dream in his way is to make it appear a pivot, a point where the beginning ends and the end begins. But surely the sight of Tadzio that occasioned the dream is the true pivot, for Aschenbach is first drawn to "origins" when he spies this "tender young god, emerging from the depths of sea and sky," a creature from "the beginning of time," an incarnate legend "of the birth of form, of the origin of the gods" (33). Even this point is not far enough back, however, as we can see by looking at the passage describing Tadzio's first appearance:

> ...the hard-worked artist's longing for rest, his yearning to seek refuge from the thronging manifold shapes of his fancy in the bosom of the simple and vast; and another yearning, opposed to his art and perhaps for that very reason a lure, for the unorganized, the immeasurable, the eternal — in short, for nothingness. He whose preoccupation is with excellence longs fervently to find rest in perfection; and is not nothingness a form of perfection? As he sat there dreaming thus, deep, deep into the void, suddenly the margin line of the shore was cut by a human form. (31)

Standing at the borderline, issuing directly from the primordial divisions of heaven and earth, land and sea, Tadzio appears a breathing god who provokes both awe and sympathy; he converts easily into a figure for Aschenbach's ancient attraction to nothingness. As we go back still farther, we note that the night before this vision, the artist's sleep had been visited by "varied and lively dreams" (28). As we have seen, no dream is innocent, for in dreams the trans-human fuses with the deeply personal, the Homeric twines around the pathological, allies against the achieving social self.

So we are constantly thrust back and back in search of the untainted, a spot where the end is not. That such a search is futile is surely the point of Mann's mentioning that Aschenbach devoted only "his best and freshest hours" to composition, when he was in full command of "the powers he had assembled in sleep" (10). The first sentences of the narrative describe his fatigue, his need for honorable rest so that he could better do homage to his own god. Sleep trammels him in dreams, the origins of "that fiery play of fancy which is the product of joy" (7). Joy — even joy is implicated! The point Mann is dramatizing is that taint, impurity, complexity are always implicit, always present. What appears to be Aschenbach's stylistic purity in fact represents a perfectly poised stalemate between opposed forces, a parody of true unity, which is always pre-creation, out of reach. He is always "born from two."

4.

Looking in the opposite direction, from the beginning to the end, we can describe the progress of the narrative as a continual conversion of elements external to the protagonist, and to the literary text, into elements "within" the protagonist and the "definite line of the book." This conversion process has the simultaneous effects of weakening the protagonist and of strengthening the text, which becomes increasingly independent of "the world," increasingly self-sufficient. I should like to focus first on this process as it applies to Aschenbach, for it is here that the notion of grotesque parody is most illuminating. Always already secretly contaminated, Aschenbach is continually "tempted," discovering affinities with the diseased outside within himself. After seeing the stranger at the cemetery, for example, he is stricken with a sudden impulse to flight: *"Und doch wusste er nur zu wohl, aus welchern Grunde die Anfechtung, so unversehens, hervorgegangen war."* Lowe-Porter translates this passage as "Yet the source of the unexpected contagion was known to him only too well" (6). "Contagion" is clearly a thematized translation, linking the present event to the artist's later contact with the plague. A translation more faithful to the "Lutheran" spirit of *Anfechtung* would be "temptation," a war of the soul.

What he is tempted to or infected by is curious — a "break, an interim existence…other air and a new stock of blood" (7–8). This is the interim that Derrida calls the "strange time" of writing. It is not too metaphysical to say that this temptation is to metaphorical identification, for metaphor occupies just this break, a "conceptual leap," discovering kinship in the foreign. To recognize the centrality of the interim is to pay particular attention to those breaks in the narrative action when nothing seems to be happening, when Aschenbach is between places, in actual transition/temptation/contagion. They are numerous, but brief: he is disturbed by something incongruous, blinks in momentary confusion, rubs his eyes, and the phantasm has vanished. The stranger at the cemetery is "not in his former place"; the gondolier "ran away, signore"; the musicians, "meanwhile, had finished and gone." After encountering the young-old man as he is boarding the ship for Venice, he feels

> not quite canny, as though the world were suffering a dreamlike distortion of perspective which he might arrest by shutting it all out for a few minutes and then looking at it afresh.… Aschenbach's brow darkened as he looked, and there came over

him once more a dazed sense, as though things about him were just slightly losing their ordinary perspective, beginning to show a distortion that might merge into the grotesque. (17–18, 19)

Recently, Susan Sontag has written of *Death in Venice* in her study of *Illness as Metaphor;* in light of this series — exertion: fatigue: relaxation: temptation: identification: infection: death — it appears more to the point to consider metaphor as illness.

Metaphor, and indeed all communication, establishes what Lévi-Strauss calls "an evenness of level, where before there was an information gap and consequently a greater degree of organization."[24] He suggests that anthropology could be called "entropology," as the name of the discipline concerned with the study of the process of disintegration. At least so far as this text is concerned, literary criticism might be another such discipline, for a grotesque parody is an entropic version, a version that fills, like a metaphor, the gap of evenness between self and other, and so constantly tends toward a lower degree of organization.

We can track Aschenbach's fate by marking the points at which he surrenders his higher degree of organization by accepting kinship. We can begin with the relatively inconspicuous incident following the Dionysian dream, in which Aschenbach visits the barber. He is tempted by the barber's arguments in favor of cosmetic rejuvenation because they mimic his own noble rejection of "the hampering and disintegrating effect of knowledge" (13). The barber's defense is moral and bourgeois, favoring action and artful discipline over nature's betrayals. He equates nature and the human soul not through the creation of extended prose narratives but by dyeing hair, powdering cheeks, and, in general, "restoring" the "natural color" that "belongs" to his client. Aschenbach succumbs to these stratagems because, in his weakened state, it seems to him as if the barber is speaking with his own voice; but this is just the beginning, for when he rises from the chair he has become in fact a grotesque parody of himself — which is to say, an image of another parody, the young-old man. When he looks in the mirror he discovers a "young man," and this mirror image encompasses both "the master" and that hideous creature of rouge and loose dentures. But the image is only the grotesque manifestation of deeper sympathies: like the young-old man, the young Aschenbach had taken away "the breath of the twenty-year-olds with...cynic utterances on the nature of art and the artist life" (12). Both teach, both provide models for youth, both are attracted to beauty. Multiplying resemblances, we can see that the barber has created not a smaller, or a false, Aschenbach, but a larger and a true one; a poet who, grotesquely but rightly, contains the young-old man.

Paradoxically, this kind of truth consists of constant dilution of the original self. In the course of the narrative Aschenbach collects attributes in a manner so crude and so mysterious that it seems at once a parody and an apotheosis of literary "devices" such as "foreshadowing" and "symbolism." We know that he goes into the barbershop sporting a straw hat, but we do not know until he leaves the shop that this hat has a "gay striped band," or that he has been wearing a red necktie. These details would be unimportant except for the fact that the young-old man and the gondolier were similarly outfitted, and the necktie and hatband now seem evidence of contamination by them. Such connections are most apparent with the three "messenger" figures who impress the artist so forcefully — the stranger at the cemetery, the gondolier, and the guitarist. It is inadequate merely to point out that these figures share a number of qualities; more accurate to say that they draw on a definable pool of characteristics or traits, to which they each contribute something: an imperious air, a "foreign" quality, an iron-shod stick, a dubious association with music, a prominent Adam's apple, crossed legs, less than middle height, a connection with the sea, an association with disease, a snub nose, pointed teeth, and a pattern of coloration that includes the three primary colors and black, white, and grey. The repetition of these attributes subverts the status of any identity in the text by implying that each individual is merely a partial incarnation, a facet, of some larger concept whose limits are unclear, but always apparently enlarging.

Surprisingly, even Tadzio draws from this well. His colors and nautical aspect are right: he wears a blue and white sailor suit, with a red breast-knot and white collar; he has yellow hair and blueish teeth. He participates, too, in his taint of illness, his foreignness, and even in his quick contempt for the Russian family whom he spies "leading their lives there in joyous simplicity" (31) — repugnant to the boy in his role as "absolute art-demon" leading Aschenbach to radical foolishness. Tadzio's mother is known as the "lady of pearls"; a pearl is a little perfection formed around a speck of dirt, the lovely product of a pathological irritation, and he is his mother's son. For he is Apollo masking Dionysus — Nietzsche's definition of Greek drama — and is recognizable both as Aschenbach's "own god" and as the "stranger god." Tadzio embraces Jaschiu, his tormentor-lover, who shares his vowel. And he embraces Aschenbach, touching through conspiratorial glances with his grey eyes. As black/white, grey is the color of mediation, of metaphor, of entropy, of the impure union of opposites. The only other grey in the text is masked, or secret: it is the color of Aschenbach's hair. Tadzio is a universal mirror and image, a glass in which everything discovers its double, especially the doubled artist whose task is to mirror both spiritual beauty and the destiny of his contemporaries.

In such ways Tadzio gathers identities unto himself; in this, he complements the last of the messenger-figures, the guitarist, who disperses himself generally. Thus the scene in which Aschenbach and Tadzio regard each other furtively while the guitarist entertains the international clientele of the hotel is especially interesting for its simultaneous and multi-leveled absorptions and dispersals. The guitarist is a truly cosmic figure, constantly breaking the frame that would limit him. First he leaves the area of performance, going up on the terrace to collect money from the assembled guests — who all contribute, even the artless Russians. While collecting, he is also dispersing, for he is drenched in carbolic and each inhales his reek. Then, having collected, he begins his performance, a rowdy song in an "impossible" dialect, with a refrain consisting only of laughter, which comes "whooping, bawling, crashing out of him, with a verisimilitude that never failed to set his audience off in profuse and unpremeditated mirth that seemed to add gusto to his own." At the height of the laughter, he reverses the frame, becoming the spectator by pointing at the audience "as though there could be in all the world nothing so comic as they; until at last they laughed in hotel, terrace, and garden, down to the waiters, liftboys, and servants — laughed as though possessed" (62). The point of his climactic scene is that they are indeed possessed; that pollution is general and as inevitable as drawing breath; that nothing is separate, nothing is outside the definite line of the poet. The smaller sympathetic contaminations I have been discussing gather here to universal taint.

The impure "type" that cannot be kept securely on the outside now engulfs everything: family resemblances have proliferated beyond control or definition. The type is scattered over the map of Europe; the pool threatens to include *all* characteristics. The protagonist has been disbanded as an individual, but has come close to achieving the condition that Northrop Frye attributes to the entire literary universe, "in which everything is potentially identical with everything else."[25]

5.

What is the center of this network, the point of this endless connectedness? Is there a type of types among the replicas, an axle from which all spokes radiate? To these questions many answers seem possible. It could be said that all the characters are "really" images of Tadzio, or that they all group around Aschenbach as manifestations of his psyche. It has been suggested that the three main tempters are images of death like those we encounter in Dürer; or that they are satyrs attendant to Tadzio-Dionysus. One critic has maintained that both Tadzio and Aschenbach are versions of Sebastian, the hero of Aschenbach's works: "The conception of an intellectual and virginal manliness, which clenches its teeth and stands in modest defiance of the swords and spears that pierce its side" (11). In finding justice in all these views I am proposing another kind of approach altogether: that we abandon the search for a center within the text, and think instead of the entire narrative as a continuing process of the foreign-becoming-intimate, the metonymic-becoming-the-metaphoric — in other words, of a movement from the center to the margin. The narrative is like a great chain of being, except that it has no definable origin, no source of order.

In making these suggestions I have extended the implications of two images that do seem, if not central, at least pervasive. The first is a metaphor for metaphor itself — the air, which passes through everything, imparting life, infecting, degrading, inspiring. The air of thought is the hateful, sultry air of the sirocco. In and through the air, everything is linked: to see the text from the point of view of the air is to see individual identity as migratory, a provisional configuration.

The second image of images is sweetness, which relates to the seepage of structure I have characterized as entropic reduction, or parody.

I am not speaking only of literal sweetnesses, such as the strawberries Aschenbach twice consumes, but as it happens these two occasions are instructive of the larger sense of sweetness I have in mind. He first eats strawberries when he sees Tadzio on the beach, early in his stay in Venice. They are delectable, but already savoring of excess (in the same way that "beaded bubbles winking at the brim" in "Ode to a Nightingale" convert instantly to the dangerous "purple-stained mouth"), for they constitute his "second breakfast." They are not fresh, but are "luscious, dead-ripe fruit" (33). Within a paragraph, sweetness is linked not with corruption but with the image of Tadzio as a young god, virginally pure and austere: the cry" 'Tadziu! Tadziu!'" with its terminal vowel, strikes Aschenbach as "sweet and wild" *(Süsses und Wildes)*. Tadzio is consistently sweet in both the senses implied in these instances; he can be considered as an epitome of sweetness itself, the kind of ambiguous delight/debauchery, fatality/fertility invoked in an Aschenbach daydream as the "sweet blood" of the slain Hyacinthus, from which the flower springs.

The second time we encounter strawberries, we know both that the food supply in Venice is the source of the plague, and that Aschenbach has emerged from the attentions of the barber with his lips colored carmine, "the color of ripe strawberries." The phrase "sweet and wild" has reappeared, too, in the account of the fearful dream, applied to the "mad rout" in the frenzied pursuit of the goats. The cry of the pursuers is accompanied by flute-notes "of the cruellest sweetness" *(alles durchsetzt und grauenhaft süss übertönt van tief girrendem)*. And we have read, and understood as a sign of the plague, of the "sweetish-medicinal smell" *(süsslich-affizinellen Geruch)* of the carbolic used to disinfect the city. This is a smell not altogether different from "that cloying, sacrificial smell" *(dumpf-süssen Opferduft)* in St. Mark's, with which it mingles. Horrid death stalks the streets in these evil vapors, much as Aschenbach stalks the delightful, "sweetly idle" Tadzio.

This pursuit is sweet stalking sweet, for Aschenbach and Tadzio are displaying the two sides of sweet: this, indeed, is the idea that unites them. Sweet things delight; and they dissolve: they rot. The strawberries are presented to him not as an assemblage of discrete items, but as a great mass, ambivalently plural and single. Sweet implies ripe, and ripe promises rot. This is precisely the course of Aschenbach's entanglement with Tadzio, which begins with baby cloudlets and images of creation and ends with corruption and death. Tadzio, with his honey-colored ringlets, rots into the stranger god, and then into Hermes, god of duplicity and ambivalence. All figures in this narrative rot. The musicians who accompany the artist's gondola to the Lido rot into the guitarist and his company; the fantasy of Socrates discoursing to Phaedrus, which occurs to Aschenbach when he first sees Tadzio, rots into the drunken dream-Socrates at the end. This version of the philosopher instructs his pupil that beauty represents a path of "perilous sweetness, a way of transgression" *(ein gefährlich-lieblicher Weg zum Geistigen durch die Sinne führt)*. Sweet things rot into their own parodies, surrendering their structure and level of organization as they do so.

We can see why "moral fiber" must be based on a renunciation of the sweet. What Aschenbach discovers is that there is no avoiding it. He had favored "lofty purity, symmetry, and simplicity" (13), opposing these to the "disintegrating effect of knowledge," but suspects from the first that simplicity itself is entropic: the very renunciation that combats rot encourages it, resulting "in its turn in a dangerous simplification, in a tendency to equate the world and the human soul..." (13). His whole aesthetic philosophy is based on entropy, in artfully disguised forms: "Thought that can merge wholly into feeling, feeling that can merge wholly into thought — these are the artist's highest joy" (46). So we cannot be taken by surprise when the scabrous Socrates tells his boy-lover that "simplicity, largeness, and renewed severity of discipline" means "a return to detachment and to form," and that this preoccupation with form leads "to intoxication and desire," and ultimately to "the bottomless pit" (73). As all communication fills in "the gap of evenness," all mergings lead to the pit.

This pit is figured by the sea, the home of largeness and simplicity, and here is the final characteristic of sweet: it dissolves into liquid, into the larger body, which absorbs it. Perhaps we call our lovers terms of endearment that summon up images of sweetness to express our desire that their singleness be fused with ours in a third thing, love. Sweet love is like a metaphor, establishing a base of sameness in difference, a sameness that necessarily involves a loss of individuality on both sides. Other sweetnesses also dissolve. Revenge is sweet because, in bringing an enemy low it destroys an odious hierarchy. That parting is a sweet sorrow means that we can blend most blissfully when we are certain of regaining our selves shortly after. Rapture precedes rupture: deep-sea divers speak of "the rapture of the deep," a form of nitrogen narcosis that is reportedly inexpressibly sweet. Aschenbach's dreams are first a delightful, and then a rank, preliminary version of his death, for they break the frame of self, permitting a free flow to the infinite. When Goffman speaks of "breaking frame" he, too, uses the image of "flooding out," and this is Aschenbach's experience — sweet love ending in liquid death.

The richest exfoliation of sweetness is the discussion of "the viscous" *(visqueux)* that concludes the enormous project of Sartre's *Being and Nothingness*.[26] The essence of the viscous is, he says, perfectly captured by the sensation of sweetness, especially in its rotting and dissolving aspects. Noting the universal and instinctive revulsion for the slimy, Sartre says that it presents us with a challenge, raising questions about the relation between the self and the world, and the way they appropriate each other. The world revealed by the viscous is "like a *leech sucking me*" (606). Slime is marginal: at the moment we touch it, it is both the world and, as it takes our impress, an outline of ourselves. So although the viscous is neither material nor psychic, neither liquid nor solid, neither subjective nor objective, it has about it a totality that embraces all these potentialities in a way no other kind of substance can. Nausea had for Sartre a similar totality; it appeared as a sickly-sweet disgust arising from the confusion of inside and outside:

"The Nausea isn't in me," he says in *La Nausée,* "I feel it *there* on the wall, on my braces, everywhere around me. It is all of a piece with the cafe; *I'm* in it."[27] As a substance in between two states, the nauseating viscous is a thing in process of becoming; and it is the terminus of a metamorphosis, for whereas liquid and solid become viscous, the viscous becomes only itself: nothing escapes the indefinite line of the slimy. Insofar as Aschenbach's career can be described as an exploration of the margin, it can be considered in light of this continual resolution into viscosity. He discovers that all figures, even those repellent or threatening to himself, can be accommodated, through metaphor, "within."

Like Adam, Aschenbach — and all fictional characters, and all narratives — "stands in the middle." The reader who regards *Death in Venice* as a "realistic" narrative will consider this marginality ethically dubious, even disreputable. In "the world," it is. As Sartre says, slime is a symbol of *"Antivalue"* (611), by which he means that value judgments follow genre-decisions, and depend upon reliable categories, strict framing. Within an "interim existence" *(eine Einschaltung not, etwas Stegreifdasein)* there can be no value. On the other hand, as Sartre says boldly, though the slimy may be repugnant, it is *being,* and embodies "the meaning of the entire world" (607). As a character, and as an emblem of writing, Aschenbach is a "true Amphibium," a creature of divided natures. His impurity, revealed at the point where the alien becomes the intimate, is the impurity of the grotesque. But it is, after all, mistaken to speak of a "point," for the range of impurity in this text reaches from noble sympathy with one's readers to utter debasement. Another student of Venice, John Ruskin, also understood how easy was the descent, how viscous the path, from the "noble grotesque," characterized by terror and pity, to the "ignoble grotesque," marked by obscenity, mockery, and grossness. According to Ruskin, Venice declined from the noble Gothic grotesque to the ignoble form when it became afflicted by a "pestilence...that came and breathed upon her beauty...."[28] In *Death in Venice,* Mann has retold this story with a terrible nobility.

CHAPTER SEVEN

To Make You Sea: Conrad's Primal Words

Who can disentangle that twisted and intricate knottiness? Foul is it: I hate to think on it, to look on it.
— Augustine

Confused things rouse the mind to new inventions.
— Leonardo da Vinci

I hate babies.
— Conrad, in conversation.

1.

Like everything else, Joseph Conrad is interesting not for his consistency but for his contradictions, of which a fair example is the following. "Work," he says in one of his most famous utterances, "is the law":

> It has a simplicity and a truth which no amount of subtle comment can destroy.... From the hard work of men are born the sympathetic consciousness of a common destiny, the fidelity to right practice which makes great craftsmen, the sense of right conduct which we may call honour, the devotion to our calling and the idealism which is not a misty, winged angel without eyes, but a divine figure of terrestrial aspect with a clear glance and with its feet resting firmly on the earth on which it was born.[1]

An inventory of Conrad's bedrock values, the passage exemplifies the "few very simple ideas" on which he insisted the world, and all his thought, were based. We may hesitate over the incongruous figure of that terrestrial angel, but for truly Conradian inconsistency we should continue reading.

> And work will overcome all evil, except ignorance, which is the condition of humanity and, like the ambient air, fills the space between the various sorts and conditions of men, which breeds hatred, fear, and contempt between the masses of mankind and puts on men's lips, on their innocent lips, words that are thoughtless and vain.

A strange conclusion: work will overcome all, except for — everything, for there is no escaping air. Moreover, words, born of and borne on this corrupt ether, are necessarily ignorant — no provision is made for any other kind — and spawn all vices. Somehow, after beginning with the "sympathetic consciousness of a common destiny," we have arrived at a vision of universal darkness against which we can only set an ideal community constituted of isolated, silent, illiterate "craftsmen."

This point of congestion is a convenient place to begin a discussion both of Conrad's beginnings and of beginnings in general. It is remarkable how many discussions, how many discoveries, how many narratives, begin with paradox, contradiction, apparent confusion. For Mann, as we have seen, the origin is always split or impure, and narratives are generated from this bifurcation. In this chapter I want to discuss the possibility of a general rule that narratives begin with such knots, whose self-interfering energies demand to be released or dissipated. To consider inaugural knots is to look at beginnings from the point of view of the grotesque.

Stories begin with something that means too much. Augustine's narrative begins with the "intricate knottiness" referred to in the epigraph above, his perverse delight in stealing pears. In the next paragraph, the opening of Book III, he goes to Carthage, commencing the process of thinking, reading, disputing, and journeying that will constitute the undoing of that knot: the renunciation of evil, the embracing of Christ, the story of his life. My second epigraph is from Leonardo's *Treatise on Beauty,* and reflects a decidedly more hospitable view of "confused things," while still recognizing their germinative powers. In this passage, he is describing his habit of observing decomposing walls, seeking out patterns, shapes, accidentally representational forms. The images produced by the effects of moisture in the plaster give rise in the generous imagination of the artist to compositional possibilities, to interpretation, to "new inventions."

Confused things frequently appear as exceptions to the rule. The artist's eye is caught by the half-formed shape for the same reason that the scientist's eye is caught by the exception: by breaking the rules, such forms imply a larger category and open onto a freer imaginative world. The subjects of Freud's early case studies, on which broad general theories are frequently based, are scarcely typical psyches — Dora, the Wolf Man, the Rat Man, Freud himself — but only extraordinary instances could provide the bases for theories as original as Freud's. He asked simple questions of little tangles, too. Where does information go when we forget it? The fateful answer: the "unconscious." The clinical study of the unconscious was born of the paradox of knowing and not-knowing, a knottiness that required an unprecedented hypothesis, a newly imagined narrative of the mind, to explain it.

Jacob Burckhardt compared the beginning of a sequence of actions to a "fundamental chord" that resonated through the entire sequence, and this simile gives us a way of conceiving many origins. For any such fundamental chord is, strictly speaking, a dissonance that must be resolved in the following progression. The only true harmony lies in the final tonic chord, beyond which no further resolution is possible: all that precedes this chord is dissonant to a greater or lesser degree. Now the more familiar we are with the conventions of a certain piece of music, the less dissonant it is likely to seem to us, but when we pass beyond a sense of dissonance altogether, we have probably also passed beyond interest, for without dissonance nothing goes anywhere. Elevator music, for example, avoids dissonance as much as possible, and, as a consequence, seems an endless middle. Like literary genres, musical forms operate by what Leonard Meyer calls "internalized probability systems"[2] which prescribe, among other things, the most likely intervals between successive notes, the most likely series of notes, the most likely chord progressions. Most often these systems leave enough room for flexibility and invention so that within any key any note can occur. But they are rigid enough so that, although no note is automatically dissonant in a given key, it can appear dissonant in improper or improbable relation. In tonal music, under normal conditions in the key of C, for example, a chord of C# cannot directly follow a chord of G7 without dissonance, but the resourceful composer might either deliberately sacrifice convention for novelty or minimize the dissonance by interposing one or more chords between the two. Those interposed chords are necessitated by the threat of dissonance.

Adrian Leverkühn, Mann's Faustus, was an exceptionally resourceful composer who

> amused himself by writing very sharp dissonances and finding all possible resolutions for them, which, however, just because the chord contained so many discordant notes, had nothing to do with each other, so that that acid chord, like a magic formula, created relations between the remotest chords and keys.[3]

In packing the chord to the point of cacophony, Leverkühn effects the "transference of the horizontal interval into the chord...the successive into the simultaneous"[4] in a manner entirely faithful to the spirit of polyphony. No chord should be valued for itself, for its moment, he insists, but only for the movement of voices converging in it. In terms of this convergence, the "polyphonic character of the chords is the more pronounced, the more dissonant it is. The degree of dissonance is the measure of its polyphonic value."[5] An atrocious chord may be the genesis of a rich, original, and profoundly polyphonic composition, and a conventional opening is more likely to yield clichés, or easy listening.

If the tradition of Aristotle is right in saying that a minimal definition of a narrative is the story of the conversion of a condition into its opposite, then dissonance would actually be a natural way to begin a progression, a way for which the grotesque would be a model. For grotesque entities contain contradictory elements, and if contraries are spun out into narrative, something will necessarily yield to its opposite. With its incongruous pieces unified by a half-perceived principle of coherence, the grotesque stands as a type of that-which-generates-progression.

The grotesque is a model for beginnings in another sense. In Chapter Three I argued that the grotesque involved a simultaneous foregrounding of mythic and historical assumptions, that it stood at the margin between the archaic and the modern. Beginnings are the same. Has it ever been noticed how many narratives begin with somebody walking? E. M. Forster advanced the sentence "The Marquise went out at five o'clock" as a typical beginning because it perfectly embodied the situation of emergence from a static past into a dynamic and uncertain present. To begin is to effect a rupture or break with a static pattern; it is to move out of what Edward Said, in his study of *Beginnings,* refers to as a sacred or original condition into a gentile or historical one.⁶ Hareton Earnshaw reads his own name and a date, locating a version of himself at the margin between a numberless, mythic time and a calibrated, progressive, and historical time. And he perceives himself as a version or copy of that original type. When Melville's narrator asks the reader to call him Ishmael, he chooses another version of himself, an alienated form. But at the same time that he surrenders inherited wholeness of being by relinquishing his given name, he is compensated, not only by assuming a legendary identity, but also by constituting himself through a free act of will. As Said says, "The beginning in writing is inaugurating and subsequently maintaining *another* order of meaning from previous or already existing writing."⁷ Recent narrators are likely to draw ironic attention to the stresses and possibilities created by this break with previous writing. The career of John Barth, for example, begins with a recognition of the conditions of an alternate existence: the first sentence of an early novel, *The End of the Road,* is, "In a sense, I am Jacob Horner." Barth's subsequent experiments in alienation move in the direction indicated by Derrida's statement that "*L'écriture universelle [serait] l'alienation absolue.*"⁸

2.

If the deconstructionists are correct in saying that writing promotes the demythologized or de-centered point of view, then it is hard to see why a man who cherished simple ideas would abandon the brotherhood of the sea and become a writer. And if I am correct in saying that the grotesque provides a model for beginnings, then it is hard to see why Conrad insisted that simple ideas provided the origin of his writing. We can begin to unravel these paradoxes by examining some permutations of simplicity in a book that seems to many Conrad readers an atypical production, *The Secret Agent.* This novel, which Mann so admired for its exemplary grotesqueness, is dedicated "affectionately" to H. G. Wells as a "Simple Tale of the XIX Century."

Conrad maintains this insistence on simplicity through to the end, when we see the "incorruptible Professor" walking the streets of London, explosives concealed in his coat, "terrible in the simplicity of his idea calling madness and despair to the regeneration of the world." Something awful has happened to simplicity between the dedication and the conclusion, a violation Conrad explains in a prefatory Author's Note by saying that the tale is written in the "ironic mode." In this useful mode, words can imply their own opposites, so simplicity can be both a simple and a complex idea.[9]

The Author's Note also reveals the simple idea which was the novel's seed crystal, its germ — an account, current in 1907, of an attempt to blow up the Greenwich Observatory which ended only in a man's being blown to smithereens. From a certain point of view (the ironic one) this is a surpassingly simple event — what could be more clear, more decisive, more final — but from another point of view, such an event is like the "storms" Leonardo drew in his notebooks, lines swirling over lines to an ultimate effect of violent confusion, lines that have cousins in *The Secret Agent* in the endless circles drawn by Stevie, the idiot boy blown to bits. Of the original incident, Conrad says it was

> a bloodstained inanity of so fatuous a kind that it was impossible to fathom its origin by any reasonable or even unreasonable process of thought.... that outrage could not be laid hold of mentally in any sort of way, so that one remained faced by the fact of a man blown to bits for nothing even most remotely resembling an idea, anarchistic or other.

Here is the crisis of confrontation between Conrad, whose world rests on simple ideas, and an event whose origin is unfathomable, and wholly un-ideal. What could Conrad see in this subject for him?

Perhaps the point of kinship lies in the "ironic mode" itself, by which the univocal utterance fractures into multiple competing statements. As the narrator says of Winnie Verloc, "it was borne upon her with some force that a simple sentence may hold several diverse meanings — mostly disagreeable." The disagreeable consequences of insight which always reveals disabling irony persuade her that "Things don't bear too much looking into," advice that is itself both serious and ironic. One of Conrad's simple ideas was that prose fiction makes word pictures, and that his whole aim, as he says in the Preface to *The Nigger of the "Narcissus,"* was to make the reader *see*. Throughout *The Secret Agent* characters peer into a moral, psychic, political, and actual fog, unable to see anything clearly or whole. Here as elsewhere in Conrad, what we see is not at all what we get, for nothing is so problematic, so doubtful, so invisible as the visible. The detonation of Stevie is only one of many enigmas the reader must try to visualize in a text that communicates a nearly comedic despair at anyone's ever being able to see anything. Irony is not merely one arrow in the storyteller's quiver, but is embedded in the world of the novel itself, which is double in essence, and hostile to the very notion of pictorialization. In this situation, language, though strained, can on rare occasions escape irony and achieve univocal adequacy: regarding Michaelis, the monstrously obese incarnation of "humanitarian passion," "The lank man, with the eyeglass on a broad ribbon, pronounced mincingly the word 'Grotesque,' whose justness was appreciated by those standing nearest him."[10]

Not even the simplest ideas are immune to ironical self-cancellation, for their advocates in this novel are Winnie Verloc, the incorruptible Professor, and, pre-eminently, Stevie, who espouses all Conrad's causes — hard work, fidelity, honesty, and a sense of common destiny, or "universal charity." Stevie is simplicity not merely made forktongued, but literally blown to bits, and yet, in his correspondence, Conrad seems almost cheerful about the novel. As soon as he finished it, in fact, he began another in a great spurt of enthusiasm on a similar theme: *Under Western Eyes* was also born from an account of a man blown to bits.[11] Conrad had found his subject.

In an essay to which I shall return, Paul de Man suggests a way of reading Locke's *Essay Concerning Human Understanding* that illuminates both Conrad's difficulties and his resolutions. Locke shared Conrad's moral preference for order and clarity of expression as opposed to mere wit, fancy, and verbal ornament which could only mislead and deceive. Furthermore, Locke based his theory of language on substances, mixed modes, and — simple ideas. Of the latter, Locke examines two, motion and light. In both cases, de Man says, Locke begins by attempting to establish a reasonable definition entirely free from arbitrariness, or what de Man calls tropological defiguration. But in both cases Locke is eventually forced into nonsense-definitions. De Man abbreviates Locke's conclusion in the following way:

To understand light as idea is to understand light properly. But the word "idea" *(eide),* of course, itself means light, and to say that to understand light is to perceive the idea of light is to say that understanding is to see the light of light and is therefore itself light.[12]

Stuck in "the repetitive stutter of tautology," de Man says, Locke concludes that "The *names of simple* ideas *are not capable of any definitions*...bk. 3, chap. 4, p. 26)." [13]

As de Man says, "This complication of the simple will run through the entire argument...."[14] The same can be said for Conrad. In his articles and prefaces Conrad always divides the world between the forces of simplicity (which can be seen, and are aligned with fidelity, work, and truth) and the forces of chaos (which cannot be seen, and are aligned with lies, adventure, subtlety, and self-interest). If either the world or Conrad were as neatly cloven as this, there would be nothing of interest to speak of at all. It is the point of contact between these poles, the chaos of simplicity and the subtlety of truth, that engages the mind, that can be captured only in writing, and that generates fictions. Conrad's novels hover around this margin, attempting to discover and create a language for it, because it is here that the simple code of the sea abuts a destabilizing and disabling awareness of the bewildering multiplicity of reality. As an explorer of this boundary line, Conrad is a perpetual beginner.

3.

Immediately after composing his first masterwork, *The Nigger of the "Narcissus",* Conrad wrote an "After-word" explaining what had been his intentions. Omitted from the first book edition of the work, this document has since appeared as a preface, achieving the status of a classic as Conrad's aesthetic credo. It is a highly revealing statement, although it reveals different things as an afterword from what it does as a preface. Before attending to this matter, however, let us approach it as tradition has presented it, as a preface.

Art, Conrad says, "may be defined as a single-minded attempt to render the highest kind of justice to the visible universe, by bringing to light the truth, manifold and one, underlying its every aspect."

Properly considered, the forms, colors, and lights of the visible world will reveal to the artist "their one illuminating and convincing quality — the very truth of their existence." In this aspect, things don't bear too much looking into. But this appeal to the visible, which informs the entire preface, immediately runs into trouble, for if vision is merely the bodily sight of external forms, colors, and textures, then no "truth" is yielded at all. We must interpret vision, therefore, to mean not only sight but insight:

> Confronted by the...enigmatical spectacle [of the visible world] the artist descends within himself.... His appeal is made to our less obvious capacities; to that part of our nature which, because of the warlike conditions of existence, is necessarily kept out of sight within the more resisting and hard qualities — like the vulnerable body within a steel armor.

So, no sooner is the visible world invoked than it is dismissed, a rejection made possible by the double meaning of *sight*.

Through a latent or secondary meaning Conrad embraces and repudiates simultaneously, a subtle verbal gesture in a document exalting univocal, or "single-minded," truth. A similar awareness of subsurface meaning enabled Conrad, a stranger in any company, to advocate "the latent feeling of fellowship with all creation; and...the subtle but invincible conviction of solidarity that knits together the loneliness of innumerable hearts...." Our similarities are more important than our differences; we're all in this boat together; we should all hang together or we will all hang separately — these seem to be appropriate paraphrases for Conrad's sentences. But even when Conrad is being bromidic he is subtle. Scrutinize, for example, the conventional-sounding statement that fiction "appeals to temperament...the appeal of one temperament to all the other innumerable temperaments whose subtle and resistless power endows passing events with their true meaning...." Whatever Conrad means by "temperament," it is clear that although everybody has one, they are all different, and "not amenable to persuasion." Temperament is the essence of individuality, of uniqueness, and a fiction that appeals to it will tend to reinforce alienation. Still, "true meaning" issues from the massed consensus of temperaments. In the very next sentence, however, Conrad relocates the truth of art by saying that literary truth consists of "an impression conveyed through the senses.... All art...appeals primarily to the senses...." Conrad treats sense-impressions as common property, and therefore the opposite of temperament, but still manages to maintain that fiction "appeals primarily" to them both. The claim for the senses is made on the basis that all art is sensuous, but this formula applies directly only to the visual, plastic, or aural arts. Literature does not appeal directly to the senses; its appeal is wholly internal or "latent": we are not meant to see the ink on the page as an aesthetic composition, except in the case of concrete poetry. Conrad tries to minimize the interiority of literature by speaking of "the shape and ring of sentences," but it is apparent that fiction's unique attraction for him was its ambivalence: as an "art," it had something of the definiteness of the sensory world — while communicating as well to that part of our nature that was "kept out of sight."

David Goldknopf has argued that Conrad seems unaware of the old problem of how "we go from the ephemeral and notoriously fallible evidence of the senses to the truth which is assumed, wishfully or not, to underlie that evidence."[15] This assessment misses the point. Conrad wanted to find the ground of truth, the substance in which confidence could be anchored. The senses, particularly sight, provided this ground. The evidence of the eyes was not fallible, but unquestionable, really real, true for everyone, something anybody could see. His problems arose from the fact that, in order for the truth of sense impressions to be shared so that solidarity could be augmented, these impressions had to be converted into language. And it is the truth of language, not the evidence of the senses, which was "notoriously fallible."

Stated in this way, the problem appears insoluble. Of course, Conrad does not state it in this way; he relies on the capacity of words to signify ambiguously through what he calls "the light of magic suggestiveness" thrown "over the commonplace surface of words," in order to blur his own logic and suggest that the problem has been transcended in a higher, synthetic vision. But it has not. Fiction, he says, must "strenuously aspire to...the magic suggestiveness of music — which is the art of arts." And, only moments later, the famous statement: "My task...is, before all, to make you *see*!" The patient reader has every right to ask not only *what* he is supposed to see (Is our vision supposed to be any clearer than that of the Russian in *Heart of*

Darkness who tells Marlow that Kurtz had "made me see — things"?), but also to ask how an art that aspires to the condition of music can make us *see* anything.

Conrad is exploiting the fracture in *see* to mediate blunt contradictions. This fracture permits him to endorse both terms of the contradiction and yet keep what he calls "a clear conscience." Having said his piece about solidarity and the visible world, he can turn to alienation and the invisible: "If I succeed, you shall find there according to your deserts: encouragement, consolation, fear, charm — all you demand; and, perhaps, also that glimpse of truth for which you have forgotten to ask." Beginning with a single-minded attempt to render high justice to the visible world, Conrad now tells readers that they will all see differently, and will forget about truth altogether.

Conrad makes a final attempt at univocal speech, evoking once again the notion of solidarity, this time "in mysterious origin, in toil, in joy, in hope, in uncertain fate — which binds men to each other and all mankind to the visible world." But whatever this sentence gives is taken away by the following paragraph, which speaks of the artist's craft. One cannot follow any of the "temporary formulas" of art, such as Realism, Naturalism, Romanticism, Conrad says, for all these will eventually pass, leaving the artist "to the stammerings of his conscience [the clear conscience stammers!] and to the outspoken consciousness of the difficulties of his work." The honest artist takes leave of all formulas, all community, all methods and standards, stripping himself down until he is alone with the cry of Art for Art itself; and this cry "has ceased to be a cry, and is heard only as a whisper, often incomprehensible, but at times, and faintly encouraging." We are back to the repetitive stutter of tautology and the collapse of simple ideas; the visible world is no consolation, and the clear strong voices of solidarity have dwindled to an incomprehensible whisper. This whisper does not merely say that it is hard to write a good book; its tininess and incoherence bear a strong and melancholy message that competes on equal terms with the manifest sense of the preface.

In the final paragraph Conrad finds himself so deflated by the difficulties of his work that he retreats from everything he has said about the goals of fiction. Now all he hopes for is to "arrest...the hands busy about the work of the earth, and compel men entranced by the sight of distant goals to glance for a moment at the surrounding vision of form and colour, of sunshine and shadows; to make them pause for a look, for a sigh, for a smile...." For Conrad, as we have seen, Work promoted Solidarity; but this passage implies that Art interrupts Work. Moreover, the achievement of this gap in the flow of life is offered as the highest goal to which Art can aspire. Most darkly, the pause of Art prefigures death: there is "a moment of vision, a sigh, a smile — and the return to an eternal rest."

This conclusion disturbs even Ian Watt, Conrad's most eloquent apologist, who worries that "Conrad inadvertently suggested that his book would die forever as soon as it had been read, or even that its readers would return, not to their 'labours at the work of the earth,' but to their 'eternal rest.' In either case the meaning was muddied...."[16] Watt is suggesting here that the imprecision of evocative language permits an interpretation Conrad would not have endorsed and one he did not intend. There are no reasons for thinking this, though there are many for wishing it.[17] Watt's comments reflect the large goal of his study of *Conrad in the Nineteenth Century,* the rescue of the texts from recent critical excesses by the application of "the literal imagination" to the task of interpretation. But throughout Watt's discussion, this method results not in greater fidelity to the text, not in greater "objectivity," but merely in the privileging of that side of things associated with the visible world, human solidarity, work, fidelity, and so on. But it is Conrad himself who subverts literalism by latency, Conrad who reveals the complexity of even the simplest ideas, and Conrad who tells us that art blows words and people to bits.

4.

I do not want to be understood as endorsing the increasingly popular view of Conrad as the poet of the heart of darkness, the laureate of nihilism. My interest in the point of conversion from seaman to writer focuses not on any estimate of Conrad's morality, but on his verbal strategies in accommodating both the simplicity of the code of the sea and the complexity of the code of language. It focuses on latencies, such as those hidden in puns. It may be significant, for example, that Conrad expresses his goal to make the reader *see* in the preface to a book about the sea. Both homonyms are simple and complex. As the simple Other, the sea unifies men, making them aware of their participation in the brotherhood of the sea, their common devotion to

Work. On land, values are relative and shifting and truth is obscured in shadows; at sea, by contrast, a man knows where he stands.

But it would be a bad mistake to assume that Conrad was of one mind about the sea. The inaugural knot of *The Nigger of the "Narcissus"* is located in the phrase from the preface that speaks of "the latent feeling of fellowship with all creation." "All creation" must include the sea, which thereby loses its status as the Antagonist. On occasion, in fact, Conrad felt very warmly toward the sea, as in the following passage from *The Mirror of the Sea:*

> Water is friendly to man. The ocean, a part of Nature farthest removed in the unchangeableness and majesty of its might from the spirit of mankind, has ever been a friend to the enterprising nations of the earth. And of all the elements this is the one to which men have always been prone to trust themselves, as if its immensity held a reward as vast as itself.[18]

This mood never lasted; in fact, a few pages later Conrad is cursing "the unstable element itself" as being "Faithful to no race after the manner of the kindly earth." Even its majesty is a temporary illusion, for Conrad characterizes the sea as a disloyal servant who "has never adopted the cause of its masters."[19] At the conclusion to this passage Conrad speaks his mind in the unmistakable accents of experience and sincerity:

> To-day, as ever, he is ready to beguile and betray, to smash and to drown the incorrigible optimism of men who, backed by the fidelity of ships, are trying to wrest from him the fortune of their house, the dominion of their world, or only a dole of food for their hunger. If not always in the hot mood to smash he is always stealthily ready for a drowning. The most amazing wonder of the deep is its unfathomable cruelty.[20]

In a letter, Conrad voiced an ultimate exasperation with this sometime friend to man: "The sea is uncertain, arbitrary, featureless, and violent. Except when held by the varied majesty of the sky, there is something inane in its serenity and something stupid in its wrath."[21] Here, the sea appears as truly inconceivable; thought is wasted on it.

In this, it resembles the human bomb at Greenwich. We begin to discern the markings of a whole class of such sea-like phenomena.

Yet Conrad broods on the sea, attributing characteristics to it. One aspect that especially confused Conrad the simple sailor (whose dress while at sea was so conspicuously and incongruously natty that his fellow officers referred to him as "the Russian Count"[22]) was its sexual identity. In the passage quoted above, the sea is a *he*; and in another passage in *The Mirror of the Sea*, Conrad says that "He [the sea] cannot brook the slightest appearance of defiance," and then qualifies his pronoun by adding that this *he* has "no display of manly qualities."[23]

But neither is the sea much of a woman, for it gives "nothing of itself to the suitors for its precarious favours."[24] With its passions, fickleness, and coyness, the sea is feminine (at least to Conrad), but she is the kind of woman who makes women of her men, and can thus be a corrupt *she* as well as a dishonorable *he*. Perhaps this explains why the sea gives nothing of *itself*. The obliterator of binary distinctions, the sea is the unmanly man, the unwomanly woman, the faithless servant, the merciless tyrant, the unchangeable, the unstable, the friendly alien.

Conrad is so routinely thought of as a writer of "mists," of adjectival insistences and rhetorical inflations, that it may seem odd to assert that he is generally trying to be precise. But the double-sexed sea is a genuinely contradictory entity, wrenching from the narrator of *The Nigger of the "Narcissus"* such contorted meditations as the following, at the beginning of Chapter Four, after the storm:

> On men reprieved by its disdainful mercy, the immortal sea confers in its justice the full privilege of desired unrest. Through the perfect wisdom of its grace they are not permitted to meditate at ease upon the complicated and acrid savour of existence. They must without pause justify their life to the eternal pity that commands toil to be hard and unceasing, from sunrise to sunset, from sunset to sunrise; till the weary succession of nights and days tainted by the obstinate clamour of sages, demanding bliss and an empty heaven, is redeemed at last by the vast silence of pain and labour, by the dumb fear and the dumb courage of men obscure, forgetful, and enduring.

Watt defends this passage against the charge of verbal mistiness by defending mistiness in general. The passage, he says, provides the reader with "relief from the immediate image, from the particularities of time and space, and this, by contrast, both brings out these particularities more clearly and at the same time reminds us that there are other less definite and yet equally real dimensions of existence" that cannot "be made real visually."[25] This seems to me a doubly mistaken defense, for the passage offers no "relief" at all, nor does it point toward "less definite dimensions of existence."

Instead, it is extraordinarily painful precisely because it is so definite. Applying even the limited interpretive freedom granted the "literal imagination," the reader discovers that the sea is disdainful yet merciful; that it is just, wise, grace-granting, and pitying (like God) — but that the existence it sanctions does not bear much looking into, for it is "complicated and acrid." Thus it is a mark of pity that the sea forces men to work, for work prevents them from thinking. At some level, "unrest" is desired for the same reason; it is even a privilege. Moreover, brutish toil is "just" because the sea commands it. Sages may clamor, but wisdom would only entail mental pain, and this would be irrelevant. At least physical pain may redeem our days and nights, but mental pain redeems nothing. The meaning of "redeem" must be unconventional, because the only reference made to heaven is contemptuous, implying that the afterlife is an illusion. In that case, redemption cannot be worth much because it happens here, on the scene of dumb suffering. There is no sense of injustice in this fate, for men are all obscure, forgetful, and enduring: their concerns do not matter, they will forget them anyway, and they will go on doing the same thing regardless.

The passage is no mere blur; it bristles with self-canceling specifics, adjectives that do not sort well with their nouns, and sentences that take a radical new turn with each phrase. It embodies its own meaning, for it is painful to try to understand, and more painful still when it is understood. And yet Conrad has discovered, through what Watt calls "continuous latent irony"[26] a way of communicating these sentiments in a quasi-religious tone, so that the passage not only embodies its own pain, but offers its own consolation as well. We feel at the end that while heaven may not be worth having, water is friendly to man. In one mood, Conrad might call the sea "inconceivable"; and insofar as anything else in Conrad is inconceivable, we can say that it is sealike.

5.

Nothing in Conrad is clearer than the opposition of the sea and the ship. Love of a ship is a manly love, reinforcing simple ideas while the sea puts them into question. The dichotomy is as clean as that between liquid and solid because the ship is a small version of the nation, especially in the grandeur and dignity of its ancient codes and traditions. In the narration of *The Nigger of the "Narcissus,"* England is

> a mighty ship bestarred with vigilant lights — a ship carrying the burden of millions of lives.... She towered up immense and strong, guarding priceless traditions and untold suffering, sheltering glorious memories and base forgetfulness, ignoble virtues and splendid transgressions. A great ship! For ages had the ocean battered in vain her enduring sides; she was there when the world was vaster and darker, when the sea was great and mysterious, and ready to surrender the prize of fame to audacious men. A ship mother of fleets and nations! The great flagship of the race; stronger than the storms! and anchored in the open sea. (101)[27]

This seems the very type of the skip-able passage, for it apparently expresses nothing more than a conventional form of patriotism. But Conrad, with his strong weakness for oxymoron, can never quite keep latent meanings out. Why does the nation-ship guard suffering, or shelter base forgetfulness and ignoble virtues? What *is* an ignoble virtue? Is Conrad nodding, or is even jingoism fractured below the surface? At the very end he slips in the fact that the nation is anchored "in the open sea." It does not require years of nautical experience to see that unless the anchor rests on the ocean floor the ship will drift and most anchors will not reach to the floor of the "open" sea. This might seem a needlessly intense reading of a single, grammatically unnecessary phrase, but its syntactic superfluity indicates a strong rather than a weak impulse behind it; this impulse corresponds to the latent sense of the passage, which is not that the ship is a miniature nation, sharing its massive solidity; but that the nation is a larger ship, sharing its instability, its dependence upon random forces.

This analysis of the latent sense of the Conrad paragraph is corroborated by another image designed to impart nobility and cosmic significance to the ship. In Chapter Two the narrator describes the ship as "a fragment detached from the earth," moving "lonely and swift like a small planet" (18). The previous passage suggests that land floats, ship-like; this image says that even the planet floats through the void. No anchor could be adequate, whether for ship, nation, or planet; for there is no ground, no substance truly solid. So the images with which Conrad achieves vastness and grandeur lead inexorably back to the sea.

Conrad constantly encourages the reader to think that the uncertainty that prevails in the vasty deeps does not pertain on board ship, where, enforced by tradition, law, and the general will, order, hierarchy, and proper distinctions rule. Or do they? On board ship, fellowship and solidarity may be manifest, but there are latencies as well; and, within a few pages of the beginning, we see the fatal sea-stain, the smudging of sexual identities. The crewmembers tend to pair up: the Swedes form a couple; the "carpenter and the boatswain sat together with crossed arms; two men friendly, powerful, and deep-chested"; and "Couples tramped backwards and forwards, keeping step and balance, without effort, in a confined space" (19). The most interesting figure in this regard is James Wait himself, who appears in the narrative, as on the roll, as a "smudge" (10).

At the moment of Wait's first appearance the narrator registers an impossible double response. Wait is "calm, cool, towering, superb," a magnificently attractive presence. But he is also repellent, with a "head powerfully misshapen, with a tormented and flattened face — a face pathetic and brutal; the tragic, the mysterious, the repulsive mask of a nigger's soul" (11). Wait is sea-like man, a huge and contradictory being who strains the powers of syntax to contain him. He is most sea-like in his androgyny, and in the confusion he creates in others. As a helpless and dependent figure who is "out of it," to recall Marlow's description of women in *Heart of Darkness,* he is "our Jimmy," "our nigger," and "Jimmy darlin'" The crew are disgusted by "his unmanly lie," but impressed that "he stuck to it manfully" (45). Jimmy is a man who makes women of the men around him. Belfast, for example, secures "universal respect" by being "as gentle as a woman" (86) with him; and in fact sympathy for him turns the entire crew into "a crowd of softies" (26).

Jimmy both is and keeps ambivalent company. His "monstrous friendship" with death is a manly comradeship, for death is a *he* (20), but when, years later, Conrad wrote a preface "To My Readers in America," he spoke of "James Wait afraid of death and making Her his accomplice,"[28] so death has latencies too. Out of a simple desire to have no such accomplice, the men become ulterior, complex, subtle in their language: "we all lovingly called him Jimmy, to conceal our hate of his accomplice" (22). Under such pressures, simple men cannot long remain simple, and within a few days the crew feel as if "all our certitudes were going; we were on doubtful terms with our fellow officers; the cook had given us up for lost.... We suspected Jimmy, one another, and even our very selves" (26).

At once embraced and outcast, a precious possession and a mortal enemy, slave and master (although he says he "belongs to the ship" when he arrives, the men spontaneously stand "behind him in a body" (10) as though they belong to him), Wait is embodied ambivalence, liquid humanity and solid sea. It is Wait who first evokes one of Conrad's key images, to which he returns in *Heart of Darkness* and *Lord Jim* when he wishes to represent corruption or tyranny:

> We served him in his bed with rage and humility, as though we had been the base courtiers of a hated prince; and he rewarded us by his unconciliating criticism. He had found the secret of keeping for ever on the run the fundamental imbecility of mankind; he had the secret of life, that confounded dying man, and he made himself master of every moment of our existence. (23)

This image not only anticipates the beginning of Chapter Four, in which the sea, Wait-like, keeps dumb men forever on the run; it is varied in a passage in *The Mirror of the Sea* in which the sea is described as having "the conscienceless temper of a savage autocrat spoiled by much adulation."[29]

We have just begun to undo Wait's knots. On a ship, as elsewhere, the "secret of life" is a familiar figure to students of the grotesque: the air. The ship goes where the wind blows, and the wind bloweth where it listeth. Jimmy has an air-like unreadability — as the narrator says, "a nigger does not show" (27) — but he is more than merely airlike. When he first appears to be ill, the narrator records the sensation that "a black mist emanated from him; a subtle and dismal influence, a something cold and gloomy that floated out and settled on all the faces like a mourning veil" (21). Air shares sea's doubleness, a duplicity brought out by darlin' Jimmy our mortal enemy. Jimmy is the "cause of head winds" (87) that, keeping the ship from land, threaten the lives of the crew; but as "Land draws life away" (90) and ships "cease to live" (102) once they dock, head winds sustain life as well. Both the sea and the wind are like Jimmy's monstrous accomplice, his lethal friend.

If we follow the drift of images we arrive at the conclusion that the essence of Wait, the nigger's soul within the splendid, repulsive mask, is simply air itself. Beginning as a dense physical presence, he becomes increasingly vaporous. He gulps continually "as if swallowing draughts of fresher air" (67) out of some obscure necessity, but the effect of such inspiration is ambivalent at the very best; for with each breath he exhales he loses himself. When he hallucinates momentarily in Chapter Four, it is said that

> All his inside was gone. He felt lighter than the husks — and more dry. He expanded his hollow chest. The air streamed in, carrying away in its rush a lot of strange things that resembled houses, trees, people, lamp-posts.... No more! There was no more air — and he had not finished drawing his long breath. (69)

This remarkable passage defies paraphrase, bordering on nonsense, but perhaps Donkin reveals an understanding of its import when he accuses the gasping, wasted Jimmy of "putting on airs," and cries, "Yer nobody! Yer no one at all!" (93)

On board the "Narcissus," nobody looks a lot like everybody. In a final paradox the narrator comments that Jimmy was "unique, and as fascinating as only something inhuman could be...," and, three sentences later, "Through him we were becoming highly humanised, tender, complex..." (85). Jimmy the inhuman humanizer is apart, yet diffused among us; we have steeped through each other because he has steeped through us: his "hateful accomplice seemed to have blown with his impure breath undreamt-of subtleties into our hearts" (25).[30] This is the form which the "subtle but invincible conviction of solidarity" assumes in the novel. Wait-air is not merely space, but nearly a space-filling substance itself: it gives life but is also kin to ignorance and, in its duplicity, to lies — which, as Marlow says in *Heart of Darkness,* have a "taint of mortality." In the latter sense, Jimmy's dismal mist is not just *his* air; it is *the* air. With his metallic cough, his panting, his labored breathing, Jimmy puts the crew in mind of a literal fact and a latent truth: that air — head winds, fair breezes, storms, and dead calms — is within, outside, and among; through it, in it, and by it, humankind is linked, breathing and being breathed by each other. Subtle concepts — or, as the narrator says, "We had the air of being initiated in some infamous mysteries" (90).

6.

Jimmy "tainted our lives," the narrator reports, because he "would never let doubt die" (29). He taints by enlisting participation in his "sham existence," his false illness. The issue is simple, and lies at the heart of Conrad's entire career: Is Jimmy sick or not? Is he lying or is he telling the truth? The question Wait raises is that of the adequacy of language to render not just the visual truth, but the truth of the inside.

In ordinary circumstances, the first voice we might attend to would be the narrator's. But in this case the "narrator" is a bundle of voices, all telling us different things. There is (1) an omniscient narrator who mostly rhapsodizes on the sea, and is indifferent to the problems of individuals. And there is (2) a philosophically inclined narrator who also meditates on the large issues (for example, at the beginning of Chapter Five), but who refers to the crew as "we." Another (3) speaks of the crew as "they." A fourth is merely a voice, but no person, for he turns up in places no person could be — in Jimmy's cabin, for instance, when Jimmy and Donkin are alone. A fifth is so air-like that he is able to enter into Jimmy's mind to record a surprisingly banal interior monologue in Chapter Four. All of these have different concerns, or "temperaments," and it is not always possible to tell which is speaking. To make things more difficult still, each is at least theoretically capable of irony, as when narrator three speaks of Jimmy as "the fit emblem of their aspirations" (75). And, of course, they contradict each other. Narrator number three speaks of "the imposture of his ready death" (64), implying that Jimmy is shamming; but narrator number two says that Jimmy was "utterly wrong about himself" (85), implying that he was not shamming but mistaken. Without belaboring the obscure, we can say that nearly every possible attitude toward Jimmy is expressed by a voice carrying some kind of authority.

Even if we ignore what the narrators tell us, which no responsible reader would do, we are simply not equipped to decide whether Jimmy is lying. Jimmy himself does not know, for he insists that he is ill when he appears well, and then insists that he is well when he is obviously dying. He tells Donkin that he has shammed before and is shamming now: "Then Jimmy coughed violently. 'I am as well as ever,' he said, as soon as he could draw breath." Donkin regards him closely and assures him that "anyone can see that" (68). The reader could simply assume that Donkin was a liar and his words were not to be trusted, if the narrator, speaking for the crew, had not said, several pages earlier, "We abominated the creature and could not deny the luminous truth of his contentions" (62).

In Donkin, Conrad has portrayed a man repellent in every aspect, not least in that he talks too much; Conrad preferred men of few words, such as Captain MacWhirr of *Typhoon*. In silence the truth is preserved from "tropological defiguration," remaining a property of the visible world. An exemplary captain, Allistoun is a man of few words, a man who can be trusted with the truth. His confrontation with Jimmy should result in a decisive victory for univocality. On this occasion, in Chapter Four, Jimmy says he is well and will return to duty, though he is obviously gravely ill. Allistoun hesitates "for less than half a second" before telling Jimmy that he has been shamming all along: "Why, anybody can see that. There's nothing the matter with you, but you choose to lie-up to please yourself — and now you shall lie-up to please me" (74). Allistoun would be well advised to confine himself to the clichés of command ("I am here to drive this ship and keep every man-jack aboard of her up to the mark."), for even this minimal utterance gets him into trouble. Donkin's words have made their way into his mouth, and with the same incongruity. "Anybody can see" that Jimmy is dying, not that he is well. A number of questions arise here. Why does Allistoun pretend to punish him? Why does he insist upon appearing to impose his will on Jimmy when he is really acting in Jimmy's interest? And why does the crew nearly mutiny in protest over Jimmy's incarceration when work would surely finish him? To these questions no satisfactory verbal reason is, or perhaps can be, given: everything is swimming. Allistoun's own interpretation of his simple exercise of authority foregrounds the questionable character not only of interpretation but of authority itself. He tells his mate that he could see plainly that Jimmy was

> three parts dead and so scared — black amongst that gaping lot — no grit to face what's coming to us all — the notion came to me all at once, before I could think.... Kind of impulse. It never came into my head, those fools.... H'm! Stand to it now — of course. (78)

We learn from this speech that Allistoun's apparent severity was actually pity; and that he had no motive other than "impulse" for acting as he did; and that he had not anticipated the consequences. In other words, where he was not ignorant of the situation, he was shamming.

Can any word ground itself in a validating source, a unified origin; is any vision unmediated, or undisfigured by bias, limitation, or desire? The plain assumption behind the character of Singleton, who enlisted the admiration of his creator long after the book was published, is that if simple ideas prevail anywhere, they prevail here, in the breast and in the speech of this ancient warrior of the sea. So sea-wise that he does not depend upon carnal or external vision, Singleton "looked at no one" but "possessed the secret of their uneasy indignations and desires, a sharper vision, a clearer knowledge" (79). Singleton's sight is identical with insight, as he is "untouched by human emotions" (25).

Issuing from this untainted source, Singleton's ideas carry great weight with the crew: "We all knew the old man's ideas about Jimmy, and nobody dared to combat them. They were unsettling, they caused pain; and, what was worse, they might have been true for all we knew" (87). This comment is itself unsettling and painful, for two reasons. The first is that the repeated phrase "we all knew" recalls another narrator's comment on Donkin: "They all knew him!" (6) Instinctively, somehow, the men "all know" both the plain talk of Singleton and the verbal charlatanism of Donkin. This brings us to the second point. The phrase "we all knew" at the beginning implies clear and full understanding; the phrase "for all we knew" at the end implies doubt. It seems simply clumsy of Conrad to get himself tangled up like this, but it is actually subtly precise, as we can see by looking at Singleton's "ideas about Jimmy." In Chapter Two, when Jimmy appears to be shamming, Singleton says, "Why, of course he will die," a judgment that is taken for prophecy until the men realize that, "after all Singleton's answer meant nothing." Then the utterance that had seemed to grant certitude is interpreted as deceitful mockery: "We were appalled.... We began to hate him for making fun of us. All our certitudes were going..." (26). So Singleton's speech, like all other speech, is susceptible to radical reinterpretation, revealing to the suspicious eye its own negation.

On one occasion Singleton actually explains himself: "Mortally sick men — he maintained — linger till the first sight of land, and then die.... It is so in every ship. Didn't we know it? He asked us with austere contempt: what did we know?" (86) No one in the crew has sufficient presence of mind to query Singleton about his conversion from skepticism about Jimmy's illness to belief — but perhaps this is because none of them is quite sure about it himself.

Singleton is at least consistent in his certainty that Jimmy will die, but this consistency is no guarantee of insight, for not only does it "mean nothing," but it could reflect penetrating psychological insight, prophetic truth, mockery, or sea-lore. What do we know, indeed, when the words "He will die" shatter in this way, revealing intentions both plain and enigmatic, superficial and subtle, literal and latent? It is a truly Conradian twist that Singleton teaches Wait's lessons for him. In fact, the only indisputable truth Singleton utters concerning Jimmy is also the conclusion he comes to about himself — that he will soon die. "'Old! old!' he repeated sternly" (60). Conrad tends to repeat his key words ("The horror! the horror!"), cracking them open so their duplicity, or multiplicity, can shine forth. *Old* here means not only feeble, near death, but also born long ago. In the first sense Singleton connects with Wait. In the second, he connects both with tradition, the unquestioned prelapsarian source of authority, and, depressingly, with Donkin. When Donkin first appears, the narrator groans, "Is there a spot on earth where such a man is unknown, an ominous survival testifying to the eternal fitness of lies and impudence" (6). Donkin's air-like omnipresence links him with ignorance and evil (c.f. the passage quoted at the beginning of this chapter), but his antiquity, as well as the "luminous truth of his contentions" bonds him with Singleton. From the first instant of creation, it seems, Donkin and Singleton have walked together,[31] a truly inaugural pedestrianism.

One of Conrad's early supporters, R. Cunninghame Graham, wrote to the author suggesting as a human ideal "Singleton with an education." About this prospect Conrad had no illusions. "Well — yes," he replied. "Everything is possible.... However I think Singleton with an education is impossible." What would he study, Conrad asks — Platonism or Pyrrhonism? But the real impossibility is not in the curriculum, but in having Singleton think at all: "Would you seriously, of malice prepense cultivate in that unconscious man the power to think. Then he would become conscious — and much smaller — and very unhappy. Now he is simple and great like an elemental force."[32] Has Conrad read his own book? The reader of this letter must feel as if all his certitudes are going, for the tragedy of Singleton is, from a certain point of view, precisely that he has become conscious — and thereby both smaller and unhappy. And how could Conrad write the following passage and then assert that it does not represent "thought":

> He looked upon the immortal sea with the awakened and groping perception of its heartless might; he saw it unchanged, black and foaming under the eternal scrutiny of the stars; he heard its impatient voice calling for him out of a pitiless vastness full of unrest, of turmoil, and of terror. He looked afar upon it, and he saw an immensity tormented and blind, moaning and furious, that claimed all the days of his tenacious life, and, when life was over, would claim the worn-out body of its slave...." (61)

Singleton's bondage to the sea also throws a horribly ironic light on Conrad's claim that he is "simple and great like an elemental force," for Singleton will soon enough in that destructive element be immersed.[33] Singleton and the sea belong together: at the end, the narrator — a sixth voice, who speaks in the first person and throws a valedictory veil over the entire narrative — comments benignly that "Singleton has no doubt taken with him the long record of his faithful work into the peaceful depths of an hospitable sea" (107). Throughout his letter to Graham, as throughout the preface, Conrad converts the acid insights of the novel into the base forgetfulness of sentiment with an ingenuity that might, in another writer, be called dishonesty, or at best, disreputable verbal cleverness. With an undoubtedly "clear conscience," Conrad, who has apparently forgotten Singleton's end, asks Graham, "Would you seriously wish to tell such a man: 'Know thyself.' Understand that thou art nothing, less than a shadow, more insignificant than a drop of water in the ocean, more fleeting than the illusion of a dream. Would you?" Conrad has left himself open here to the charge of sentimentalization, or of forgetfulness, a charge that, for all we know, may be true. After all, Conrad did forget that Singleton was literate when, at the end, he has the old man sign his name with an X. But this charge also leads to a relatively uninteresting view of Conrad and the kind of truth he was trying, even against all his inclinations, to tell.

Singleton is the key to this truth. Watt expresses the conventional — indeed, nearly unanimous — view of him as a "lonely relic of an earlier, heroic age of seamen," an example, he adds, of Herbert Spencer's law of the "evolution of the simple into the complex, through successive generations."[34] Though Conrad, Watt, and many other intelligent readers have held such a view, it cannot be right. It depends upon a dichotomy between Singleton and the crew that Conrad labors to undermine by revealing points of kinship that place Singleton on a sliding scale with the others, in the same order of discourse. Conrad's constant method is to begin by reducing manifold visible reality to a polarity — land/sea; light/dark; Singleton/Donkin; Allistoun/Wait; ship/sea; the list could be extended and reorganized greatly — and then to reduce the polarity to a unity. But while this procedure seems to be intended to expose the complex as a form of the simple, it also, as we have seen, exposes the simple as a form, an especially subtle form, of the complex. Albert Guerard has guided many Conrad critics in seeing Wait "*as something the ship and the men must be rid of before they can complete their voyage.*"[35] But this is what Conrad would call an illusion — desirable, perhaps, from the sentimental point of view, but impossible and perhaps even destructive. Wait belongs to the ship, to the nation, to the planet. Even the Singletons will join him in the hospitable sea, sharing with him the sympathetic consciousness of a common destiny.

Conrad wrote before Freud introduced "narcissism" into the psychoanalytic lexicon, but he had a profound and surprisingly particular intuitive understanding of the concept. According to Freud, "primary narcissism" was characterized by an "oceanic" sensation occurring in earliest infancy, before consciousness had made its mark. In this happy condition, no distinction is drawn between the self and the total environment; "object-libido" is identical to "ego-libido." "Secondary narcissism," which Jacques Lacan has called the "mirror-stage," occurs most typically during the "latency" period, but can occur at any time after that as well. A postlapsarian attempt to return to the bliss of primary narcissism, it is not a perversion, but simply "the libidinal complement to egoism."[36] It is characterized by the withdrawal of the libido from all external objects and its corresponding displacement onto the ego, so that the total environment is seen as an extension or projection of self. Conrad's crew, simple children of the sea, innocent in their latency, begin as secondary narcissists. The figure for their projections is Wait, who is seen by Donkin as deceitful, skulking and subtle; by Belfast as a test of orthodoxy; by Allistoun as the pretext for an exercise of authority; and by Singleton as the man who will die. Conrad's "fellowship with all creation" is one way of describing a condition which, if Freud is right (as he surely is), can never, once lost, be attained again — except, we can theorize, in death. This theory, latent in many forms of Romanticism, helps account for the funereal conclusion of the novel, when the narrator greets a crew of Shades on the sea of death; and it accounts, too, for the abrupt introduction of "eternal rest" at the end of the preface. (Conrad habitually spoke of the book in deathly terms, as in a letter where he says that he wrote the book in order to "enshrine my old chums in a decent edifice."[37]) Like Heathcliff, Wait is more maelstrom than character; other figures circle into him, and into the sea. Looking at Wait is like looking into the "enigmatic spectacle" of life. Initially, one sees the object, then realizes that it is a mirror. The surface of this mirror is deep, revealing the secrets of the observing self. Simple observation converts to subtle interpretation, then to ambivalence and self-doubt; and we are made sea.

Now we can appreciate the urgency of the preface in the matter of subtle latencies. Those words are the agents of the sea, with their open faces and mirror-like surfaces revealing their meanings plainly, while the depths move silently beneath. Conrad is, I believe, trying to be sincere, that is, to speak in a language that is faithful to both sight and insight, as well as to those impulses "kept out of sight," perhaps even from himself. With such masters to serve, no wonder writing was such an agony for him. He is trying, as well, to redeem the language of the text: the subtleties of the preface constitute an apology for those of the narrative. In fact, the entire preface is an attempt to reclaim the text from the inconceivable sea by applying its key terms to a statement of plain intentions and reliable observations. The preface actually renounces language — hence the reference to the "musical" character of prose. It was wise of Conrad's publishers to print it as a preface. As an "after-word" it seems as ironic as the professor's explosive simplicity in *The Secret Agent*, but as a preface, it has the effect, for most readers, of limiting irony by circumscribing the interpretative activity of the reader.

Conrad never abandoned this impossible struggle. In 1912, in "A Familiar Preface" to *A Personal Record*[38] — how poignant his desire for trust and intimacy with those strangers, his readers! — he recalls writing *The Nigger of the "Narcissus"* in an attempt to "render the vibration of life in the great world of the waters, in the hearts of the simple men who have for ages traversed its solitudes...." In order to preserve "the exact notion of sincerity," he says, he had sacrificed any presentation of extreme emotional states; he had always counted himself among those "to whom an open display of sentiment is repugnant." Never mind that he says later that this preface is "the place and the moment of perfectly open talk" — there are opens and opens, and the reader will surely understand how the truth is served by masking the emotions rather than by laying them indecently "bare to the world." After all he says, "We have all heard of simple men selling their souls for love or power to some grotesque devil," and "the fact is that I have a positive horror of losing even for one moving moment that full possession of myself which is the first condition of good service." A familiar difficulty: the exhortation to simple-heartedness and open talk, and the recognition that simplicity is the prey of grotesque devils. And the familiar solution of bivocality: In *A Personal Record* he will try to present the "vision of a...coherent, justifiable personality" as well as to give the "record of personal memories." The final sentence of this familiar preface is Conrad in a nutshell: "In the purposely mingled resonance of this double strain a friend [*mon semblable, mon frère*] here and there will perhaps detect a subtle accord." [*Hypocrite lecteur!*] This double-voiced persona who seeks only to be understood is reminiscent of the narrator at the end of *The Nigger of the "Narcissus,"* at last an *I*, who cries a greeting to his shadow friends, beseeching them, "Haven't we, together and upon the immortal sea, wrung out a meaning from our sinful lives?" (107) The tone of desperation actually begs the question — Which meaning did we wring out after all? It is a question we are not supposed to ask, for although the preface entreats us to *see,* the novel initiates us into shadows, mists, fogs, smudges; it educates us in air, and constitutes a constant "reminder of the dependence upon the invisible" (90).

7.

In writing "A Familiar Preface" Conrad was introducing one book, but he was also going back over several others whose memory continued to disturb him, especially those connected with his decision to abandon the sea and become an author. *The Nigger of the "Narcissus"* is one of these. But it is in *Heart of Darkness* that we find simple men selling their souls to grotesque devils, and where "moving moments" of abandon are recalled in horror.[39] The central issues of this novel, as well as of this chapter, are condensed into a single incident, the interview with Kurtz's Intended, where Marlow "lies," telling her that the last words Kurtz spoke were her name. Conrad wrote that "The interview of the man and the girl locks in — as it were — the whole 30,000 words of narrative description in one suggestive view of a whole phase of life, and makes of that story something quite on another plane than an anecdote of a man who went mad in the Center of Africa."[40] Before the interview, the central problem of the text can be represented as a crisis in the definition of "the human," a crisis manifest in such passages as the following:

> It was unearthly, and the men were — No, they were not inhuman. Well, you know, that was the worst of it — this suspicion of their not being inhuman. It would come slowly to one. They howled and leaped, and spun, and made horrid faces; but what thrilled you was just the thought of their humanity — like yours — the thought of your remote kinship with this wild and passionate uproar. (36-37)

In the interview, experience is converted into narrative, and a potentially disabling insight into the nature of man is transfigured into a potentially liberating discovery about language. In this episode we can, therefore, observe Conrad reproducing the moment of transition from seaman to artist, from (in his own words) a "perfect animal" to (tentative, doubting, anguished) man of letters.

The crystal of Kurtz's being and the germ of Marlow's fictional narrative to the Intended is the terminal utterance, the two — or rather, four — words, "The horror! The horror!" I suggested earlier that the doubling of the phrase encourages the suspicion that what appears to be one statement may actually be two, or that multiple meanings may be intended. Of these there is no shortage, for, as others have asserted, the "horror" could be Kurtz's betrayal of the Intended; or his betrayal of the savage queen he is leaving; or even himself, in whom, monstrously enough, the two women have a common share.

The most durable interpretation is that Kurtz is horrified by his own reversion to savagery, his abandonment of European civilization, his participation in unspeakable rites and the base raptures of the jungle. Analyses based on this premise commonly discuss the dialectical play of contraries running through the narrative, especially the opposition of images of light and darkness. The conservatives argue that Conrad's message is that while the darkness may be tempting, our better nature impels us to seek the light, and that to revert as Kurtz does is to become less human. The radical approach would insist on the ultimate primacy of the darkness, maintaining, as Hillis Miller does, that Conrad is a nihilist. The moderate path, certainly the road least traveled by, also has its adherents, who speak of mystery or paradox, and whose statements are all questions.[41] That "horror," acontextual and unmotivated by immediate circumstance, demands to be attached to something; and, coming at the end of an unusual life, it seems to have special moral status as a deathbed recognition. This is a temptation no interpreter can resist, despite the inevitable banality, and the suspicious finality, of interpretations that seek to settle the matter of Conrad's values through an aggressive reading of Kurtz's words.

Kurtz's words themselves tend to be highly aggressive. His report for the International Society for the Suppression of Savage Customs, for example, makes Marlow "tingle with enthusiasm," despite the fact that the first paragraph strikes him as "ominous." In it, Kurtz says that whites must necessarily appear to savages "in the nature of supernatural beings — we approach them with the might as of a deity." What is ominous here is that these words, though appearing to prescribe a missionary morality, also describe Kurtz's actual activities.

The report concludes that whites can "exert a power for good practically unbounded" — another ominous sign from a man who, in a practical sense, became un-bound. Marlow, whose thrill of response to these words is very similar to his reaction to the sound of jungle drums, praises the report for its "unbounded power of eloquence" (51). Eloquence is radically interpretable: it is possible to follow its precepts and still commit horrors. Kurtz's language, we could say, sanctions horrors as it proclaims intentions.[42]

In other words, horror may be as legitimate as any other word for the Intended. This would be a justifiable inference even if Conrad had not been so careful to provide evidence for the view that horror is at least a pun. The Intended lives in Brussels, the "sepulchral city" that recalls Babylon, the "whited sepulchre" in Revelation, full of all uncleanness and dead men's bones. The existence of its inhabitants is a similar horror, for Belgian prosperity depends upon the flow of ivory, a tension neatly symbolized by the piano in the Intended's parlor, with its ebony — black and ivory — white keys. If we read Kurtz as a mediation (or *short for*) Christ and cursed, or Christ and Antichrist,[43] then we can read the Intended as a Bride of Christ and the Whore of Babylon. Like other whores, the Intended has her price. Her family had forbidden her marriage to Kurtz because of his inadequate fortune, and his whole venture in the Congo had been undertaken as a means of making money so he could marry her. Perhaps this perversely ingenious but bluntly literal circuit of logic accounts for Conrad's caginess both in ignoring the translation problem involved in Kurtz's speaking French, and in his giving the Intended no name at all, so that although we know that Marlow lies, we could not prove it in a court of law.

Marlow says before meeting Kurtz that "Kurtz was just a word for me" (27). This could mean that he has not yet been introduced; or that Kurtz's existence is exclusively verbal; or that Kurtz is a "double" for Marlow himself; or that Kurtz is word-like. It can mean all these, though the last is the richest and most inclusive. As a species of word, Kurtz demonstrates that no two concepts are so remote from each other that they cannot be brought within the compass of a single phoneme: his own "horror" is a persuasive demonstration of such condensation. As a citizen, and not as a writer, Conrad surely would have scorned such a conclusion, for it would require that we abandon the very notions of truth and lie, or verbal certitude of any kind.

If one would tell this truth, one must commit oneself to such devices as irony and punning. Given this commitment, it seems unfair that the interview with the Intended should be attacked for its "cheap irony" and "melodramatic tricks."[44] Irony was never cheap for Conrad, as this scene reveals. In it, every utterance is fractured — in fact, tripled. The Intended conducts her conversation, bearing away her consolation; Marlow conducts his, discharging his responsibility; and somehow they speak to each other. The form the conversation takes is that she says something ("He died as he lived"), then he makes a response that appears synonymous but is actually antonymous ("His end was in every way worthy of his life"). In a letter to his publisher Conrad spoke of "A mere shadow of love interest just in the last pages — but I hope it will have the effect I intend."[45] He does not say what he intended — perhaps only that we should see — but it is good that he does not, for the lack of specificity permits us to see that the shadow of love may fall between the Intended and Kurtz, Kurtz and Marlow, and the Intended and Marlow. The simplicity of their statements to each other enables all three currents to run through the same wires.[46] The situation Conrad is dramatizing is his own discovery that not only do certain primal words such as "see," "simple," "subtle," "illusion," and "horror" contain their own negations, but that under the pressure of necessities all civilized people feel, any word can ramify.

Conrad was so attracted to the English language that at times he attributed his decision to write to his encounter with the language itself. He was "adopted by the genius of the language," he says; and speaks of "the sheer appeal of the language, my quickly awakened love for its prose cadences, a subtle and unforeseen accord of my emotional nature with its genius.... You may take it from me that if I had not known English I wouldn't have written a line for print, in my life."[47] No matter how intense his admiration for Flaubert and Maupassant, Conrad must have been wary of French precision and drawn toward English, with its remarkable richness in puns and homonyms. English is especially rich in the kind of "abuse of language" that Locke called "mixed modes," linguistic tropes that have no equivalent in nature. De Man calls these tropes "catachreses," and says they are

> capable of inventing the most fantastic entities by dint of the positional power inherent in language. They can dismember

the texture of reality and reassemble it in the most capricious of ways, pairing man with woman or human being with beast in the most unnatural shapes. Something monstrous lurks in the most innocent of catachreses: when one speaks of the legs of the table or the face of the mountain, catachresis is already turning into prosopopeia, and one begins to perceive a world of potential ghosts and monsters.[48]

Language as catachresis is language as grotesque, a prospect repugnant to Conrad and Locke alike. But as de Man points out, Locke's own analysis demonstrates that all of language summons up "chimeras" that have no equivalence in nature, even propositions stating simple ideas and words denoting substances. At no point, de Man concludes, "can the empirical entity be sheltered from tropological defiguration."[49] In his own way, Conrad arrived at a similar conclusion, and this accounts for his characteristic ambivalence, his simultaneous sympathy/antipathy toward language, his silent words we are supposed to see and hear.

In his family circle, Conrad wrote, his book was "familiarly referred to as The Nigger."[50] As a fraud with the secret of life, or a lie that speaks truly, the book-as-Nigger aligns with other Conradi as images of special importance, including the Mint at the end of "The Nigger," the San Tome mine in *Nostromo,* the Inner Station in *Heart of Darkness,* even the Greenwich Observatory in *The Secret Agent.* These are all value-factories, or sites of the origin of worth. They may be attacked and defended with guns, bombs, or spears, but the value itself is wholly immaterial and air-like. Recognizing this, we might say that the very thing-ness of these structures is a mark of their imposture, and perhaps they should be blown to bits. But a tolerant, or ambivalent, attitude would be wiser. For value must be localized or contained in something — in the imposture of art, for example, even an art created by a man who has willingly chosen to leave the sanctified existence of the seaman in favor of the ethically dubious life of the writer. The curious "sheltering" of "base forgetfulness" in the passage quoted earlier from *The Nigger of the "Narcissus"* has its source in Conrad's realization of the problematic origin of value. Nietzsche voices Conrad's darkest suspicions in considering truth and lies in their "ultramoral sense":

Only by means of forgetfulness can man ever arrive at imagining that he possesses "truth" in that degree just indicated. If he does not mean to content himself with truth in the shape of tautology, that is, with empty husks, he will always obtain illusions instead of truth.[51]

Hence Conrad's insistence on illusion as central to art, though fatal to truth. There are, as it happens, no artists in Conrad's cast of characters to whom we might turn for a direct representation of his thoughts on art, but there is, in "The Nigger," a striking image — especially considering that Conrad was at this time in the process of deciding to become a writer: "Our contempt for [Donkin] was unbounded and we could not but listen with interest to that consummate artist. He told us we were good men" (61).

CHAPTER EIGHT

Conclusion: Doodles, Dragons, Dissonance, and Discovery

1.

It has always fascinated art historians that Leonardo, who devoted so many years of passionate and inspired labor to the representation of human beauty, should have filled his notebooks with figures of such deformity that they have come to be called "grotesque heads." Lacking the constant and reliable justification of simple attractiveness, these figures have been moved in to the center or out to the margins of the picture of Leonardo's genius as conceptions of him have changed. The grotesque heads accorded well with Vasari's unpredictable wizard, who once, Vasari tells us, equipped an already bizarre lizard with wings made of the scales of other lizards, false eyes, horns, and beard, and exhibited the freak to universal dismay and astonishment. In our time, however, more moderate views have been advanced by Kenneth Clark and A. E. Popham, who have argued that Leonardo's "doodles" were like random flotsam of the unconscious mind. In Clark's words: "The mind throws up fragments of weeds and dirt which float about on its surface and betray us into tuneless humming or stupid reiterated words: and such, it seems to me, was the origin of most of Leonardo's caricatures."[1] In a brilliant essay written in 1952, E. H. Gombrich advanced another theory, that Leonardo was so drawn to grotesques because they were not re-presentations at all, but true creations, with no original or type in nature: "the doodle could become the instrument and token of the freely creative imagination."[2] In this context, Leonardo's famous meditation in the *Treatise on Beauty* is especially significant:

> In what way the painter is the lord of all varieties of man and of all things: if a painter desires to see beautiful women who make him fall in love, he has the power to create them; and if he desires

to see monstrous things which frighten or are clownish, laughable, or really arouse compassion, he is their Lord and God.[3]

For Gombrich, the marginal doodle becomes the center of a "new conception of art" as a creation to satisfy the creator, and also the signature of an art independent of nature. There is something, he says, of Prospero in Leonardo, conjuring up storms — and his "storms" are but more grotesques — and lording it over Caliban.[4]

Attractive as Gombrich's analysis is, it is incomplete, and contradicted by Leonardo himself. Although these figures may seem to represent an autonomous art, they are nevertheless also representations of human monstrosities of a kind that were far more prevalent in Leonardo's day, before modern hygiene, reconstructive surgery, and orthodonture, than now. And, as Gombrich says, Leonardo would sometimes spend entire days shadowing people with particularly interesting deformities, imprinting their features on his mind so he could reproduce them on paper. Moreover, though he developed a scheme for classifying the features of the normal face according to type, he said that no such system was necessary in the case of "grotesque heads" because their features impressed themselves on the mind without effort, eliminating the need for such an aid to memory. These facts suggest that the "grotesque heads" are not pure or autonomous art, not creatures wholly of the artist's fancy, but precisely the opposite — they are representations taken directly from nature, independent of the artist's preconceptions or representational habits. Their monstrosity is a guarantee of their dense actuality, their resistance to idealization or generalization, their proximity to what Baudelaire called "innocent life." The artist who draws them is humbly reproducing what only nature could produce, not boldly bringing forth a new species of his own making. That honor, or curse, would now fall on the figures of beauty, nobility, courage, or virtue, whose creation required such massive investments of labor; grotesque forms, on the other hand, would stand as a reminder of the inability of the artist to rival the inexhaustible abundance and ingenuity of nature, or of God.

Is it possible that Leonardo could have held both positions? More to the point, is it possible for us to regard the grotesque as a designation for both positions? If we could, then we could see the grotesque as a sign neither of a pure not an impure art, but of a total conception of an art that recognized its own paradoxical character, pure and impure, autonomous and dependent, image and mirror. If this hypothesis were true, it would serve to organize many previously unconnected arguments. For example, in the first chapter I said that the grotesque image consisted of a medley of recognizable forms in unrecognizable combinations, with no dominant principle, so that representation was simultaneously invoked and discredited. In the second chapter I demonstrated how meaningless ornament became grotesque with the introduction of meaning-bearing forms, especially human forms which, because of their interpretability, rivaled the center. In Chapter Three I suggested that the grotesque involved the foregrounding of archaic and modern elements. In each instance the grotesque was defined not as the mediation of oppositions but as the presentation or realization of a contradiction central to art itself. This, I believe, is the key to the grotesque: it denotes the essence of art when art is conceived as contradiction, operating by laws peculiar to itself and faithfully representing the visible world.

This is the spirit in which I have, from time to time, mentioned metaphor as a particularly helpful way of looking at the grotesque. Once considered an ornament of language, metaphor is more often perceived these days as identical to figuration, so that it shares with the grotesque the capacity of appearing both marginal and central Both metaphor and the grotesque give a dominant impression of unity, though they are manifestly constructed of pieces. And both operate by means of self-abolishing incongruity. We interpret the metaphor in such a way as to minimize the referentiality of its language, and we interpret the grotesque form, filling in its gaps and reading it as a symbol, or a "sign of the times." In both cases, the act of interpretation we perform with all language, and with all images, is intensified to the point where it rises above our threshold of awareness so that we can, as it were, catch ourselves in the act.

Finally, in the case of both metaphor and the grotesque, the form itself resists the interpretation that it necessitates. We remain aware of the referential absurdity of the metaphor despite our attempts to transcend it, and the discord of elements in the grotesque form remains discordant. But this is precisely the reason that both are capable of standing for the entire field of art. For if the interpretation supplanted the form that gave rise to it, there would be no need for art. Art lives by resisting interpretation as well as by inviting it, and it is this double movement that is figured in both the metaphor and the grotesque.

Because the grotesque form stands independently, with the presence of a thing of nature, it confuses the distinction between art and the ground or subject of art. And because it calls forth contradictory interpretations, and interpretations to which it refuses to yield, it disrupts the relationship between art and the meaning of art. We should expect it, therefore, to cause consternation in many camps — among those concerned to relate art and reality, those concerned to establish the basis of "pure art," those who deny that art has any non-artistic meaning, and those who believe that the moral status of art is grounded in reliable and true interpretations. No matter what kind of case one wants to make on these basic aesthetic issues, one runs up against the problem of grotesque art as the final obstacle to a universal and internally consistent theory of aesthetics.

2.

Kant's aesthetic theory begins with a clear, sharp line drawn between art and nature on the basis that aesthetic judgment is free of all "interest," whereas all other forms of judgment are, first, based on interest; second, expressed in logical terms; and third, referable to the object rather than solely to the apprehending subject. On this basis, Kant distinguishes between the agreeable, which responds to aesthetic appreciation, and the good, which is admired not in itself but for its end, or teleology. The essence of the agreeable, or the aesthetic, is that it is independent of concept or use, which Kant calls "objective finality." His examples recall the Domus Aurea designs:

> So designs *à la grecque,* foliage for framework or on wallpapers, &c., have no intrinsic meaning; they represent nothing-no Object under a definite concept-and are free beauties. We may also rank in the same class what in music are called fantasias (without a theme), and, indeed, all music that is not set to words.[5]

Kant is describing here an ornamental art that has thrown off its ornamental function, adorning no center, and existing purely as itself. Thus he is led to the grotesque:

But where all that is intended is the maintenance of a free play of the powers of representation (subject, however, to the condition that there is to be nothing for understanding to take exception to), in ornamental gardens, in the decoration of rooms, in all kinds of furniture that shows good taste, &c., regularity in the shape of constraint is to be avoided as far as possible. Thus English taste in gardens, and fantastic taste in furniture, push the freedom of imagination to the verge of what is grotesque — the idea being that in this divorce from all constraint of rules the precise instance is being afforded where taste can exhibit its perfection in projects of the imagination to the fullest extent.[6]

It is especially interesting here, that although Kant seems to endorse a view of the grotesque as pure unencumbered art, he actually stops just short of such a statement. The freedom of imagination can be pushed to the verge of the grotesque, at which point pure art encounters a mysterious bar and further progress is impossible. What is the problem; why is the grotesque somehow beyond license?

The reason for Kant's reluctance to identify the grotesque with a pure art can be found later, in paragraph 48 of the *Critique of Judgment* (from which the above quotations have been taken), when he draws back from the notion that art can ever be entirely free from concept and a sense of objective finality. In this section he says that a beauty of nature need not be attended by a concept of what sort of thing it is supposed to be in order to be judged beautiful, but a beauty of art always presupposes such a concept. Moreover, when nature is judged to be beautiful, it is judged as art, though "superhuman art." So when Kant says that if a thing is beautiful, it is art; and if a thing is art, it is the result of the execution of some intention, purpose, or concept, he is dealing a deathblow to the dream of pure art, and to purely aesthetic judgment as well. Even ornament must be appreciated *as ornament*, and thus as the expression of some concept. Grotesque ornament both recognizes and resists the sense of meaning. It cannot be fully understood through logic, but it cannot truly be appreciated by the faculty of taste either, for it clings to the non-aesthetic world.

Kant has his own idea about why the grotesque resists being classed as art. There is "one kind of ugliness alone," he says, which "is incapable of being represented conformably to nature without destroying all aesthetic delight, and consequently artistic beauty, namely, that which excites *disgust*."⁷ The grotesque is preeminently the art of disgust; we can think, for example, of Poe's definition of the grotesque as involving "much of the beautiful, much of the wanton, much of the *bizarre,* something of the terrible, and not a little of that which might have excited disgust." According to Kant, the disgusting form has taken leave of the realm of art because the "representation of the object is no longer distinguishable from the nature of the object itself in our sensation, and so it cannot possibly be regarded as beautiful."⁸ In other words, we feel precisely the same emotion concerning a painting of something disgusting as we do concerning the disgusting object itself, and so we lose the distinction between art and reality. This must be why pure art can be pushed to the verge of the grotesque, but can never be grotesque itself. Paradoxically, although the grotesque is closer to pure art than any other art form, it is also utterly opposed to pure art. We begin to see what Leonardo was getting at.

An adequate figure for Kant's scheme might be a line representing the possibilities of artistic expression, at one end of which lies nonrepresentational art wholly divorced from any prior reality, and communicating no meaning accessible to logic; and at the other end of which lies wholly representational art that accepts both the goal of mimesis and the burden of meaning. The grotesque, in Kant's scheme, would lie just beyond both terminal points of that line; or perhaps it would be more accurate to say that the very tips of the line would be called grotesque. We might more easily imagine a curved line with the tips almost meeting, separated by a space of art/non-art, the grotesque, in which the disgusting mingles with the ultra-aesthetic, the brutish with the freely playing fancy, a realm in which art is manifest primarily as sensation. We know that Leonardo took very seriously the "power of his art to stun, to overwhelm and to make the flesh creep,"⁹ to make a sensation, and his profound affinity with the grotesque can be seen in this light, as a part of his attempt to create an art that moves the passions and participates fully in the nonaesthetic world. Perhaps Kant's concept of the relation between art and the grotesque also enables us to understand the otherwise puzzling tendency of various forms of "aestheticism" to embrace the grotesque. Aubrey Beardsley, whose statement, "If I am not grotesque I am nothing" summed up either his life or his work, or the conjunction of the two, deliberately created images that fused the disgusting and the beautiful, images that tested our categories, especially those of "art" and "nature" by existing impossibly in both modalities at once.

This entire problem is reframed in the work of Hegel, whose dream of pure art was one of the most compelling fantasies of his century. For Hegel, as for Kant, pure art issues from "no personal longing, obsession, or desire, but only a pure pleasure in the thing itself." In this happy condition of innocence the soul is raised "through the serenity of form, above any painful involvement in the limitations of reality.[10] As he says in the preface to *Vorlesungen über die Ästhetik,* art becomes truly genuine only when it brings "to consciousness and expression the divine meaning of things, the deepest interests of mankind, and the most universal truths of the spirit."[11] The artistic impulse comes from a supra-sensuous world altogether beyond immediate consciousness, and beyond form; so, although the spirit manifests itself through forms accessible to the senses, this manifestation is a kind of fall of the spirit, for there is always a discontinuity, even an antipathy between the spirit and the form, the impulse and the vehicle.

Hegel's difficulty is similar to Kant's, for in locating the essence of art outside of any given artifact, he has conceived of art as inevitably incongruous and impure, and rendered the quest for pure art hopeless from the outset. And, like Kant, he has also made it inevitable that he should engage with the grotesque. He does this in a way familiar to readers of this book, who will recall the discussion in Chapter Two of how Vitruvius's condemnation of the grotesque was used to attack both primitive and decadent art, both Gothic and Baroque. For Hegel, art is a quest of the spirit for a form adequate to its essence. There are three phases to this quest, represented by symbolic, classic, and romantic art. The grotesque, as might be expected, figures in the first and last phases. In symbolic art, the spirit is rudimentary, indefinite, and obscure, groping not so much for adequate form as for any form at all. As it is ill-formed itself, all natural forms will be foreign to it:

> And the spiritual idea, having no other reality to express its essence, expatiates in all these natural shapes, seeks itself in their unrest and disproportion, but finds them inadequate to it. It then exaggerates these natural phenomena and shapes them into the huge and the boundless. The spiritual idea revels in them, as it

were, seethes and ferments in them, does violence to them, distorts and disfigures them into grotesque shapes, and endeavors by the diversity, hugeness, and splendor of such forms to raise the natural phenomena to the spiritual level.[12]

The spiritual idea in the symbolic phase is a kind of Gargantua, whose crude needs overwhelm form. If symbolic art is "bizarre, grotesque, and without taste," it is because the infinite substance disdains the perishing mass of appearances through which it must express itself.

In classical art this impulse, now matured and tamed, is able to find adequate form because it is itself less unruly, and capable of achieving a completed and fully expressive form. But in romantic art the union between spirit and form is again destroyed; and again we find disjunction between the inside and the outside. Romantic art represents the triumph of the spirit, which in this phase disdains form not because of its own confusion but because it has transcended all form.

The external side of things is surrendered to accident and committed to the excesses of the imagination, whose caprice now mirrors existence as it is, now chooses to distort the objects of the outer world into a bizarre and grotesque medley, for the external form no longer possesses a meaning and significance, as in classical art, on its own account and for its own sake.[13]

In the case of both symbolic and romantic art, the word that arises to describe the incongruity between spirit and form is *grotesque,* which serves to describe the poles of the process, as Kant used it to describe art of the highest tastefulness and of the most utter tastelessness. If we have gotten no closer to discovering what it is about "the grotesque" that enables it to stand as a description of such antithetical forms, at least we are beginning to establish a pattern of such usage.

Ruskin approached the phenomenon of the grotesque directly with a concern for explaining precisely this element of internal inconsistency that enabled the grotesque somehow to stand for the essence both of human creation and of human degradation. He was able to advance on his predecessors by dividing the grotesque into two main branches, the sportive and the terrible, depending upon whether the element of the ludicrous or the fearful, which are found in all grotesques, predominates. Having said this, however, he immediately says that it is impossible to discuss the forms of the grotesque according to this scheme, for all its forms combine the two elements. It is easier to discuss the kinds of minds that produce the grotesque, for here precision is possible. Although Ruskin's scheme is extravagantly complex, involving many subdivisions, the basic pattern remains dualistic, consistently resolving itself into the true and the false, the noble and the ignoble. The true grotesque, he says in "Grotesque Renaissance," is "the expression of the *repose* or play of a *serious* mind," whereas the false grotesque "is the result of the *full exertion* of a *frivolous* one." Ruskin approves of grotesques created by "good and ordinarily intelligent men," but on the work of the other sort he is very hard. Of a monstrous, leering, stone head on the tower of a Venetian church, he comments that it is the evidence "of a delight in the contemplation of bestial vice, and the expression of low sarcasm, which is, I believe, the most hopeless state into which the human mind can fall." And of Raphael's form of *grottesche,* though it is utterly different in character, he has a similar appraisal: "It is almost impossible to believe the depth to which the human mind can be debased in following this species of grotesque."[14]

Ruskin is, in fact, constantly astonished by the dimensions of human character revealed by the grotesque, and in the midst of an elaborate taxonomy it is possible to see this one consistent element, the element so important to Leonardo, of sensation. For Ruskin, as for Kant and Hegel, the grotesque disdains the middle ground, and can perhaps only be defined as the art of moral extremes; the grotesque is any kind of art that stands at the margins of experience and that, as a consequence, enlarges our conception of human capacities. If anything, such a definition surrenders rather than gains precision, for there is absolutely no attempt made to define the formal properties of grotesque art. In place of such a description Ruskin gives us a rogue's gallery on the one hand, and Michelangelo, Tintoretto, Dante, Spenser, and Gothic cathedrals on the other, all linked by a common share in the grotesque. He has no notion of pure art, but he does express overtly a concept latent in Leonardo, Kant, and Hegel, that of a total art. For Ruskin, grotesque is the only one of art's modes that can serve as an emblem of the entire field of art, from the depths to the heights. In "Grotesque Renaissance," he states "one most important conclusion":

that wherever the human mind is healthy and vigorous in all its proportions, great in imagination and emotion no less than in intellect, and not overborne by an undue or hardened pre-eminence of the mere reasoning faculties, there the grotesque will exist in full energy. And, accordingly, I believe that there is no test of greatness in periods, nations, or men, more sure than the development, among them or in them, of a noble grotesque; and no test of comparative smallness or limitation, of one kind or another, more sure than the absence of grotesque invention, or incapability of understanding it.[15]

Grotesque is the name Ruskin gives to a "monotheistic" art that, although it takes many forms, issues from a single source. Because of this comprehensive unity, it stands, even in its most debased forms, close to some originating creative power that might be called the divine. This proximity to a unified source compelled Ruskin always to be if not respectful at least humble before the awesome power of the grotesque, which was capable of bringing mankind near to God or to bestial cretinism. The power of art to ennoble or to degrade was always astonishing to Ruskin. What is even more astonishing is that he should have discovered that both movements are phases of a single activity. The categorical excess described earlier derived from the unrecognized fact that, although he was only seeking to describe the grotesque, he was in fact describing all of art.

3.

The concept of the grotesque may imperil the orderliness of a system of aesthetics, but it need pose no such problem to artists themselves. As an example of an artist who discovered in the grotesque the kind of creative potency that might be expected from an emblem of a total art, I would like briefly to discuss the theory and practice of Flannery O'Connor, perhaps the most articulate of all recent artists who have spoken of the subject. O'Connor provides an especially illuminating comment on Ruskin, as they share an extraordinary sensitivity to the extremities of art, exaltation and debasement.

A committed Catholic, O'Connor was also committed to what she regarded as realism, and so produced, and, in a number of essays and introductions, described, an art anchored firmly both in the visible world of reality and in the invisible world of Reality. Insofar as she sustains this sense of two worlds, all referents are split, nothing is unified or pure, and her art is an art of the margin marked by constant interpenetration. Her subject, she says, is "the almost imperceptible intrusions of grace" in "territory held largely by the devil." Her deliberately crafted motley and discordant art is an attempt to render a total realism that takes into account the antithetical worlds in which human existence occurs. According to her prescription, the novelist is a "realist of distances," whose business it is to reveal the operation of the far within the near, "and it is this kind of realism that you find in the best modern instances of the grotesque."[16]

If what I described as Conrad's verbal grotesque involved an apparently unconscious strategy of masking antithetical meanings in simple utterances, then O'Connor's grotesque is very similar. Moreover, she was, though a less great artist, substantially shrewder, for she courted the grotesque as an expression of a truth constantly before her eyes, not a truth she would deny if she could. She quotes Conrad's phrase about making the reader see, but, unlike him, immediately adds that carnal sight is inadequate and even a form of temptation that must be resisted. There is something in her position of an attitude, as old as Augustine, in which sense experience in general is but "the lust of the eyes," and she is conventionally distrustful of the sensory world. But if she regarded the carnal eye as capable only of perceiving illusions and contributing to evil, her art would not be grotesque, for whatever monsters might appear would be easily interpretable by appeal to the overruling truth of the spiritual eye. Her art is grotesque precisely because she never completely denies the carnal eye; she recognizes the realities people see as well as the Reality they often don't. "The novelist," she says, is defined "not by his function but by his vision, and we must remember that his vision has to be transmitted and that the limitations and blind spots of his audience will very definitely affect the way he is able to show what he sees. This is another thing which in these times increases the tendency toward the grotesque in fiction."[17] O'Connor recognizes not only that the visible is the damned, but also that it is a true temptation, and that the impulse to look is itself a sign of an obscure awareness that there is something to see. If her characters pursue the invisible with carnal eyes, they may be grotesque, but they are nonetheless saved.

Such a judgment, of course, is never manifest or assured, but only interpreted. O'Connor's fictions are distinguished by the amount of interpretive energy they require. Interpretation is encouraged by the author, who would have her readers recognize that they too believe that there is something to see, some connection between the apparent or the referential story, which may amuse or appall, and a shadow-story mysteriously inhering in the apparent one. Her fictional practices, her enticements to interpretation, go well beyond mere allusions to the Bible, and achieve considerable complexity. When Haze Motes, the protagonist of her novel *Wise Blood,* who is setting out to preach that the mere sight of the "new jesus" will save people, buys a car, he asks how much it costs, and is told "Jesus on the cross.... Christ nailed." A moment later, he is advised, "I wouldn't trade me a Chrysler for a Essex like that." If Haze is indeed trading Christ for the car, then he may be making a bad deal, but the reader who recognizes it will be rewarded by the sense of an interpretation that fits. But other signals indicate that the car may be more complex than we had suspected. Essex is a breed of swine, and so the car is potentially connected, in an unpredictable way, to any of the swine-figures that abound in the story. Perhaps the pig-car is one of the Temptations of St. Haze, for the pig is a recurrent figure among Anthony's temptations. Following this track, we might see the pig as a demon or tormentor, a connection reinforced by the figure of Hoover Shoats, a disguised pig who parodies Haze. Perhaps something can be made of a possible connection between the car and an early reference to a man who "got the cholera from a pig." But the richest vein of possibilities is afforded by the Biblical incident of the Gerasene demoniac as related by Mark and Luke,[18] in which Christ drives devils out of a possessed man and into a herd of swine who plunge off a cliff to their destruction. Haze's car, it turns out, suffers a similar fate, after which Haze immediately blinds himself.

By such split references and clues the reader is continually directed out of the carnal story, and into another story, or to many other stories, eventually to discover that he is not out of the story at all, for "the story" is not only Haze's, but Christ's, Anthony's, and, incidentally, ours. The proliferating connections between pig, man, demon, car, and God encourage a kind of interpretation that recognizes that all these entities are within the others, a kind of interpretation that recognizes the grotesque. The important point to be made is that this sort of interpretation is not different in kind from any other. Meaning is made through connections, by linking something with something else outside itself; it is made by establishing relations both within and outside the text, by ascribing intentionality to things that do not inherently possess it, by seeing elements in contexts other than the ones in which they occur, by seeing one thing as another. These operations are carried out at high intensity when we encounter grotesque forms, which is why O'Connor used the grotesque so often, but they are in a broader sense the marks of all interpretation, the methods by which any meaning is made.

O'Connor's fierce dedication to the grotesque has caused her to be regarded as unique when her goal was to reveal not only that salvation was constant and universal, but also that this impetus toward fulfillment manifested itself continually, even in the secular act of interpretation directed toward her own fictions. The grotesqueness of these fictions is commonly described as an aspect of her "Gothic" style, but this term is widely misunderstood as indicating no more than a general air of degradation and degeneracy, and a certain slack or random freakishness in her cast of characters. The essence of O'Connor's Gothic is to be found in the various cripples and amputees who people her works, but they are merely symptomatic of a much larger expression of what Paul Frankl described as the "principle of dependency" which informs all medieval Church Gothic.[19] O'Connor might have argued that all fiction is "Gothic" insofar as it demands, or depends upon, the fulfillment of interpretation, and insofar as it embodies or fosters progress toward an end. She might have added that all such progress, whether moral or interpretive, can be seen in the category of the grotesque:

> Most of us have learned to be dispassionate about evil, to look it in the face and find, as often as not, our own grinning reflections with which we do not argue, but good is another matter. Few have stared at that long enough to accept the fact that its face too is grotesque, that in us the good is something under construction.[20]

For Ruskin, the Gothic represented the highest development of the noble grotesque; he was disgusted by the necessity of placing it in the same class as the "artistical pottage" of the ignoble grotesque. O'Connor felt no such embarrassment. For her, the grotesque did not come in noble and ignoble forms; the essence of her grotesque is that the noble is mingled with the ignoble. At the beginning of her collection of stories, *A Good Man Is Hard to Find,* she quotes St. Cyril of Jerusalem: "THE DRAGON IS BY THE SIDE OF THE ROAD, WATCHING THOSE WHO PASS. BEWARE LEST HE DEVOUR YOU. WE GO TO THE FATHER OF SOULS, BUT IT IS NECESSARY TO PASS BY THE DRAGON." In this parable, the dragon (the discordant world-in-the-making) stands apart from and opposed to the Father of Souls, but is also a phase of the Father, just as the griffin can be a phase of Christ. The goal is beyond the grotesque, but once you have arrived at the grotesque, you have also arrived at the goal.

4.

What is meant by the threat that the dragon would "devour" us? What sort of dragon is it? How is it appeased? How do we pass by? And, most important, what lies beyond it? D. H Lawrence, from whom O'Connor probably got the phrase "wise blood,"[21] struggled with the dragon, and sought the father, all his life, before asking questions like these in his final book, *Apocalypse*[22] Throughout this chapter the grotesque has been discussed as the margin between art and something else, but the character of that something else has escaped definition, for it has always been "beyond." The Book of Revelation is the one book in the Bible that takes as its subject precisely that "beyond." In confronting this book directly, Lawrence sought not to examine the dragon, but to stand in the very presence of the Father. His results should tell us a great deal.

Originally conceived as a preface for Frederick Carter's *The Dragon of the Apocalypse,* Lawrence's book quickly grew into an independent piece as he began to examine in detail the document with which he had been intimate all his life. His first response to this task, registered in the opening pages, was a powerful feeling of nausea regarding the entire Bible, especially Revelation, toward which his instinctive reaction "is one of dislike, repulsion, and even resentment" (4). Freud's formula for repulsion, which was mentioned in Chapter One — the piercing into the conscious mind of elements of the unconscious — applies in Lawrence's case, for he is studying at close quarters a relic from his nearly preconscious or precritical childhood. But it applies as well to the text itself, which Carter had decided,[23] and Lawrence felt in his bones, was corrupt, speaking in several voices. At the deepest level, Lawrence heard the voice of a pagan initiation ritual deriving from an ancient religion of solar worship: its images of collectivity and connection are still there in Revelation, though they are at war with the "repellent," power-hungry individualistic spirit of later religions. In the first half of Revelation, the pagan voice dominates, but in the later parts of the text, the reader loses contact with the old, centered cosmos, and moves into a phase dominated by a "jewish" hatred of the world and a lust for the End. Lawrence's quick, incisive mind moves directly to an exciting conclusion:

> What we feel about the Apocalypse is that it is not one book but several, perhaps many. But it is not made up of pieces of several books strung together, like Enoch. It is one book, in several layers: like layers of civilisation as you dig deeper and deeper to excavate an old city. Down at the bottom is a pagan substratum, probably one of the ancient books of the Aegean civilisation: some sort of book of a pagan Mystery. This has been written over by Jewish apocalyptists, then extended, and then finally written over by the Jewish-Christian apocalyptist John: and then, after his day, expurgated and corrected and pruned down and added to by Christian editors who wanted to make of it a Christian work. (53–54)

Even in his "modern" role as teacher, Jesus retains traces of the ancient Kosmokrator. But in enlarging the story, the later writers masked what had been plain and manifest, creating secrets, breaking up a design that had been complete and whole. The scribes, Lawrence says, "smashed up the patterns"— other words are "disfigured," "mutilated," "smeared," and "mangled" — to "make it safe" (89).

The problem with modern man, Lawrence says for the last time, is that he makes everything safe, passing by the dragon on tiptoes. The great "splendid divine dragon within a man" is slumbering, waking only rarely as in a Dempsey or a Lindbergh (145). In its place is the democratic, "frictional" spirit of individualism, which has succeeded in casting the dragon of the origin in the role of the Beast of the Apocalypse. The work of renovation must begin, he says, with the stripping away of sophistication, commentary, and moralizing, getting back to the initiation ritual told in the Ur-text. This is his appeal in the final sentences of his final book: "What we want is to destroy our false, inorganic connections, especially those related to money, and re-establish the living organic connections, with the cosmos, the sun and earth, with mankind and nation and family. Start with the sun, and the rest will slowly, slowly happen" (200).

This conclusion seems to me dismal and tragic. Having sought factual truth and imaginative nourishment, he concludes with a metaphor — Start with the sun — that is both insipid and infernally vague. And his recommendation that we wake the dragon within does not sort well with his scholarly technique, which entails a suspicious eye, a constant distrust of the text, a relentless skepticism — all forms of alienated academicism that reinforce the tendencies of individualism and sink the dragon deeper in its slumbers. It is conventional to regard this book as one more "illustration of how intellect contributed to the discoveries of Lawrence's imagination."[24] But such an estimate takes an antithesis for a synthesis, ignoring the fact that the intellect achieved its insights by breaking connections, by dismantling and dislocating a traditional text. In this case, the method of the intellect is itself "jewish"; it does not contribute to, but simply cancels out, the program of the imagination.

Even more important than the discord in Lawrence's mind is the discord of the text, which he finds to be split, disfigured, impure, grotesque. With the most powerful sense of an ending of his century, Lawrence was forced to admit that closure offered no rest, and that the end was just as incongruous as the middle he had been trying to escape. Instead of the stasis and clarity of a true end, he finds a corruption, with a spirit of world-hatred disfiguring the only trace of the pure origin left to us. Beyond the grotesque lies...the grotesque.

Whatever this conclusion may have done to Lawrence, it need not cause dismay among us, even considering the possibility that the grotesque may harbor the essence, or symbolize the totality, of art. Admittedly, we yearn to achieve certainty, to complete circles, in short to renounce the grotesque. And admittedly, art sometimes seems to conspire in establishing this fiction of reliable and final knowledge, not only by concluding but also by providing us with resting-points along the way where things seem to make sense and our interpretations seem to fit. For these resting-points the grotesque is no model; it is more commonly associated with incomplete or open works such as *Gargantua and Pantagruel, Tristram Shandy,* and Aubrey Beardsley's *The Story of Venus and Tannhäuser* than it is with closed or more conventional forms. Many works, such as Montaigne's *Essays,* indulge in the grotesque only to leave it behind at the end out of an honorable belief that, although life would be poorer if there were no dragons to pass by, it would be a terrifying and bewildering affair if there were no Father of Souls to pass on to. But the grotesque implies discovery, and disorder is the price one always pays for the enlargement of the mind. Art, perhaps, is measured by its ability to enrich our understanding, but it is also measured by its capacity to provide evidence for the falsification of whatever theories we arrive at. It is this capacity that insures a text's continued life by guaranteeing that there is something left to discover. One sign of this "something left" is contradiction, or dissonance. As William Carlos Williams said (speaking of the Curies) in *Paterson IV,*

A dissonance
in the valence of Uranium
led to the discovery

Dissonance
(if you're interested)
leads to discovery

NOTES

Notes to Preface

1. Princeton: Princeton Univ. Press, 1960.
2. Harmondsworth, England: *Penguin History of Art*, trans. Dieter Pevsner, 1962.
3. *The Gothic*, p. 828.
4. Kayser, trans. Ulrich Weisstein (Toronto and New York: McGraw–Hill, 1966), orig. pub. as *Das Groteske: seine Gestaltung in Malerei und Dichtung* (1957). Bakhtin, trans. Hélène Iswolsky (Cambridge, Mass. and London: The M.I.T. Press, 1968), orig. pub. as *Tvorchestvo Fransua Rable* (1965). The "lesser lights" include Frances Barasch, *The Grotesque: A Study in Meanings* (The Hague and Paris: Mouton, 1971); Arthur Clayborough, *The Grotesque in English Literature* (London: Oxford Univ. Press, 1967); Lee Byron Jennings, *The Ludicrous Demon* (Berkeley and Los Angeles: Univ. of California Press, 1965); and Philip Thomson, *The Grotesque* (London: Methuen & Co., The Critical Idiom Series, 1972).
5. Hugh Kenner, *A Homemade World: The American Modernist Writers* (New York: William Morris and Co., 1975), p. 41.
6. *Mystery and Manners,* ed. Sally and Robert Fitzgerald (New York: Farrar, Straus & Giroux, 1969), p. 40.
7. A. D. Coleman (New York: Ridge Press, 1977).
8. III. iii. 48.
9. *Robert Browning* (London: Macmillan and Co., 1903), p. 150. Bagehot's defense of Browning occurs in "Wordsworth, Tennyson, and Browning; or, Pure, Ornate, and Grotesque Art in Poetry," in ed. R. H. Hutton, *Literary Studies,* 2 vols. (London: Longmans, Green and Co., 1879), II, p. 375.

Notes to Chapter One

1. Susan Stewart, *Nonsense: Aspects of Intertextuality in Folklore and Literature* (Baltimore: The Johns Hopkins Univ. Press, 1979), p. 61. Leach has advanced this theory in several publications, but most fully in "Anthropological Aspects of Language: Animal Categories and Verbal Abuse," in *Reader in Comparative Religion,* ed. William Lessa and Evon Vogt (New York: Harper and Row, 3rd ed., 1972), pp. 206–20.

2. Giorgio Vasari, *Lives of the Most Eminent Painters, Sculptors and Architects,* trans. Gaston Du C. de Vere, 3 vols. (New York: Harry Abrams, 1979), vol. III, p. 1879. This admirable edition is extremely handsome and especially valuable in being unabridged, but the translation is often inelegant. For this passage I have used the translation of George Bull in *Lives of the Painters* (Harmondsworth: Penguin, 1975), p. 374.
3. *Art and Illusion: A Study in the Psychology of Pictorial Representation* (Princeton: Princeton Univ. Press; XXXV in the Bollingen Series, 1972; orig. pub. 1960), pp. 217–20.
4. New York: G. B. Putnam's Sons, 1966, pp. 289–90.
5. *The Pound Era* (Berkeley and Los Angeles: Univ. of California Press, 1971), p. 232.
6. "The Essence of Laughter," in *The Painter of Modern Life and Other Essays,* ed. and trans. Jonathan Mayne (London: Phaidon, 1964), p. 189.
7. *Robert Browning,* p. 148.
8. *The Metamorphoses of the Circle,* trans. Carley Dawson and Elliott Coleman (Baltimore: The Johns Hopkins Univ. Press, 1966), p. 35.
9. Trans. Maria Jolas (Boston: Beacon Press, 1969; orig. pub. 1958), p. 351.
10. It is this structure that accounts for Ruskin's otherwise surprising estimate that Jacob's ladder was a grotesque: "Thus, Jacob's dream revealed to him the ministry of angels; but because this ministry could not be seen or understood by him in its fullness, it was narrowed to him into a ladder between heaven and earth, which was a grotesque." *The Stones of Venice* III. iii. 62.
11. *Hell,* in *The Divine Comedy,* 3 vols., trans. Dorothy Sayers (Harmondsworth: Penguin, 1977), vol. I, XXV: II. 49–78; p. 229.
12. "Making Love to Music," in *Phoenix,* ed. Edward D. McDonald (New York: Viking, 1972), p. 161.
13. Thus Octavio Paz's complaint that "One of the most grotesque consequences of Stalinist obscurantism was the introduction of the pejorative adjective 'formalist' into artistic and literary discussions." In *Claude Lévi Strauss: An Introduction,* trans. J. S. Bernstein and Maxine Bernstein (New York: Dell, 1974), p. 145.
14. "A Note on the Unconscious in Psycho-Analysis," in *The Standard Edition of the Complete Psychoanalytical Works of Sigmund Freud,* ed. James Strachey, 24 vols. (London: Hogarth Press, 1958), vol. 12, p. 264.
15. *Rabelais and His World,* pp. 25–26.
16. *The Poetics of Space,* pp. 108–109. The work Bachelard cites is Jurgis Baltrušaitis, *Le moyen–âge fantastique.*
17. *A Homemade World,* p. 220.
18. New York: Barnes and Noble, 1966, pp. 10–11.

19. First explored by Arnold van Gennep and others in the first decades of this century, the notion of liminality has more recently been developed by Victor Turner. See *Dramas, Fields and Metaphors; Symbolic Action in Human Society* (Ithaca: Cornell Univ. Press, 1974).
20. Pt. IV (Expression), sec. 64 (The Grotesque) (London: Adam and Charles Black, 1896), pp. 256–58.
21. *Metamorphoses,* trans. Rolfe Humphries (Bloomington and London: Indiana Univ. Press, 1955), XIV: 11. 59–69, p. 340.
22. Loren Eiseley, *Darwin's Century: Evolution and the Men Who Discovered It* (Garden City: Anchor Books, 1961), p. 202.
23. See *The Structure of Scientific Revolutions* (Chicago and London: Univ. of Chicago Press, 1968; orig. pub. 1962), esp. chaps. VII and VIII, pp. 66–90.
24. In *Other Criteria: Confrontations with Twentieth-Century Art* (London, Oxford, New York: Oxford Univ. Press, 1972), Steinberg asserts that "Gombrich's conviction that alternatives cannot be seen in simultaneity is argued on the evidence of trivial diagrams. It ignores the fact that the most powerful visual imagination of our century has labored precisely to make ambiguity visible, to create the illusion of simultaneous alternative readings" (p. 411, n. 27; see also chap. 6, *passim).*
25. *Wheel of Fire* (London: Oxford Univ. Press, 1930), p. 192.
26. Quoted and trans. in Kayser, p. 205.
27. "Grotesque Renaissance," in *The Stones of Venice* III. iii. 58.
28. *Ibid.,* III. iii. 59.
29. *Modern Painters,* III. viii. 4.
30. *Ibid.*
31. Although paradox presents an implicit criticism of absolute judgment, it is self-abolishing, and so actually tends to reinforce absolute judgment. As Rosalie Colie has observed, "Like a tight spring, the implications of any particular paradox impel that paradox beyond its own limitations to defy its categories." *Paradoxia Epidemica: The Renaissance Tradition of Paradox* (Princeton: Princeton Univ. Press, 1966), p. 11.
32. Cambridge, Mass.: Harvard Univ. Press, 1979. See esp. chap. 1, "Carnal and Spiritual Senses," pp. 1–22.
33. The problematics of such "gaps" have been explored most thoroughly by Wolfgang Iser. See "Indeterminacy and the Reader's Response in Prose Fiction," *Aspects of Narrative* (English Institute Essays), ed. J. Hillis Miller (New York Columbia Univ. Press 1971), pp. 1–45; and *The Implied Reader: Patterns of Communication in Prose Fiction from Bunyan to Beckett* (Baltimore and London: The Johns Hopkins Univ. Press, 1974), esp. chap. 11, "The Reading Process: A Phenomenological Approach," pp. 274–94.

34. This phrase, equally as Ruskinian as the concept of "gaps," is from chap. 2 of "On Celestial Hierarchies" by the "Pseudo-Dionysius," a Syrian monk of the late fifth century whose writings on mysticism were extraordinarily influential during the Middle Ages.
35. Roland Barthes begins *The Pleasure of the Text* by asking his reader to "imagine someone (a kind of Monsieur Teste in reverse) who abolishes within himself all barriers, all classes, all exclusions, not by syncretism but by simple disregard of that old spectre: *logical contradiction;* who mixes every language, even those said to be incompatible; who silently accepts every charge of illogicality, of incongruity.... Now this anti-hero exists: he is the reader of the text at the moment he takes his pleasure. The text of pleasure is a sanctioned Babel" (New York: Hill and Wang, 1975; orig. pub. in French, 1973), trans. Richard Miller, pp. 3–4.
36. New York: Norton, 1958.
37. *Ibid.,* p. 237.
38. *Ibid.,* p. 238.

Notes to Chapter Two

1. Pliny, *Natural History* XXXIII, XXXV; Tacitus, *Annals* XV; Suetonius, *Nero* 31; Giuseppe Lugli, *Roma antica. Il centro monumentale,* Rome, 1946; H. P. L'Orange, *Domus Aurea, der Sonnenpalast* (Oslo: Serta Eitremiana, 1942), esp. pp. 68 ff.; Nicole Dacos, *La Découverte de la Domus Aurea et la Formation des Grotesques à la Renaissance* (London: Studies of the Warburg Institute, Univ. of London, 31, 1969). See also Samuel Ball Platner, *A Topographical Dictionary of Ancient Rome* (London: Humphrey Milford, Oxford Univ. Press, 1929); and Ernest Nash, *Pictorial Dictionary of Ancient Rome,* two volumes (New York, Washington: Frederick A. Praeger, 1961), which has not only an excellent bibliography but a magnificent collection of photographs of the ancient sites; and Axel Boëthius, *The Golden House of Nero. Some Aspects of Roman Architecture* (Ann Arbor: Univ. of Michigan Press, 1960).
2. L'Orange has also written on Nero's conception of himself after the great fire as a sun-god in *Apotheosis in Ancient Portraiture,* trans. A. G. Jayne (Oslo: W. Nygaard, Instituttet fur Sammenlignende Kulturforskning, Serie B: Skrifter XLIV, 1947), pp. 57 ff.
3. *Annals* XV. 42. According to Platner (see note 1 above), the grounds of the Domus Aurea extended from the Palatine to the Esquiline; one authority is cited as saying that the total area was about 125 acres, while another puts the area at 370 acres (Hyde Park being 390) (pp. 166–68).
4. *Domus Aurea, der Sonnenpalast;* see note 1 above.
5. *The Gothic,* pp. 200–202.

6. For a chronology of these developments, see Platner, *A Topographical Dictionary of Ancient Rome*, pp. 171–72.
7. Courtesy of Pliny, *Natural History* XXXV. 120.
8. *Ibid.*
9. Lugli, *Nero's Golden House and the Trajan Baths*, trans. John Tickner (Rome: Bardi Editore, 1968), p. 9. This is a pamphlet issued by the Bureau of Tourism in Rome, consisting of material in *Roma antica;* see note 1 above.
10. See Nicolas Ponce, *Descriptions de bains de Titus* (Fol. Paris, 1786). This work was reprinted in Ponce, *Collection des tableaux et arabesques antiques, trouves a Rome, dans les ruines des Thermes de Titus* (Paris: Ponce, 1805).
11. There are no known representations of Horace's mermaid in antiquity, but Figure 15, by Lucas van Leyden, may be a knowing representation of this figure.
12. *De Architectura,* trans. and ed. Frank Granger (Cambridge, Mass.: The Loeb Classical Library, Harvard Univ. Press, 1934), vol. II, p. 105. Ruskin followed the vitruvian line in his chapter on "Grotesque Renaissance" in *The Stones of Venice* (III. iii. 39), characterizing the grotesque ornamental style as "an elaborate and luscious form of nonsense" which "developed itself among the enervated Romans."
13. *Norm and Form; Studies in the Art of the Renaissance* (London: Phaidon, 1971), pp. 84–85.
14. *Ibid.*
15. *Domus Aurea*, pp. 139–60.
16. This etymology is given in Arthur Clayborough, *The Grotesque in English Literature*, p. 2.
17. Pinturicchio was one of the earliest painters to adapt the new style, his most famous work being the Piccolomini Library in the Cathedral at Siena. For a generous estimate of Pinturicchio's importance in this regard see J. Schulz, "Pinturicchio and the Revival of Antiquity," *Journal of the Warburg and Courtauld Institutes*, 25 (1962), pp. 35–55.
18. The studio of Domenico Ghirlandaio (1449–94) produced the most complete contemporary sketches of the designs of the Domus Aurea. See H. Egger, ed., *Codex Escurialensis. Ein Skizzenbuch aus der Werkstatt Domenico Ghirlandaio* (Vienna, 1906).
19. The story is recounted in Vasari's life of Giovanni da Udine:

> Whereupon, Giovanni going with Raffaello, who was taken to see them, they were struck with amazement, both the one and the other, at the freshness, beauty, and excellence of those works, for it appeared to them an extraordinary thing that they had been

preserved for so long a time; but it was no great marvel, for they had not been open or exposed to the air. These grotesques—which were called grotesques from their having been discovered in the underground grottoes—executed with so much design, with fantasies so varied and so bizarre, with their delicate ornaments of stucco divided by various fields of colour, and with their little scenes so pleasing and beautiful, entered so deeply into the heart and mind of Giovanni, that, having devoted himself to the study of them, he was not content to draw and copy them merely once or twice.

Vasari (de Vere translation), vol. III, p. 1673. Raphael may also have seen the *villa di Livia,* a house from approximately the same era as the Domus Aurea, with similar designs.
20. See Dacos, *Domus Aurea,* p. 51.
21. See C. A. Patrides, *The Grand Design of God; the literary form of the Christian view of history* (London: Routledge and Kegan Paul, 1972), pp. 54–57. Patrides discusses Raphael's Loggias as part of a tradition that includes *The Tryptich of the Redemption* by the School of Rogier van der Weyden, ca. 1470; Bosch's *The Garden of Earthly Delights,* 1500–05; and Michelangelo's Sistine Chapel, 1508–12. Patrides argues that the method of depicting a narrative in a series of scenes reflects a linear view of history as opposed to the mythic, cyclical view. The tradition in which Raphael's frescoes participate grew out of medieval illuminations of the Bible; also in that tradition are the Great East Window of the York Minster, 1405—08; the choir screen at Exeter Cathedral, done in the early fourteenth century; and the Bedford Book of Hours, from the fifteenth century.
22. The translation is by Fabio Calvo and now resides in the Library in Munich *(Cod. Ital.,* 37). Raphael undertook the study of Vitruvius in order to learn, as he wrote to Leo X on July 1, 1514, "if he has some beautiful secrets in architecture." He later wrote to Castiglione that "Vitruvius gives me a lot of explanations but not quite enough." See V. Golzio, *Raffaello nei documenti...* (Vatican City, 1936), pp. 31, 30. Quoted and translated in Fernando Castagnoli, "Raphael and Ancient Rome," in *The Complete Works of Raphael* (New York: Harrison House, 1969), p. 572 (no author or editor given). Golzio has recently been reissued (Westmead: Gregg, 1971).
23. "In my Journal the place and moment of conception are recorded; the fifteenth of October 1764, in the close of evening, as I sat musing in the Church of the Zoccolanti or Franciscan fryars, while they were singing vespers in the temple of Jupiter on the ruins of the Capitol." *Memoirs of*

My Life, ed. Georges A. Bonnard (London: Thomas Nelson and Sons, 1966), p. 136.

24. F. de la Guertiere, *Miscellanae picturae vulgo grotesqves in spelaeis Vaticanis à Raphaele Vrbinate* (Paris: Chez Mariette, 165–?); Giovanni Volpato, *Le Logge di Raffaele, incise da Giovanni Volpato* (Rome, 1772–1777); Agostino Valentini, *I freschi delle Loggie Vaticane*(Rome: A. Valentini, 1851); and Marcello Ferraro, *Les ornaments de Raphaël*(Paris: J. Marie, 1860).
25. Trans. A. B. Hinds, ed. William Gaunt (London: Dent, 1966), vol. 4 of 4, p. 10 (De Vere III, p. 1675).
26. *The Stones of Venice* III. iii. 39.
27. *Ibid.,* III. iii. 49.
28. *Ibid.,* III. iii. 50.
29. In "The Image Made by Chance in Renaissance Thought," H. W. Janson concludes a discussion of random or chance images, which had been mentioned prominently by Pliny, Philostratus, and Cicero, and in the Renaissance by Leonardo and Alberti, by suggesting that, for us, photography has taken over the task of representation, leaving painting free to pursue *fantasia,* or free form. "Perhaps," writes Janson, "we have thus at last resolved the ancient Greek dichotomy by assigning each of them to its own separate domain." In Millard Meiss, ed., *De Artibus Opuscula XL Essays in Honor of Erwin Panofsky* (New York: New York Univ. Press, 1961), vol. 1 of 2, p. 266. Janson wrote before the publication of *The Grotesque in Photography.*
30. Translated by B. Hogan and G. Kubler as *The Life of Forms in Art* (New York, 1948), p. 18; original French edition, 1934.
31. *The Nude: A Study in Ideal Form* (New York: Anchor, 1959), pp. 36970.
32. Ed. Sir Thomas Dick Lander (London, 1842); quoted in Angus Fletcher, *Allegory: The Theory of a Symbolic Mode* (Ithaca: Cornell Univ. Press, 1964), p.256.
33. Quoted without reference in Robert J. Clements, *Michelangelo's Theory of Art* (London: Routledge and Kegan Paul, 1963), p. 217.
34. See C. R. Dodwell, *Painting in Europe 800 to 1200* (Baltimore: Penguin, 1971). The student interested in this tradition will find an excellent introduction in the works of Jurgis Baltrušaitis; see *Aberrations: quatre essais sur la légende des formes* (Paris: O. Perrin, 1957); *Reveils et prodiges, le gothique fantastique* (Paris: A. Colin, n.d.), esp. pp. 119 ff.; and *Le moyen âge fantastique* (Paris: A. Colin, 1955), esp. chap. Four, "Arabesques Fantastiques," pp. 103–50.
35. Migne, Patrologia Latina, 182, coll. 915/6; a full translation is in Elizabeth G. Holt, *A Documentary History of Art,* 2 vols. (Garden City, N.

Y.: Doubleday, 1957–58), vol. I, pp. 19–22. For a study of the influence of Bernard's position, see Jean Adhémar, *Influences Antiques dans l'Art du Moyen Age Francais* (London: Studies of the Warburg Institute, 7, 1939), pp. 270–71; and Meyer Schapiro, *Romanesque Art* (New York: G. Braziller, 1976), chap. One, "On the Aesthetic Attitude in Romanesque Art."
36. See M. R. James, *"Pictor in Carmine," Archeologia* XCIV (1951), pp. 141–66. The passage here cited is p. 141 of this translation, which is accompanied by the Latin original. Bernard's position was reiterated in the mid-fifteenth century by the Archbishop St. Antonio in the *Summa Theologica* III, tit. 8, sec. 4, chap. 11: "It seems superfluous and vain in the stories of saints or in churches to paint oddities, which do not serve to excite devotion, but laughter and vanity, such as monkeys and dogs chasing hares, and the like, or vain adornments of clothing." Excerpt published by C. Gilbert, "The Archbishop on the Painters of Florence, 1450," *Art Bulletin* XLI (1959), p. 76.
37. *Painting in Britain; The Middle Ages* (Baltimore: Penguin, Pelican History of Art, 1965; orig. pub., 1954), p. 100.
38. The Rutland Psalter, f. 87 v. This is figure 502 from Lillian M. C. Randall, *Images in the Margins of Gothic Manuscripts* (California Studies in the History of Art, vol. IV, Berkeley and Los Angeles: Univ. of California Press, 1966).
39. Rickert, *Painting in Britain,* p. 100.
40. Rickert, *Painting in Britain,* p. 134.
41. Eric George Millar, introduction to *The Luttrell Psalter* (London: Trustees of the British Museum, 1932), p. 16.
42. On "reluctance," see Schapiro, "On the Aesthetic Attitude in Romanesque Art," note 35, above.
43. See note 38, above.
44. From *Speculum* XLV:4 (October 1970); reprinted in Schapiro, *Late Antique, Early Christian and Mediaeval Art* (New York: Braziller, 1979), pp. 197–98.
45. Randall, *Images in the Margins of Gothic Manuscripts,* p. 19.
46. Schapiro discusses many instances of such bowmen in "The Religious Meaning of the Ruthwell Cross," in *Late Antique, Early Christian and Mediaeval Art,* p. 182.
47. See H. W. Janson, *Apes and Ape Lore in the Middle Ages and the Renaissance* (London: Studies of the Warburg Institute, XX, 1952).
48. *Late Antique, Early Christian and Mediaeval Art,* p. 198.
49. *The Stones of Venice* III. iii. 23.
50. "The Joseph Scenes on the Maximianus Throne," in *Late Antique, Early Christian and Mediaeval Art,* p. 43.

51. Ithaca: Cornell Univ. Press, 1979. Page references are to this edition, and are given in the text.
52. See David DuBon, "A Spectacular Limoges Painted Enamel," *The Bulletin,* Philadelphia Museum of Art 76: 329, pp. 3–17, which describes a recent acquisition of a Limoges enamel by Jean de Court (French, active c. 1555-85) with grotesques inspired by Jacques Androuet Ducerceau and Etienne Delaune.
53. *Grottesche* re-emerged a final time at the end of the nineteenth century as a mode of interior decoration. See the Gamble Room at the Victoria and Albert Museum, London.
54. Gombrich says that "It may be argued that the very possibility of reproducing and spreading these designs through the medium of engraving changed the status and function of the grotesque.... The grotesque has moved from the margin to the centre and offers its inconsequential riddles to focused vision" *(The Sense of Order,* p. 281). Printing may have been able to do the same for drollery—a number of books of drollery prints exist—but the moment had passed.
55. See Rudolf Berliner, *Ornamentale Vorlagebliitter des 15. bis 18. Jahrhunderts, 4* vols. (Leipzig: Klinkhardt and Biermann, 1925), I, p. 115.
56. This is the title of one such book by B. Th. de Bry. See Berliner, I, p. 115.
57. See *Œuvres de Jacques Androuet dit Du Cerceau: 62 petites arabesques* (Paris: Librairie de l'Art, 1884).
58. Since I wrote this, that book has actually appeared. See Janet S. Byrne, *Renaissance Ornament Prints and Drawings* (New York: The Metropolitan Museum of Art, 1981).
59. There are a surprising number of books of grotesque prints by these and other artists. These include, in addition to those mentioned in notes 56 and 57, above, Lucas Kilian's *Newe Gradisco Buch* (1624), Ducerceau's *Grotesques* (1550), *Aus der Groteskenfolge* (1623), and *Folge von Grotesken* (1607). For a more complete list, see Berliner, vol. 1, *passim;* and Peter Jessen, *Meister des Ornamentstichs,* 4 vols.; see vol. 1, *Gotik und Renaissance im Ornamentstich* (Berlin: Verlag fur Kunstwissenschaft, 1922), *passim.* For the development of the Netherlandish grotesque, see Sune Schéle, *Cornelius Bos: a study of the origins of the Netherland grotesque* (Stockholm: Almquist and Wiksell, 1965).
60. *Neuw Grottesken Buch Nürnberg 1610,* ed. H. G. Franz (Graz, Austria: Akademisch Druck, 1966). See Peter Wick, "A New Book of Grotesques by Christoph Jamnitzer," in *Bulletin,* Museum of Fine Arts, Boston 60: 321 (1962), pp. 83–104, which discusses not only Jamnitzer's book but also the work of other Dutch exponents of *knorpelwerk,* or the "cartilage" style, "which produced the dissolution of tectonic tradition in

the kneading, pulling, twisting and softening of forms as if it were dough or putty, giving rise to a distinct Dutch style of ornament and goldsmith's work which flourished in the second half of the seventeenth century" (pp. 96, 99).
61. Roben-Dumesnil, *Le Peintre-Graveur francais*, 11 vols. (Paris: G. Waree, 1835–71); Ume, *L'art Decoratif* (Liege: Claesen, n.d.).
62. For Jessen, see note 59, above; for Berliner, see note 55, above.
63. For an introduction to later French versions of the *grottesche* style, see George Savage, *French Decorative Art 1638–1793* (London: Allen Lane, The Penguin Press, 1969); on Bérain in particular, see pp. 48 ff.
64. See *Classical Ornament of the Eighteenth Century, Designed & Engraved by Michelangelo Pergolesi* (New York: Dover, 1970). This work draws on Pergolesi's designs before 1793.
65. *Le Logge di Raffaello* (Rome: Instituto Poligrafico dello Stato, Libreria delia Stato, 1977). See also Rumer Godden, *The Raphael Bible* (London: Macmillan, 1970), which reproduces the entire series of panels on the Loggia ceiling.
66. See Gombrich, "Raphael's Stanza delia Segnatura" in *Symbolic Images: Studies in the Art of the Renaissance* (London: Phaidon, 1972), pp. 85–101.
67. Giulio Romano, who executed several of the main panels of the Loggias, finished the painting after Raphael's death. It is said (sometimes critically) that he worked especially on the figure of the youth.
68. *Painting in Italy, 1500 to 1600* (Harmondsworth: Pelican, 1971), p. 83.

Notes to Chapter Three

1. Frogmore, St. Albans, Herts.: Chatto, Bodley Head & Jonathan Cape and Granada Publishing Ltd., 1977. Originally published 1963; all page references in the text are to the 1977 edition.
2. *Die Wandmalerei Pompejus* (Hildesheim: George Olms Verlagbuchandlung, 1963), p. 138. Originally published 1929.
3. Lévi-Strauss describes deerskins "illuminated with arabesques" by the Caduveo Indians living in the lowlands on the left bank of the Rio Paraguay, in *Tristes Tropiques,* trans. John and Doreen Weightman (New York: Pocket Books, 1977), p. 174. And E. O. James writes in *From Cathedral to Cave; temples and shrines of prehistoric classical and early christian times* (London: Thames and Hudson, 1965) that Paleolithic caves bear similar markings: "Intermingled with these...designs are interlacings and arabesques with animal silhouettes, naturalistic in style and technique," p. 25. The arabesque may represent man's earliest artistic

expression. In *Prehistoric and Primitive Art,* trans. Harry Mins (New York: Abrams, 1967), Luis Péricot-Garcia, John Galloway and Andreas Lommel assert that "The oldest of these [wall engravings] are the meanders and arabesques traced by fingers on the dry walls of the cave," p. 61. The difference between grotesque and arabesque in postclassical art is that, as a result of a Moslem injunction against representing the human figure, the arabesque is exclusively vegetal. For further distinctions, see chap. Five, below.

4. This function of myth is eloquently stated by Roland Barthes in *Mythologies,* trans. Annette Lavers (New York: Hill and Wang, 1972). Noting the capacity of myth to make its subject appear inevitable, so that it "goes without saying," he comments that

> Myth does not deny things, on the contrary, its function is to talk about them; simply it purifies them, it makes them innocent, it gives them a natural and eternal justification, it gives them a clarity which is not that of an explanation but that of a statement of fact.... In passing from history to nature, myth acts economically: it abolishes the complexity of human acts... It establishes a blissful clarity: things appear to mean something by themselves. (p. 43)

5. The discussion that follows is not intended as an anthropological study, but simply as an attempt to formulate a consensus view of the dominant aspects of the mythological mind. Among primitive cultures, this view applies more to "cold" societies, which resist change, than to "hot" societies, which embrace change as a source of cultural energy.

6. *Late Antique, Early Christian and Mediaeval Art,* p. 198.

7. *Domus Aurea,* p. 73: "*Ces prodiges déconcertants sont entrâinés dans des mouvements tellement fébriles qu'ils semblent appartenir àun monde en perpétual le metamorphose, où les animaux s'unissent et se changent en acanthe et où les monstres s'humanisent.*"

8. Lévi-Strauss, *The Savage Mind* (Chicago: Univ. of Chicago Press, 1966), p.5.

9. See *The Notebooks on Primitive Mentality,* trans. P. Riviere (Oxford: Basil Blackwell, 1975), p. 104. Originally published as *Carnets* in 1949.

10. *The Savage Mind,* p. 36.

11. "The Structural Study of Myth," in Thomas Sebeok, ed., *Myth: A Symposium* (Bloomington and London: Indiana Univ. Press, 1974), p. 105. This article first appeared in *Structural Anthropology,* trans. C. Jacobson and B. G. Schoepf (New York: Anchor, 1967); originally published 1958.

12. "Genesis as Myth," in *"Genesis as Myth" and Other Essays* (London: Jonathan Cape Ltd., 1969), p. 11.

13. C. G. Jung, trans. R.F.C. Hull, *Four Archetypes: Mother Rebirth Spirit Trickster* (Princeton: Princeton Univ. Press, 1973), pp. 143–44. This is a reprint from *The Collected Works of C. G. Jung,* Bollingen xx (Princeton: Princeton Univ. Press, 1972), vol. 9, pt. 1.
14. *The Savage Mind,* p. 22.
15. Trans. John and Doreen Weightman (New York: Pocket Books, 1977), p.50.
16. "Categories," 5.4a.10–12. In Richard McKeon, ed., *The Basic Works of Aristotle* (New York: Random House, 1941), p. 13.
17. The term *illud tempus* was introduced by Mircea Eliade, and can be found throughout his works.
18. "Prologemena," in C. G. Jung and K. Kerenyi, trans. R.F.C. Hull, *Essays on a Science of Mythology: The Myth of the Divine Child and the Mysteries of Eleusis,* Bollingen XXII (Princeton: Princeton Univ. Press, 1973), p. 8. Originally published 1949.
19. Jung offers the following account of the mythic connection between the symbolic and the material:

> The symbols of the self arise in the depths of the body and they express its materiality every bit as much as the structure of the perceiving consciousness. The symbol is thus a living body, *corpus et anima*... The uniqueness of the psyche can never enter wholly into reality, it can only be realized approximately, though it still remains the absolute basis of all consciousness. The deeper "layers" of the psyche lose their individual uniqueness as they retreat farther and farther into darkness. "Lower down," that is to say as they approach the autonomous functional systems, they become increasingly collective until they are universalized and extinguished in the body's materiality, i.e., in chemical substances. The body's carbon is simply carbon. Hence "at bottom" the psyche is simply "world".... The more archaic and "deeper," that is the more *physiological* the symbol is, the more collective and universal, the more "material" it is. *(Ibid.,* p. 93)

20. Eliade summarizes the practice of alchemy as an attempt to project onto inanimate matter ceremonies which primitive man had performed on himself. The alchemist's innovation was to project *"on to Matter the initiatory function of suffering.* Thanks to the alchemical operations, corresponding to the tortures, death and resurrection of the initiate, the substance is transmuted, that is, attains a transcendental mode of being; it becomes gold. Gold, we repeat, is the symbol of immortality.... Alchemical transmutation is therefore equivalent to the perfecting of matter or, in Christian terminology, to its redemption." From *Myths, Rites, Symbols: A*

Mircea Eliade Reader, ed. Wendell C. Beane and William G. Doty, 2 vols. (New York, Evanston, San Francisco, London: Harper and Row, 1975), vol. 2, p. 429. The passage is taken from *Shamanism, Archaic Techniques of Ecstasy*, trans. Willard R. Trask, Bollingen LXXVI (Princeton: Princeton Univ. Press. 1964), pp. 165–68.
21. "The Life of Milton," in *The Lives of the Most Eminent English Poets* (London, 1783), p. 220.
22. Leach, *Genesis as Myth*, p. 11.
23. This ritual transformation of the outcast is particularly true of those mythological systems in which the human body is seen as the archetype for the entire world, a model for the cosmos. The psychology of such systems is discussed by Erich Neumann, *The Origins and History of Consciousness*, trans. R.F.C. Hull, Bollingen XLII (Princeton: Princeton Univ. Press, 1973). Originally published in 1954. See especially chap. 1, "The Uroboros."
24. On the connections between domestic ritual and cosmogony, see Lévi-Strauss, *The Raw and the Cooked*, trans. John and Doreen Weightman (New York: Harper and Row, 1975), pp. 337 ff.; and *The Savage Mind*, pp. 130 ff.
25. *Purity and Danger: an analysis of concepts of pollution and taboo* (London: Routledge and Kegan Paul, 1966).
26. *Ibid.*, p. 167.
27. *Ibid.*, p. 35.
28. *Ibid.*, p. 168. Mary Douglas has written on this cult at greater length in *The Lele of the Kasai* (London: Oxford Univ. Press, 1963). See also Roy Willis, *Man and Beast* (London: Hart–Davis, MacGibbon, 1974), esp. chap. 2, "The Paradox of the Pangolin." A giant pangolin is on display in London's Museum of Natural History in Kensington. It must be seen.
29. *Purity and Danger*, p. 169.
30. "A meditation. . . ." *ibid.*, p. 173; "which invite their . . ." *ibid.*, p. 170.
31. *Ibid.*, p. 53.
32. *Ibid.*, p. 55. This taxonomic strictness is the context for Christ's saying, "Not that which goeth into the mouth defileth a man, but that which cometh out of the mouth, this clefileth a man" (Matthew 15:11).
33. Neumann, *Origins and History of Consciousness*, p. 227.
34. See G. Rachel Levy, *The Gate of Horn: A study of the religious conceptions of the stone age, and their influence upon European thought* (London: Faber and Faber Ltd., 1948), pp. 14–15.
35. See E. O. James, *From Cave to Cathedral*, p. 37. On brain-eating as a means of acquiring the identity of the dead and simultaneously granting him new life, see F. M. Bergounioux, "Notes on the Mentality of Primitive Man," in Sherwood 1. Washburn, ed., *Social Life of Early Man*

(Chicago: Aldine, 1961), p. 14; and Alberto C. Blanc, "Some Evidence for the Ideologies of Early Man," in the same volume, p. 126.

36. Eliade discusses the cave in these terms in *Myths, Dreams, and Mysteries: The Encounter between Contemporary Faiths and Archaic Realities*, trans. Philip Mairet (New York: Harper and Row, 1967), p. 171; and in *Rites and Symbols of Initiation*, trans. Willard R. Trask (New York: Harper and Row, 1965), pp. 51–53, 61–66.

37. Centre d'études et de documentation préhistorique: Montignac, 1952.

38. Trans. Norbert Guterman (New York: Abrams, 1967).

39. For a representative and persuasive demurrer, see Ann Sieveking, *The Cave Artists* (London: Thames and Hudson, 1979), p. 61:

> Basically this sexual division depends upon the human representations themselves, but the number of these is small, not, in fact, sufficient to determine any sexual grouping. Leroi-Gourhan therefore resorted to signs to extend his categories and while the female signs are fairly acceptable as a group, the male are much less so. The attribution of arrows, lines and dots, for example, to the masculine principle is simply a matter of opinion. On this structure, which is already somewhat hypothetical, is built the division into masculine and feminine animals. Here again the evidence is not conclusive....

40. *Treasures of Prehistoric Art*, p. 173.
41. *Ibid., p.174.*
42. See Sieveking, *The Cave Artists*, p. 149.
43. The critic is Sieveking, *The Cave Artists*, p. 148.
44. On "anthropomorphic figures" see H. Bégouën and H. Breuil, "*De quelques figures hybrides (mi-humaines, mi-animales) de la caverne des Trois Frères (Ariège),*" *Revue Anthropologique* XLIV (1934), pp. 115–19. For "têtes humaines grotesques" see L. Capitan, H. Breuil, and D. Peyrony, *Les Combarelles aux Byzies (Dordogne)* (Paris: Masson, 1924), pp. 69 ff.
45. E. Ripoll Perelló, "Las Representaciones antropomorfas en el arte paleolítico español," *Ampurias* (Barcelona), XIX–XX (1957–58), p. 172. Quoted and translated in Siegfried Giedion, *The Eternal Present: A Contribution on Constancy and Change* (New York: Pantheon, 1962–64), 2 vols., vol. 1, *The Beginnings of Art* (1962), p. 487.
46. *Treasures of Prehistoric Art*, p. 131.
47. *Ibid.,* p. 132.
48. Giedion, *The Beginnings of Art,* p. 511. Giedion concludes his discussion of the use of the human figure in cave art with a bold suggestion:

"Perhaps the eternal figure of the creative artist, with his ability to find an approach to spheres that are inaccessible to the average man, comes nearest to the meaning of the shaman, first projected in the form of the hybrid figure" (p. 512).
49. See Levy, *The Gate of Horn*, pp. 43–44.
50. *The Eternal Present*, vol. 2 of 2, *The Beginnings of Architecture (1964)*, p.61.
51. *The Savage Mind*, p. 37.
52. See Jane Harrison, *Prologemenon to the Study of Greek Religion* (Cambridge: Cambridge Univ. Press, 1903), p. 537: "The conjecture lies near to hand that in bygone days there was a marriage to a sacred bull." On this subject, Herbert Schneidau comments in *Sacred Discontent The Bible in Western Tradition* (Berkeley and Los Angeles: Univ. of California Press, 1977) that "Queen Pasiphaë, along with Io, Leda, Europa, and other heroines, becomes more interesting by the moment, and the 'ox-eyed' Hera of Homer deserves new scrutiny, for her epithet may as easily mean 'ox-faced.' If so she is clearly the Greek equivalent of the Egyptian Hathor, who had the body of a woman and the head of a cow" (p. 93).
53. Margaret W. Conkey, "A Century of Paleolithic Cave Art," in *Archeology* 34:4 June 1981), p. 23.
54. *The Gate of Horn*, p. 70.
55. *Ibid.*, p. 35.
56. "The word 'grotesque' is one of the keys to Flaubert's vocabulary and thought," according to Benjamin Bart in *Flaubert* (Syracuse: Syracuse Univ. Press, 1967), p. 51.
57. *The Beginnings of Art*, p. 511.
58. Even for prehistoric man the caves were considered places of great antiquity, according to Kerényi, who has traced a series of myths involving the Primordial Child, a rubric under which he gathers Apollo, Hermes, Dionysus, and others. All these myths, Kerenyi points out, involve the grotto, which was connected with "primal waters" and summoned up a time when even the gods were children. See *Essays on a Science of Mythology*, esp. chap. 1, "The Primordial Child in Primordial Times."
59. See note 52 above.
60. See *Mythologies*.
61. *The Savage Mind*, p. 219.
62. See *The Child's Conception of the World*, trans. Joan and Andrew Tomlinson (Frogmore, St. Alban's: Paladin, 1973): "It may be that the child's idea of 'participation' differs from that of the primitive, but they resemble one another..." p. 157. Piaget was writing, of course, before Lévi-Strauss's attacks on Levy-Bruhl.

63. In the "Preface" to the third edition, written in 1911, Freud says, "I may even venture to prophesy in what other directions later editions of this book—if any should be needed—will differ from the present one. They will have...to afford closer contact with the copious material presented in imaginative writing, in myths...." See *The Interpretation of Dreams,* trans. and ed. James Strachey (New York: Avon, n.d.), pp. xxvii–xxviii. Originally published 1899.

64. In *Totem and Taboo,* originally published in 1913, Freud argues that the primitive mind, like that of the neurotic, is characterized by a higher than normal level of ambivalence; moreover, that the mind of the obsessional neurotic is akin to the savage's in sustaining feelings of taboo, which can be viewed as extreme forms of desire/prohibition, or attraction/repulsion. In fact, taboo is simply a highly aggressive form of "conscience," the internal perception of the rejection of a wish. Neurotics therefore have inherited an archaic constitution as an atavistic vestige. The grotesque, I have been arguing, is the same—a collision between the unusually virulent primitive and an enfeebled but still operative modern.

65. It follows that the "cure" of psychoanalysis parallels the archaic attempt to return, through ritual and myth, to the primordial past and repeat the cosmogonic birth. Or, as Eliade says, "We might translate the operative procedure into terms of archaic thought, by saying that the cure is to begin living all over again; that is, to repeat the birth, to make oneself contemporary with 'the beginning.' . . . for the modern man, personal experience that is 'primordial' can be no other than that of infancy." In *Myths, Dreams, and Mysteries,* pp. 53–54.

66. Originally published 1920.

67. From "The Dissection of the Psychical Personality," in *New Introductory Lectures on Psychoanalysis,* trans. and ed. James Strachey (London: Hogarth Press, 1974), The International Psycho-analytical Library, vol. 24, pp. 73–74.

68. *Totem and Taboo: Some Points of Agreement between the Mental Lives of Savages and Neurotics,* trans. and ed. James Strachey (New York: Norton, n.d.), p. 154.

69. *New Introductory Lectures on Psychoanalysis,* p. 74.

70. "Metalogue: What Is an Instinct?" in *Steps to an Ecology of Mind* (New York: Ballantine Books, 1977), p. 57.

71. A fascinating, and tragic, example of such binary definition exercised by a dominant social group is the case of the Sierra Leone Creole, as described by Lemuel A. Johnson in *The Devil, the Gargoyle, and the Buffoon: The Negro as Metaphor in Western Literature* (Port Washington, N. Y., and London: National University Publications, Kennikat Press, 1971), chap. 1.

72. Freud's most interesting discoveries in this line are contained in his 1919 essay "On the Uncanny."
73. For Ruskin, see "Grotesque Renaissance" in *The Stones of Venice* III. iii. 39; Scott: "The Novels of E.T.A. Hoffmann," in *Miscellaneous Prose Works of Scott,* ed. Robert Cadell (London: Whittaker & Co., 1834–36), vol. 18, Article X; Baudelaire: "The Essence of Laughter," in *The Painter of Modern Life and Other Essays,* ed. and trans. Jonathan Mayne (London: Phaedon, 1964), p. 154; Symonds: "Caricature, the Fantastic, the Grotesque," in *Essays Speculative and Suggestive* (London: Smith, Elder and Co., 1907), originally published 1890. Symonds makes the interesting point that the grotesque is a form of white man's disease because it always contains an element of caricatural mockery, a quality peculiar to "the Teutonic section of the Aryan family" (p. 159); the "Asiatic and Greek minds" lack this quality. To this list should also be added Friedrich Schlegel, who noted in *Gesprach über die Poesie* that the arabesque was "the oldest and most primitive form of the imagination" and was linked with mythology as "works of art produced by nature." Quoted and translated in Wolfgang Kayser, *The Grotesque in Art and Literature,* p. 50.
74. "The Essence of Laughter," note 73 above, pp. 154, 155, 156, 157.
75. Kayser, *The Grotesque in Art and Literature,* p. 21.
76. *Ibid.,* p. 157.
77. Bakhtin, *Rabelais and His World,* p. 9. Any emotional monotone, including gay merriment and exuberant acceptance of all of life, quickly becomes a caricature of itself, and Bakhtin is not exempt from this. As a demonstration of the regenerative ambivalence of the Roman carnival, he gives the following example:

> In the world of carnival all hierarchies are cancelled. All castes and ages are equal. During the fire festival a young boy blows out his father's candle, crying out, *sia ammazzato it signor Padre!* "Death to you, sir father!" This admirable carnivalesque interjection of the boy merrily threatening his father with death and blowing out his candle needs no further comment. (251)

I believe I speak for fathers everywhere in suggesting that his admirable interjection would, in any context other than carnival, require an energetic comment of an unambivalent nature.
78. *Ibid.,* p. 48.
79. "Structure, Sign, and Play," in Richard Macksey and Eugenio Donato, eds., *The Languages of Criticism and the Sciences of Man: The Structuralist Controversy* (Baltimore: The Johns Hopkins Univ. Press, 1970), p. 264.
80. (Princeton: Princeton Univ. Press, 1968, originally published in German, 1946.)

81. *Ibid.,* p. 151.
82. *Ibid.,* pp. 54,55,56,57.
83. *Ibid.,* pp. 194, 272, 276.
84. "Of friendship," see chap. 2, note 14, above; p. 135.
85. "Of experience," *ibid.,* p. 857.
86. *Ibid.,* p. 539.

Notes to Chapter Four

1. *The Classic* (London: Faber and Faber, 1975), p. 131.
2. *Ibid.,* p. 130.
3. *Ibid.,* p. 119.
4. All page references are to the critical edition edited by William M. Sale, Jr. (New York: W. W. Norton & Company, 1972).
5. *The Gothic Cathedral* (Princeton: Princeton Univ. Press, Bollingen Series XLVIII, 1974), p. 53. But, Dionysius added,

> ...it must be said that the reason for attributing shapes to that which is above shape, and forms to that which is beyond form, is not only the feebleness of our intellectual power which is unable to rise at once to spiritual contemplation, and which needs to be encouraged...but it is also most fitting that the secret doctrines, through ineffable and holy enigmas, should veil and render difficult of access for the multitude the sublime and profound truth of the Supernatural Mind: for, as the Scripture declares, not everyone is holy, nor have all men knowledge. (Chapter Two, *On Celestial Hierarchies*)

6. T. Tindall Wildridge, *The Grotesque in Church Art* (London: Andrews, 1899), p. 2.
7. This strategy is explicit in instructions given to Augustine by Pope Gregory:

> Do not pull down the fanes. Destroy the idols: purify the temples with *holy water:* set relics there, and let them become temples of the true God. So the people will have no need to change their places of concourse, and where of old they were wont to sacrifice cattle *to demons,* thither let them continue to resort on the day of the saint to whom the Church is dedicated, and slay their beasts, no longer as a sacrifice but for a social meal in honour of Him whom they now worship.

Quoted in Ronald Sheridan and Anne Ross, *Grotesques and Gargoyles:*

Paganism in the Medieval Church, Newton Abbot, Devon: David and Charles, 1975, p. 14; no source given.

8. *The Consolation of Philosophy,* trans. V. E. Watts (Harmondsworth: Penguin, 1978), IV. III, p. 125.
9. *Preface to Chaucer* (Princeton: Princeton Univ. Press, 1962), p. 154.
10. *Ibid.,* p. 152.
11. See note 7, above.
12. Trans. Dora Nussey, *The Gothic Image: Religious Art in France of the Thirteenth Century* (New York, Evanston, and London: Harper and Row, 1958; orig. pub. in French, 1913), p. 49.
13. *Ibid.,* p. 50.
14. *Ibid.,* p. 51.
15. *Ibid.,* pp. 60–61.
16. Ed. Harald Busch and Bernd Lohse, *Gothic Sculpture* (London: B. T. Batsford, 1963), p. iv.
17. *Psychoanalytic Explorations in Art,* p. 213.
18. *The Old Curiosity Shop* (Harmondsworth: Penguin, 1977), p. 276 (chap. 27).
19. From an unsigned review in *Douglas Jerrold's Weekly Newspaper,* January 15, 1848, p. 77. Reprinted in Miriam Allott, ed., *The Brontes: The Critical Heritage* (London and Boston: Routledge and Kegan Paul, 1974), p. 228. 20. *Aspects of the Novel* (New York: Harcourt, Brace & World, n.d.), pp. 125, 136.
21. "A Fresh Approach to *Wuthering Heights,*" in Sale, *Wuthering Heights,* p. 306. Originally printed in F. R. and Q. D. Leavis, *Lectures in America* (New York: Pantheon Books, 1969).
22. "Introduction" to *Wuthering Heights,* ed. V. S. Pritchett (Boston: Houghton Mifflin, 1956), p. 3.
23. "Coherent Readers, Incoherent Texts," the *Critical Inquiry,* III, 4 (summer, 1977), pp. 781–80.
24. Margaret Homans, "Repression and Sublimation of Nature in *Wuthering Heights,*" *PMLA* 93 (1978), p. 10.
25. See "The Structural Study of Myth," in *Structural Anthropology,* see chap. 3, n. 11, above.
26. *Aspects of the Novel,* p. 146.
27. "The Structure of *Wuthering Heights,*" in Sale, *Wuthering Heights,* pp. 286–98.
28. *Ibid.,* p. 289.
29. See the diagrams in discussions by Kermode, Kincaid, and Inga-Stina Ewbank, *Their Proper Sphere: A Study of the Bronte Sisters as Early-Victorian Female Novelists* (Cambridge, Mass.: Harvard Univ. Press, 1966), p. 136; reprinted in Sale, p. 329.

30. This contrast is inescapable for anybody who has visited the Bronte parsonage at Haworth, where Emily lived in a small house backing up to the moors with her brother, sisters, father, and sometimes a maid. Her room measures approximately 6' x 9'.
31. *The Savage Mind*, p. 10.
32. In *A Future for Astyanax: Character and Desire in Literature* (London: Marion Boyers, 1978), Leo Bersani argues that Heathcliff embodies the "fantasy of existence without origins" (p. 205), a creature who calls into question the nature of the self by existing outside the family circle of inherited being. It is closer to the truth to say that he embodies the fantasy of existence without *human* origins, for with his evocation of autochthony, he represents origin itself.
33. *The Raw and the Cooked: Introduction to a Science of Mythology*, I, trans. J. and D. Weightman (New York: Harper and Row, 1969).
34. *Structural Anthropology*, p. 212.
35. "Genesis as Myth," in *Genesis as Myth and Other Essays* (London: Cape, 1969).
36. "La connaissance du bien et du mal et le péché du paradis," in *Analecta Lovaniensia Biblica et Orientalia*, 1948; trans. and quoted in Paul Ricoeur, *The Symbolism of Evil* [trans. Emerson Buchanan] (Boston: Beacon Press, 1969), p. 249.
37. *Ibid.*, p. 255.
38. *Ibid.*, p. 256.
39. *Genesis as Myth*, p. 8.
40. *Symbolism of Evil*, p. 258.
41. *Ibid.*, p. 343.
42. *Enchiridion* 11; trans. Marcus Dods, *The Works of Aurelius Augustinus* (Edinburgh: T. & T. Clark Co., 1871–76); excerpted in Vernon J. Bourke, ed. *The Essential Augustine* (New York: New American Library, 1964), p. 65.
43. Trans. R. S. Pine-Coffin, *Confessions* (Harmondsworth: Penguin, 1979), p.103.
44. *Ibid.*, p. 104.
45. *Symbolism of Evil*, pp. 25–26.
46. *Ibid.*, p. 25.
47. Bersani, *Astyanax*, p. 222.
48. Geoffrey Hartman, "The Voice of the Shuttle: Language from the Point of View of Literature," in *Beyond Formalism: Literary Essays 1958–1970* (New Haven and London: Yale Univ. Press, 1970), pp. 342–43.

Notes to Chapter Five

1. Disorder can be defined as "the extent to which the elements of a given order are distributed outside that order among the elements of other orders," according to James K. Fiebleman. See "Disorder," in Paul G. Kuntz, ed., *The Concept of Order* (Seattle and London: Univ. Washington Press, 1968), p. 11.
2. *The Poetics of Space*, p. 211.
3. H. G. Wells has rendered in an amusingly literal way the consequences of *p* and *not–p* occupying the same space. In the following passage from *The Time Machine,* the Time Traveller is seated in his machine, whirring through the ages, when it occurs to him that perhaps his house has been torn down and the space previously occupied by his study is now occupied by the wall of another building:

> So long as I travelled at a high velocity through time, it scarcely mattered; I was, so to speak, attenuated — was slipping like a vapour through the interstices of intervening substances! But to come to a stop involved the jamming myself, molecule by molecule, into whatever lay in my way; meant bringing my atoms into such intimate contact with those of the obstacle that a profound chemical reaction — possibly a far-reaching explosion — would result, and blow myself and my apparatus out of all possible dimensions — and into the Unknown.

4. *The Poetics of Space*, p. 214.
5. New York: Avon, 1969, pp. 19–20.
6. This point is stressed (to the breaking-point) by Jean Starobinski: "No inside is conceivable...without the complicity of an outside on which it relies. Complicity mixed with antagonism, for the unfriendly outside makes the membrane deploy in order to contain and then secure the constancy of the 'internal milieu' against the vicissitudes of the *Umwelt."* "The inside and the Outside," in *The Hudson Review,* XXVII: 3 (autumn 1975), p. 342.
7. *Western Attitudes toward Death: From the Middle Ages to the Present,* trans. Patricia M. Ranum (Baltimore and London: The Johns Hopkins Univ. Press, 1976; orig. pub. 1974), p. 42. Nesson's lines are quoted in A. Tenenti, *Il senso della morte et l'amore della vita nel Rinascimento* (Turin, 1957), p. 147.
8. In *Rabelais and His World;* "[The grotesque body] is not a closed, completed unit...," p. 26; "phenomenon in transition...," p. 24; "not separated from the world...," p. 27; "going out to meet the world...," pp. 39–40.

9. Quoted in Angus Wilson, *The World of Charles Dickens* (New York: Viking, 1970), pp. 9–10.
10. Trans. John Linton (London: The Hogarth Press, 1972), pp. 97, 100–101.
11. See *Poe Newsletter* I, 1968, pp. 9–10.
12. *Poe Poe Poe Poe Poe Poe Poe* (Garden City: Doubleday, 1972), pp. 207–08.
13. *Poe Studies* VIII: 2 (December 1974), pp. 42–45.
14. "The Angelic Imagination," *Kenyon Review,* summer 1952; in *Collected Essays,* 1959. Here Tate quotes Jacques Maritain, *The Dream of Descartes* (New York, 1944), pp. 179–80.
15. "The Colloquy of Monos and Una."
16. Poe, however, was drawing not on accounts of plagues long past for his material, but on one quite recent, the cholera epidemic originating in India in 1826, which spread over Europe, finally crossing the Atlantic on boats of Irish immigrants in 1832. A friend of Poe's, Ebenezer Burling, was one of its victims in Richmond, Poe's home town. A special newspaper, *The Cholera Gazette,* was published in Philadelphia beginning in 1832, documenting the progress of the disease from the ports into the interior, and it is certain that Poe was familiar with its symptoms. It is in fact likely that his direct inspiration was a newspaper account of an outbreak in Paris on March 29, 1832. This is Heinrich Heine's account, given in a letter dated April 9, 1832, as summarized in Fielding H. Garrison in *An Introduction to the History of Medicine:*

> On the twenty-ninth of March, the night of *mi-carême,* a masked ball was in progress, the *chahut* in full swing. Suddenly, the gayest of the harlequins collapsed, cold in the limbs, and, underneath his mask, "violet–blue" in the face. Laughter died out, dancing ceased, and in a short while carriage–loads of people were hurried from the *redoute* to the Hotel Dieu to die, and, to prevent a panic among the patients, were thrust into rude graves in their dominoes.

The translation is apparently Garrison's (4th ed., Philadelphia: W. B. Saunders Company, 1929). The Heine letter is cited as: Franzosische Zustande, letter of April 9, 1832 *(Sämmtliche Werke,* Cotta ed., xi, 88–102). The festival of *mi-carême* is a day of Carnival riot held the third Thursday (the exact middle) of Lent, to celebrate the fact that half the season of penitence is over. It has a ritually tragic conclusion.
17. *The Grotesque in Art and Literature,* p. 78.
18. See Bonaventura, "On the Reduction of All Arts to Theology"; and Augustine, "Of the perfection of the number six, which is the first of the

numbers which is composed of its aliquot parts" and "Of the seventh day, in which completeness and repose are celebrated," XI. 30, 31 in *The City of God.*

19. See "The Poetic Principle."

20. There is no distinction between the seventh day as the day of rest and the seventh room as the room of death. As Poe says in "The Colloquy of Monos and Una, "by sleep and its world alone is *Death* imaged."

21. Matthew 24:43–44; Luke 12:39–40; 1 Thessalonians 5:2; 2 Peter 3:10; Revelation 3:3, 16:15.

22. Trans. Gayatri Chakravorty Spivak (Baltimore and London: The Johns Hopkins Univ. Press, 1978), p. 303.

23. This self–annihilation, Rousseau would say, is the condition of the actor, who displays "other sentiments than his own, saying only what he is made to say, often representing a chimerical being, [and who] annihilates himself, as it were . . . ." By contrast, the Red Death is what Rousseau would call the orator, who "represents only himself...the man and the role being the same... . " See *Essay on the Origin of Languages,* quoted in *Grammatology,* p. 305. In Rousseau's terms, Poe's story dramatizes the encounter between the actor and the orator, or the re-presenter and the presence.

24. *Grammatology,* p. 313.

25. *Ibid.,* p. 313.

26. In Richard Macksey and Eugenio Donato, ed., *The Languages of Criticism and the Sciences of Man: The Structuralist Controversy* (Baltimore and London: The Johns Hopkins Univ. Press, 1970), pp. 155–56.

27. "The Facts in the Case of M. Valdemar." In an interesting article, J. Hillis Miller employs the image of the margin to argue for a pluralistic or deconstructive approach to literary criticism, as opposed to the univocal approach through the "obvious" meaning. All texts and all readings, he maintains, are both parasites and hosts, with their borders continually compromised:

> "Para"...[signifies] at once proximity and distance, similarity and difference, interiority and exteriority, something simultaneously this side of the boundary line, threshold, or margin, and at the same time beyond it.... A thing in "para"...is also the boundary itself, the screen which is at once a permeable membrane connecting inside and outside, confusing them with one another, allowing the outside in, making the inside out, dividing them but also forming an ambiguous transition between one and the other.

"The Critic as Host," in *Critical Inquiry* XIII: 3 (spring 1977), p. 447.

Notes to Chapter Six

1. See "Two Aspects of Language and Two Fundamental Types of Disturbance," in *Fundamentals of Language,* ed. Roman Jakobson and Morris Halle (The Hague: Mouton, 1956), pp. 67–96.
2. According to Jakobson, "The primacy of the metaphoric process in the literary schools of romanticism and symbolism has been repeatedly acknowledged, but it is still insufficiently realized that it is the predominance of metonymy which underlies and actually predetermines the so-called 'realistic' trend, which belongs to an intermediary stage between the decline of romanticism and the rise of symbolism and is opposed to both. Following the path of contiguous relationships, the realistic author metonymically digresses from the plot to the atmosphere and from the characters to the setting in space and time." *Ibid.,* p. 78.
3. *Schriften,* ed. Th. W. Adorno, Gretel Adorno, and F. Podszus (Frankfurt: Suhrkamp Verlag, 1955), 2: 464–65. Quoted and trans. in Edward Said, *Beginnings: Intention and Method* (Baltimore and London: The Johns Hopkins Univ. Press, 1975), p. 231.
4. *Revelations of Divine Love,* trans. Clifton Wolters (Harmondsworth: Penguin, 1976), pp. 87–88, 89.
5. *Jokes and their Relation to the Unconscious,* trans. and ed. James Strachey (New York: Norton, 1963), p. 201.
6. Ernst Kris and E. H. Gombrich, "The Principles of Caricature," in Kris, *Psychoanalytic Explorations in Art* (New York: Schocken, 1971), p. 199.
7. C. I. Scofield, *The New Scofield Reference Bible* (New York: Oxford Univ. Press, 1967), p. xvi; and Alexander Heidel, ed., *The Babylonian Genesis: The Story of Creation* (Chicago and London: Univ. of Chicago Press, 1965), p. v.
8. This passage is from the *Memoirs of Dr. Burney,* 1832, printed as an appendix to *Diary and Letters of Madame d'Arblay,* ed. Charlotte Barret (London: Macmillan, 1904), vol. 1 of 6, pp. 509–10. In another passage, however, we learn that even Boswell can be outdone in his admiration of Dr. Johnson, by one Mr. Musgrave, of whom "Mrs. Thrale has extremely well said that he is a caricature of Mr. Boswell, who is a caricature, I must add, of all other of Dr. Johnson's admirers" vol. 2, p. 28.
9. Trans., H. T. Lowe-Porter (New York: Vintage, 1971), pp. 19–20.
10. *Ibid.,* p. 181.
11. *Ibid.,* p. 181.
12. "A Parodying Novel: Sterne's *Tristram Shandy,*" in John Traugott, ed. *Laurence Sterne: A Collection of Critical Essays* (Englewood Cliffs, N.J.: Prentice-Hall, 1968), pp. 68–89.

13. See "Sufferings and Greatness of Richard Wagner," in *Essays of Three Decades,* trans. H. T. Lowe–Porter (New York: Knopf, 1965). Wagner fascinated Mann for the multitude of contradictions he was able to turn to creative purposes. These contradictions are the theme of this essay, which explores the polarities of German and European, and reactionary and revolutionary.
14. "Freud and the Future," in *Essays of Three Decades.*
15. "The Old Fontane," in *Essays of Three Decades,* 305.
16. *Mythology and Humanism: The Correspondence of Thomas Mann and Karl Kerenyi,* trans. Alexander Gelley (Ithaca and London: Cornell Univ. Press, 1975), p. 100.
17. *The Wheel of Fire,* p. 160. The passage on Conrad is from a review essay of *The Secret Agent* reprinted in *Past Masters,* trans. H. T. Lowe-Porter (London: Martin Secker, 1933), in which Mann says: "For I feel that, broadly and essentially, the striking feature of modern art is that it has ceased to recognise the categories of tragic and comic, or the dramatic classifications, tragedy and comedy. It sees life as tragicomedy, with the result that the grotesque is its most genuine style—to the extent, indeed, that to-day that is the only guise in which the sublime may appear" (240–41).
18. *Betrachtungen eines Unpolitischen,* xii. 564; trans. and quoted by T. J. Reed in *Thomas Mann: The Uses of Tradition* (Oxford: Clarendon Press, 1974), p. 35.
19. *Of Grammatology,* p. 271.
20. *Death in Venice and Seven Other Stories* (New York: Vintage, 1963); All page references are to this edition.
21. *Of Grammatology,* p. 271. See also 216 ff., where Derrida discusses Rousseau's north/south division between languages.
22. See the review of *Death in Venice* reprinted in Edward D. McDonald, ed. *Phoenix* (New York: Viking, 1968), pp. 308–313.
23. *A Sketch of My Life,* trans. H. T. Lowe-Porter (New York: Knopf, 1960), p. 46. Of the various candidates, Goethe seems uppermost in Mann's mind, for he mentions the connection in at least three letters —describing the story of Goethe's last love in each of these letters as "grotesque." See *Letters of Thomas Mann, 1889–1955,* selected and trans. Richard and Clara Winston (New York: Knopf, 1971), pp. 76, 102; and *Letters to Paul Amann,* ed. Herbert Wegener, trans. Richard and Clara Winston (Middletown: Wesleyan Univ. Press, 1960), letter of 9/15/21.
24. *Tristes Tropiques,* p. 472.
25. *Anatomy of Criticism* (Princeton: Princeton Univ. Press, 1957), p. 124.
26. *Being and Nothingness: An Essay on Phenomenological Ontology,* trans. Hazel E. Barnes (New York: Philosophical Library, 1956). Page references in the text are to this edition.

27. *Nausea,* trans. Lloyd Alexander (London: New Directions, 1949), p. 34.
28. "Grotesque Renaissance," in *The Stones of Venice* III. iii. 15.

Notes to Chapter Seven

1. From "Tradition" (1918), in *Notes on Life and Letters* (London: J. M. Dent & Sons, Ltd., 1921), pp. 194–95. Quoted in Robert Kimbrough, ed., *Heart of Darkness* (New York: W. W. Norton & Company, 1971), pp. 140–41. This edition hereafter referred to as HD.
2. *Music, the Arts and Ideas* (Chicago: Univ. of Chicago Press 1967), p. 8.
3. *Doctor Faustus,* p. 73.
4. *Ibid.,* p. 73.
5. *Ibid.,* p. 74.
6. P. 357.
7. *Ibid.,* p. 357.
8. *Of Grammatology,* p. 303. *De la Grammatologie* (Paris: Les Editions de Minuit, 1967), p. 429.
9. Simplicity is actually an extraordinarily complex idea. For a survey of recent work, as well as an extremely interesting original contribution to thinking about simplicity, see Elliott Sober, *Simplicity* (Oxford: Clarendon Press, 1975), which begins by noting:

> The diversity of our intuitions about simplicity is matched only by the tenacity with which these intuitions refuse to yield to formal characterization. Our intuitions seem unanimous in favour of sparse ontologies, smooth curves, homogeneous universes, invariant equations, and impoverished assumptions. Yet recent theorizing about simplicity presents a veritable chaos of opinion. Here one finds arguments that simplicity is high probability, that it is low probability, and that it is not a probability at all. Indeed, the complexities of the problem of simplicity have led some to question the possibility and the fruitfulness of trying to define the notion of simplicity that seems to be involved in hypothesis choice. (p. 3)

10. *The Secret Agent A Simple Tale* (Garden City: Doubleday Anchor, 1953; orig. pub., 1907), p. 99.
11. Conrad, who rarely used a device just once, blew up an entire ship in "Youth."
12. "The Epistemology of Metaphor," in *On Metaphor,* ed. Sheldon Sacks (Chicago and London: Univ. of Chicago Press, 1980), pp. 15–16.

13. *Ibid.,* p. 15.
14. *Ibid.,* p. 16.
15. *The Life of the Novel* (Chicago and London: Univ. of Chicago Press, 1972), p. 82.
16. *Conrad in the Nineteenth Century* (Berkeley and Los Angeles: Univ. of California Press, 1979), p. 85.
17. Jocelyn Baines quotes a decidedly morbid comment by Conrad to the effect that his desire in writing the book was to "enshrine my old chums in a decent edifice." See *Joseph Conrad: A Critical Biography* (London: Weidenfeld and Nicholson, 1960), p. 186.
18. HD, p. 143. From *The Mirror of the Sea (1905)*.
19. *The Mirror of the Sea* (London: Dent, 1923, 1946), p. 135. Quoted in *The Nigger of the "Narcissus,"* ed. Robert Kimbrough (New York: W. W. Norton & Company, 1979), p. 192. This edition hereafter referred to as NN.
20. NN, p. 194. From *The Mirror of the Sea.*
21. Quoted in Watt, p. 97.
22. See Baines, p. 96.
23. NN, p. 193; see note 19, above.
24. NN, p. 193.
25. "Conrad Criticism and *The Nigger of the "Narcissus,"* from *Nineteenth Century Fiction,* 12 (March 1958), pp. 257–83. See NN, p. 244. In adapting this article for his book, Watt deleted the passage quoted here.
26. Watt, p. 98. Paul de Man draws the connection between irony and Baudelaire's concept of the grotesque. Speaking of the notion of self-duplication lying at the heart of *De l'essence du rire,* de Man says that "the nature of this duplication is essential for an understanding of irony. It is a relationship, within consciousness, between two selves, yet it is not an intersubjective relationship." De Man points out that Baudelaire uses the terms "le comique absolu" and "irony" interchangeably to designate a relationship that is "not between man and man, two entities that are in essence similar, but between man and what he calls nature, that is, two entities that are in essence different." See "The Rhetoric of Temporality," in Charles S. Singleton, ed., *Interpretation: Theory and Practice* (Baltimore: The Johns Hopkins Univ. Press, 1969), p. 195. Conrad's irony, and Conrad's grotesque, results from a triadic relationship between truth, language, and humanity. Conrad, I have been arguing, wishes for these three to be unitary, that is, incapable of self–multiplication; but one or more of them always fractures, revealing a being that is "in essence different."
27. All page references are to the Kimbrough edition.
28. NN, p. 168.

29. See NN, p. 193.
30. In a letter to Stephen Crane written on November 16, 1897, Conrad draws again on the image of contaminated air to describe the doubt he experienced while writing the book itself:

> I am no more vile than my neighbors but this disbelief in one's self is like a taint that spreads on everything one comes in contact with: on men—on things—on the very air one breathes. That's why one sometimes wishes to be a stone breaker. There's no doubt about breaking a stone. But there's doubt, fear—a black horror, in every page one writes. See NN, p. 184.

31. Singleton is described as "very old; old as Father time himself" (NN, p. 14) at one point, and, at another, as resembling "a cannibal chief" (NN, p. 2). Thus Singleton shares antiquity not only with Donkin but also with the savages of *Heart of Darkness* who "still belonged to the beginnings of time (HD, p. 41). In the letter quoted in note 30 above, Conrad takes Crane into his confidence by saying "You at any rate will understand and therefore I write to you as though we had been born together before the beginning of things. "
32. See NN, p. 185. The letter is dated December 14, 1897.
33. Singleton is not immune from contamination by air either: "Taciturn and unsmiling, he breathed amongst us—in that alone resembling the rest of the crowd" (25). In that alone—but it is everything.
34. Watt, p. 123.
35. NN, p. 226. Originally, this sentence appeared in the chapter on *The Nigger of the "Narcissus"* in *Conrad the Novelist* (Cambridge, Mass.: Harvard Univ. Press, 1958).
36. See "The Libido Theory and Narcissism," Lecture XXVI in James Strachey ed. and trans., *The Standard Edition of the Complete Psychological Works of Sigmund Freud* (London: The Hogarth Press, 1975), vol. XVI, *Introductory Lectures on Psycho-Analysis* (Part III), p. 417. See also the often–reprinted essays "On Narcissism: An Introduction" and "Leonardo da Vinci and a Memory of His Childhood." Conrad's repeated attempts to locate a unified ground altogether beyond question are sometimes desperate, sometimes touching, sometimes humorous. In one of his last essays, a preface to his wife's "Handbook of Cookery for a Small House," he says that "Of all the books produced since the most remote ages by human talents and industry those only that treat of cooking are, from a moral point of view, above suspicion." While "the intention of every other piece of prose may be discussed and even mistrusted," the "purpose of a cookery book is one and unmistakable...to increase the happiness of mankind." Good cooking, Conrad says grandly, is "a

moral agent. By good cooking I mean the conscientious preparation of the simple food of everyday life, not the more or less skilful concoction of idle feasts and rare dishes." The conscientious cook is the natural enemy of the quack without a conscience...." Singleton and Donkin may breathe the same air, but at least in the kitchen a "genuine form of optimism" prevails that is "altogether above suspicion." See "Cookery" in *Almayer's Folly* ∗ *Last Essays* (Edinburgh, London, Melbourne: Nelson, n.d.), pp. 370–72.

37. See note 17 above.

38. (London: Dent, 1923, 1946), pp. xiv–xxi. See NN, pp. 194–95.

39. Conrad's first biographer, G. Jean-Aubry, maintained that Conrad's journey up the Congo at the age of 35 was the decisive event in his gradual decision to become a writer. In his words, "Africa killed Conrad the sailor and strengthened Conrad the writer." From *Life and Letters* (London: William Heinemann, Ltd., 1927), I, p. 142; see NN, p. 125. Edward Garnett, Conrad's friend and literary advisor, the man who persuaded Conrad to abandon the sea once and for all, agreed, saying that "Conrad's Congo experiences were the turning–point in his mental life and…its effects on him determined his transformation from a sailor to a writer. According to his emphatic declaration to me, in his early years at sea he had 'not a thought in his head.' 'I was a perfect animal,' he reiterated." Garnett speculates that while in the Congo Conrad heard a "sinister voice…with its murmuring undertone of human fatuity, baseness and greed," and that this voice "had swept away the generous illusions of his youth, and had left him gazing into the heart of an immense darkness." From "Introduction," *Letters from Conrad* 1895–1924 (London: The Nonesuch Press, 1928), p. xii. See NN, 125. This is a tidy analysis, but there is little to suggest that Conrad, a gun-smuggler at 19, had any such "generous illusions" before his Congo venture.

40. From a letter to his publisher, William Blackwood, written in May 1902. See HD, p. 124, 236.

41. For a conservative approach, see Florence Ridley, "The Ultimate Meaning of Heart of Darkness," in *Nineteenth-Century Fiction* (June, 1963), pp. 43–53. The radical view of Conrad as nihilist is most eloquently represented by J. Hillis Miller in his *Poets of Reality* (Cambridge: Belknap Press of Harvard Univ., 1966). Watt is the chief spokesman for what I call the moderate path (although his readings are far too intelligent to be taken simply as a compromise between extremes). Still, whenever Conrad seems too "dark" altogether, he is driven to the question as a substitute for a statement he would rather not make: "which perspective is more alarming? that people such as the Intended should be so blinded by their certitude of being the bearers of light that they are quite unaware of the darkness that surrounds them? or, on the other hand, that those who,

like Marlow, have been initiated into the darkness, should be unable to illumine the blindness of their fellows to its omnipresence?" (249)

42. In his section on "Backgrounds and Sources" for *Heart of Darkness,* Robert Kimbrough has juxtaposed passages describing the reality of the Belgian presence in the Congo with a statement by King Leopold II on "The Sacred Mission of Civilization." The effect of the juxtaposition is, needless to say, ironic. In the course of an illuminating discussion of the confrontation between speaker and hearer in Conrad, Edward Said quotes an interesting passage from *Lord Jim* on the subject of what Derrida would call the "saturated" statement which so fully speaks itself that the only possible interpretation is also the only correct interpretation: "And besides, the last word is not said—probably shall never be said. Are not our lives too short for that full utterance which through all our stammerings is of course our only and abiding intention?" See *Lord Jim* (Boston: Houghton Mifflin, 1958), p. 161. Compared to that full utterance, even eloquence is but a stammering, a fractured and incomplete statement that requires interpretation, and therefore indeterminacy, in order to be made complete. My argument that Conrad is a "perpetual beginner" complements Said's assertion that "Every text that Conrad wrote, whether formally, aesthetically, or thematically considered, presents itself as unfinished and still in the making." See his article on "Conrad: The Presentation of Narrative," *Novel,* 7 (winter 1974), pp. 116–32.

43. Kurtz is more apparently a compromised Christ figure than a compromised Antichrist, but the evidence is there. As the Beast, Kurtz has as his totems horns and heads (d. Revelation 17:7 in which the angel tells John, "I will tell thee the mystery of the woman, and of the beast that carrieth her, which hath seven heads and ten horns"). Kurtz's shack is surrounded by skulls on poles and, as he is taken away on the steamer, his natives gather on the shore, nodding "their horned heads."

44. These charges are leveled by Marvin Mudrick in the course of a discussion of "The Originality of Conrad" in *The Hudson Review,* 11 (winter 1958–59), pp. 545–53. Some portions of this article are reprinted in HD, pp. 185–88.

45. Letter to David S. Meldrun, dated January 2, 1899; HD, p. 130.

46. Even the simple word *lie* is cloven, and can be punned: as Marlow says slyly, speaking of the interview, "I laid the ghost of his gifts at last with a lie" (49). Conrad himself was far from innocent on the subject of lies. In one incident, Jocelyn Baines relates, the youthful Conrad was wounded by a pistol shot, and gave it out that the occasion was a duel fought over the honor of one "Rita." As Baines's research establishes, no woman was directly involved, and the duel was actually a single: depressed over finances and other difficulties, Conrad had shot himself.

Conrad maintained the lie, which indeed has "a taint of death, a flavour of mortality" (HD 27), for the rest of his life, while portraying nine leading characters who commit suicide. See Baines, pp. 53–56.
47. Letter to Hugh Walpole written in 1918, quoted in *The Portable Conrad*, ed. Morton Dauwen Zabel (New York: Viking, 1975), p. 113.
48. "The Epistemology of Metaphor," p. 19.
49. *Ibid.*, p. 20.
50. From "To My Readers in America"; see NN, p. 168.
51. "On Truth and Falsity in their Ultramoral Sense," in *The Complete Works of Friedrich Nietzsche*, ed. Oscar Levy (London: Allen & Unwin, 1911), II, p. 177.

Notes to Chapter Eight

1. Quoted from a catalogue of Leonardo's Windsor drawings in E. H. Gombrich, *The Heritage of Apelles* (Ithaca: Cornell Univ. Press, 1976), p. 64.
2. Gombrich, *Ibid.*, p. 74.
3. Ed. A. Philip McMahon (Princeton: Princeton Univ. Press, 1956), No. 35, p. 69.
4. Leonardo's "storms" or "deluges" are comparable to the "grotesque heads" in representing the capricious figures made by furious, uncorrected nature; but there is a deeper similarity as well, in the relation between the representation and the referent. In the case of the "deluge" series, it is nature itself that is represented, a force that overwhelms everything human. But, paradoxically, the composition of these drawings is necessarily entirely Leonardo's own: there could be no original, no model, no possible point of view for these images in nature. To portray a "deluge" is to be overwhelmed by *nature,* and to be deprived of *subject.* It is to be stripped of art and to be left with only art. The same paradox, as I argue here, applies to the "grotesque heads. "
5. *Critique of Judgment,* par. 16.
6. *Ibid.,* Concluding remarks after par. 22.
7. *Ibid.,* par. 48. See also Derrida's discussion of this notion in Kant, "Economimesis," trans. R. Klein, in *Diacritics* 11:2 (summer 1981), pp. 21–25; originally published, 1975.
8. *Ibid.*
9. Gombrich, *Apelles,* p. 75.
10. *Ästhetik,* 2 vols., ed. H. G. Hotho (Berlin: Duncker und Humblot, 1835), II, p. 239. My translation.
11. In *Hegel: Selections,* ed. J. Loewenberg (New York: Charles Scribner's Sons, 1957), p. 314.

12. *Ibid.,* p. 321.
13. *Ibid.,* p. 328.
14. In *The Stones of Venice,* "expression of the repose…," III. iii. 49; "good and ordinarily intelligent men," III. iii. 33; "of a delight in the contemplation…," III. iii. 16; "It is almost impossible…," III. iii. 39.
15. III. iii. 67.
16. *Mystery and Manners,* ed. Sally and Robert Fitzgerald (New York: Farrar, Straus & Giroux, 1969), "the almost imperceptible intrusions of grace," p. 112; "territory held largely by the devil," p. 118; "realist of distances," p. 44.
17. *Ibid.,* p. 47.
18. Mark 5:1–20; Luke 8:26–39.
19. In *The Gothic,* Frankl suggests that the two-part arch expresses a spiritual principle of dependency as opposed to the unified Romanesque arch.
Iconographists, cultural historians, and historians of ideas have long since stressed the difference between God the Lord and God the Son of Man. In Romanesque sculpture

> God appears as the stern judge, the Lord and Ruler at the Last Judgment, the Crucified One, unmarked by suffering, who actively wills His lot. In Gothic sculpture He appears as the mild, all–pitying, and all–loving One, the God suffering on the Cross…. On Romanesque crucifixes Jesus stands upright and alive; nailed to his cross, he is independent. On Gothic crosses he droops in weakness or death; he is dependent. (pp. 827–28)

20. *Mystery and Manners,* p. 266.
21. One well-known letter from Lawrence to Ernest Collings says, "My great religion is a belief in the blood, the flesh, as being wiser than the intellect." See *The Collected Letters of D. H. Lawrence,* ed. Harry T. Moore (New York: Viking, 1962), p. 180.
22. New York: Viking Press, 171. Page references are to this edition, and are given in the text.
23. According to Frank Kermode, it made little difference to Lawrence that, while Lawrence was working on his introduction, Carter decided that his own manuscript was unsound. See *D. H. Lawrence* (New York: Viking, 1973), p. 127.
24. Kermode, *D. H. Lawrence,* p. 131.

INDEX

Numbers in italics indicate references to illustrations

Abel, Karl, 96
Adam, 15, 128, 158, 179
Adamic myth, 129
Adam, Robert, 69
Addison, Joseph, 103
Adhémar, Jean, 240 n35
aestheticism, 219–220
"A Familiar Preface" (Conrad), 207–208
A Farewell to Arms (Hemingway), 26
A Good Man Is Hard to Find (O'Connor), 228
air, 108, 176, 182, 199–200, 260 n33
Alberti, Leone Battista, 239 n29
Alice's Adventures in Wonderland (Carroll), 26
Altamira (Paleolithic cave), 84, 87
ambiguity of the sacred, *see* myth (sacred uncleanness), and taboo
Ammianus Marcellinus, 101
Antonio, St. (archbishop), 240 n36
Apocalypse (Lawrence), 228–230
Aquinas, St. Thomas, 132
arabesque, 75; distinguished from grotesque, 141–142, 153
Arcimboldo, 16
Ariès, Philippe, 138
Aristotle, 78, 80, 184
Assumption of the Virgin (Titian), 70
Auber, Abbë, 109
Auerbach, Erich, 101–103, 159

Augustine, 41, 133, 182, 225, 250 n7, 254–255 n18
autochthony, 78–79; in *Wuthering Heights*, 123–127

Babylonian Genesis, the, 161
Bachelard, Gaston, 11, 14, 137
Bagehot, Walter, xxv
Baines, Jocelyn, 259 n17, 262–263 n46
Bakhtin, Mikhail, xiii–xiv, xxiii, 13; on grotesque realism, 99–101; on Rabelais, 99–100, 139–140
Baltrušaitis, Jurgis, 234 n16, 239 n34
Barasch, Frances, 233 n4
baroque, 92, 221
Bart, Benjamin, 247 n56
Barth, John, 120, 185
Barthes, Roland, 93, 236 n35, 243 n4
Bateson, Gregory, 95
baths of Titus, 29–30
Baudelaire, Charles, 10, 15, 21–22, 89–91, 97–99, 160, 163, 259 n26; on significative and absolute comic, 97
Beardsley, Aubrey, 5, 231
Bedford Book of Hours, 238 n21
beginnings, 182–185, 187
Bégouën, H., 246 n44
Benjamin, Walter, 158
Bergounioux, F. M., 245–246 n35
Bérain, Jean, 68
Berliner, Rudolf, 68, 241 n59
Bernard of Clairvaux, 39–40, 45, 49, 109, 114
Bersani, Leo, 135

bestiaries, 39
Bible: Exodus, 37; Genesis, 153, 161 *(see also* Adam, Adamic myth, Eve); II Isaiah, 132; Leviticus, 83; Luke, 137, 226, 255 n21; Mark, 69, 226; Matthew, 69, 255 n21; II Peter, 255 n21; Psalms, 109, 133; Revelation, 153, 167, 228, 255 n21, 262 n43; Thessalonians, 255 n21; as model for Vatican Loggias, 32, 36; influence on Western culture, 93; medieval illuminations of, 238 n21; Old estament attacks on mythic deities, 133, 160. *See also* Gerasene demoniac
Bible of Clairvaux, 114
Bichat, Marie, 150
Black Death, the, 144
Blackwood, William, 261 n40
Blake, William, 95, 98, 128
Blanc, Alberto C., 246 n35
Boethius, 111, 132
Boëthius, Axel, 28, 236 n1
Bonaventura, St., 254–255 n18
Bos, Cornelius, *13*, 48, 68
Bosch, Hieronymus, xxii, 238 n21
Boswell, James, 161, 256 n8
Breuil, Abbé Henri, 86–88, 246 n44
Brontë, Emily, 117, 135
Browne, Thomas, xxv, 103
Browning, Robert, xxv–xxvi
Bruegel, Pieter, 98
Burckhardt, Jacob, 183
Burke, Edmund, 22
Burling, Ebenezer, 254 n16
Burney, Fanny, 161
Byrne, Janet S., 241 n58

Caesar Augustus, 76
Calvo, Fabio, 238 n22
Capitan, L., 246 n44
caricature, 160
Carnival, 99–101
Carroll, Lewis, 95
Carter, Frederick, 228
Castiglione, Baldassare, 238 n22
catachresis, 211–212
cathedral, 29, 42–43, 109–110, 223. *See also* Gothic
Catherine of Siena, St., 159
cave, 75, 84–85; as sacred enclosure, 60. *See also* Paleolithic art
Chesterton, G. K., xxv–xxvi, 10
chimeras, 42
Christ, 22, 69–70, 81, 182, 226, 229; Kurtz as, 262 n43; and metaphor, 159; as parody, 158–159
Christian hermeneutics, play of analogy in, 44–45
Cicero, 239 n29
Clark, Kenneth, 37, 215
Clayborough, Arthur, 233 n4, 237 n16
Clements, Robert J., 239 n33
Coleman, A. D., 233 n7
Coleridge, Samuel Taylor, 104
Colie, Rosalie, 235 n31
Collings, Ernest, 264 n21
Conkey, Margaret W., 247 n53
Conrad, Joseph, 180–213 *passim*, 225
Coppens, J., 127–128
Cotgrave, R., xxx
Cranach, Lucas, *1*, 6–7, 23
Crane, Stephen, 260 n30
Cruickshank, George, xxiv, 10, 98
Curies, the, 231

Dacos, Nicole, 31, 69, 77
danse macabre, 16, 145–146
Dante Alighieri, 12–13, 15, 17–18, 102, 161, 223
Darwin, Charles, 20
Daumier, Honoré, xxiv
De Bry, B. Th., 241 n56
De Court, Jean, 241 n52
Delaune, Etienne, 68, 241 n52
De Man, Paul, 187–188, 211–212, 259 n26
demons, 7, 42
Dempsey, Jack, 230
De Nesson, Pierre, 138
Dente, Marco, *12*
Derrida, Jacques, 100, 151–152, 165–166, 262 n42
Dickens, Charles, 115, 139–140
Dionysius the Areopagite, 109, 132, 236 n34
Divine Comedy, The (Dante), 12, 17
Dodwell, C. R., 239 n34
Doge's Palace, 49
Domus Aurea, 27–32, 75, 85, 98, 218
Doré, Gustave, 7
Dostoevsky, Feodor, 117, 164
Douglas, Mary, 82–83, 245 n28
drollery, 38–42, 49, 110, 114, 241 n54
Dubon, David, 241 n52
Ducerceau, Jacques Androuet, 68, 241 n52, 241 n59

Eiseley, Loren, 235 n22
El Escorial, 49
Eliade, Mircea, 85, 244 n17, 244 n20, 246 n36, 248 n65
Eliot, Thomas Stearns, 15, 98
entropy, 173–175

Escher, M. C., 36
Essay Concerning Human Understanding (Locke), 187–188
Essay on the Origin of Languages (Rousseau), 166
"etc. principle," 7
Eve, 15, 128
Exeter Cathedral, 238 n21
Ewbank, Inga-Stina, 251 n29

Fabullus, 29–31, 68
fantasia, 35, 91
Ferrari, Marcello, 34
Fiebleman, James K., 253 n1
Fitzgerald, F. Scott, xxiv
Flaubert, Gustave, 91, 211
Fletcher, Angus, 239 n32
Floris, Cornelius, *16*, 68
Flötner, Peter, *14*
Focillon, Henri, 37
Fontainebleau, 49
Font-de-Gaume (Paleolithic cave), 84
Forster, E. M., 117, 120–121, 184–185
framing, 46
Francis of Assisi (St.), 102, 159
Frankl, Paul, xxii–xxiii, 28, 227
Frazer, Sir James, 82
Freedburg, J. E., 71
Freud, Sigmund, 17, 85, 120, 183, 228–229; comparison of id with myth, 95; on narcissism, 164, 205–206; on the Oedipal crisis, 94; "The Antithetical Meaning of Primal Words," 96; *Beyond the Pleasure Principle*, 94; *The Interpretation of Dreams*, 94; *Totem and Taboo*, 94

Frye, Northrop, 162, 176

Gaddis, William, 15
Galloway, John, 243 n3
gaps, 14; and absence of being, 132–133; of indeterminacy, 107. *See also* interval
Gargantua and Pantagruel (Rabelais), 231
gargoyles, 37, 42, 109–115
Garnett, Edward, 261 n39
Garrison, Fielding H., 254 n16
Gautier, Théophile, xxv
Gerasene demoniac, 226
Ghiberti, Lorenzo, 36
Ghirlandaio, Domenico, 32, 237 n18
Gibbon, Edward, 33
Giedion, Siegfried, 88, 92, 246 n45
Gilbert, C., 240 n36
Giovanni da Udine, 32, 34–36. *See also grottesche* and Raphael
Godden, Rumer, 242 n65
Goethe, J. W. von, 162, 257 n23
Goffman, Erving, 179
Golden Palace, *see* Domus Aurea
Goldknopf, David, 190
Golzio, V., 238 n22
Gombrich, E. H., 7, 21, 30–31, 47–49, 74, 92, 241 n54, 242 n66, 263 n1
Gothic, the, xxii, –xxiii, 30–31, 74, 114, 221; in O'Connor, 227; principle of dependency in, 227. *See also* cathedral
Goya, Francisco, 98
Graham, R. Cunninghame, 204–205
Grandville, J. J., xxiv, 95
Gregory, Pope, 37, 250 n7

grotesque conception of the body (Bakhtin), 14
grotesque, etymology of, 31–32
"Grotesque Heads" (Leonardo), 11, 215
grottesche, xxii, xxiv, 31–50 *passim.*, 110, 223; as combination of realism and fantasy, 34; compared to drollery, 44; compared to Paleolithic cave art, 91–92; and corruption of meaning, 36; origin of word, 31–32; Raphael's use of, 32–34; replaces gargoyles, 115; and representation, 44; Ruskin's attack on, 36
Guerard, Albert, 205

Hartman, Geoffrey, 135
Heart of Darkness (Conrad), 198, 208–211
Hegel, Georg Wilhelm Friedrich, 221–223
Heine, Heinrich, 254 n16
Henry Esmond (Thackeray), 26
Herodotus, 85
Hoffman, Daniel, 142
Hoffmann, E.T.A., 142
Hogarth, William, xxi, 98
Holt, Elizabeth G., 239 n35
Homans, Margaret, 251 n24
Hopkins, Gerard Manley, 43
Horace, 30
Hugo, Victor, 24
Hunt, Holman, 11

images, Christian attitude towards, 37
Inferno, The, see Divine Comedy
interval, grotesque as, 17–20,43–46. *See also* gaps

irony, 186–187, 259 n26
Iser, Wolfgang, 235 n33
Jakobson, Roman, 156
James, E. O., 242 n3, 245 n35
James, M. R., 240 n36
Jamnitzer, Christoph, *17*, 68
Janson, H. W., 239 n29, 240 n47
Jarry, Alfred, 17
Jaspers, Karl, 11
Jean-Aubry, G., 261 n39
Jennings, Lee Byron, 233 n4
Jessen, Peter, 68, 2241 n59
Johnson, Lemuel A., 248 n71
Johnson, Samuel, 161, 256 n8; on *Lycidas,* 81, 96
Julian of Norwich, 159
Jung, C. G., 80, 164, 244 n19

Kant, Immanuel, 218–221
Kayser, Wolfgang, xxii, 99, 144, 249 n73
Kenner, Hugh, 10, 14–15, 233 n5
Kerenyi, Karl, 80, 164, 247 n58
Kermode, Frank, xii, xvi, 24, 107–108, 156, 251 n29, 264 n23
Kilian, Lucas, *9,* 44, 68, 2241 n59
Kimbrough, Robert, 262 n42
Kincaid, James, 117, 251 n29
King Lear (Shakespeare), 22, 164
Knight, G. Wilson, 22, 164
knorpelwerk, 241–242 n60
Kris, Ernst, 49, 115, 159
Kubin, Alfred, 95
Kuhn, T. S., 20

Lacan, Jacques, 206
Lascaux (paleolithic cave), 87, 93
Lawrence, D. H., 13, 117, 167, 228–230
Leach, Edmund, 4, 79, 81, 127
Leavis, Q. D., 117

Leo X, Pope, 33, 238 n22
Leonardo Da Vinci, 164, 181, 186, 215–216, 220, 239 n29
Leroi-Gourhan, André, 86–87
"Les Amants Tréspassés," *see* "Pair of Lovers"
Les Trois Frères (Paleolithic cave), 86–87
Lévi-Strauss, Claude, 77–79, 88–89, 93, 100, 120, 125–126, 155, 242–243 n3, 247 n62
Levy, G. Rachel, 88–91
Levy-Bruhl, Lucien, 77, 247 n62
Lewis, Wyndham, 10
Lippi, Filippino, 32
Locke, John, 187, 211
Loggias, *5, 6,* 32–36, 69. *See also* Raphael, and Vatican
Lommel, Andreas, 2243 n3
Loos, Adolphe, 73
L'Orange, H. P., 28, 236 n2
Lowe-Porter, H. T., 172
Lugli, Giuseppe, 28, 237 n9
Luther, Martin, 6, 24
Luttrell Psalter, The, 7, 40

Mâle, Émile, 113
Manichean heresy, 133
Mann, Heinrich, 164
Mann, Thomas, xxiv, 162–171, 182, 184
Marx, Karl, 95
mask, 139–141, 150
masque, 147–150, 150
Maupassant, Guy de, 211
Meditations of a Nonpolitical Man (Mann), xxiv, 164–165, 170
Melville, Herman, 117, 185
metamorphosis, 76–77
metaphor, 15, 77, 156–160, 162, 166–168, 176, 217–218; and metonymy, 157, 176; and

self–parody, 124
metonymy, 156–60; becoming
  metaphor, 159, 176; and
  realism, 156
Meyer, Leonard, 183
Michelangelo, 6–7, 38, 128, 223,
  238 n21
Millar, Eric George, 240 n41
Miller, J. Hillis, 209, 255 n27, 261
  n41
Milton, John, 98
mimesis, 35, 91
Mirror of the Sea, The (Conrad),
  193–194, 198
misericords, 38, 103
"Monchskalb," the, 24
Mondrian, Piet, 36
Montaigne, Michel de, 32, 36,
  103–104, 231
Morgenstern, Christian, 22
Mudrick, Marvin, 262 n44
Murdoch, Iris, 74, 78
myth; and autochthony, 124–
  127; and fatality-fertility
  complex, 84; and mediation
  of contradictions, 77–80;
  and metaphor, 77, 95, 156;
  and metamorphosis, 77–78;
  and narrative, 80; and
  ornament, 109–110; and
  "participation," 77–79; and
  sacred uncleanness, 82–84; in
  Wuthering Heights, 117–127

Nabokov, Vladimir, 7, 25, 138
narcissism, 164
narrative, 134–135, 155–156,
  182–185
Nash, Ernest, 236 n1
Nebuchadnezzar, palace of, 28
Nero, 28–29, 31, 76
Neumann, Erich, 84, 245 n23

Neuw Grottesken Buch
  (Jamnitzer), 68
Niaux (Paleolithic cave), 84
Nietzsche, Friedrich, 95, 164, 175,
  212–213
Nigger of the "Narcissus," The
  (Conrad), 193–208, 212;
  "Preface" to, 187, 152–56, 169
nonnons, 25
non-things, 4, 6

O'Connor, Flannery, 224–228
Oedipus myth, 78, 127
ornament, 30, 32, 36–38, 40;
  on cathedrals, 109–110;
  grottesche as, 36; and
  hybrid forms, 38; and
  interpretation, 40–43; Kant's
  view of, 218–221; origins
  of, 73–76; and paganism,
  69; and representation, 42;
  and "roughness," 38, 42; and
  tendency to abstraction, 47
ornamental prints, 68–69
*Ornamentale Vorlageblätter
  des 15, bis 18. Jahrhunderts*
  (Berliner), 68
Orphic disguise, 25
Osiris, 84
Ovid, 17, 19–20, 75

"Pair of Lovers," 15–18
Paleolithic art, xxvii, 84–93;
  and archaic religion, 89;
  compared to *grottesche,* 691–
  92; and hunting magic, 87;
  hybrid figures in, 88; sexual
  symbolism in, 86–87
pangolin, 82–83
paradigm crisis, 20–21, 70. *See
  also* Kuhn, T. S.
Paradiso, see Divine Comedy

paradox, 23–24, 103, 164, 235 n31
parody, 153, 157–164, 171; and the grotesque, 157–158, 160; and metaphor, 157–158
Patrides, C. A., 238 n21
Paz, Octavio, 234 n13
Peche-Merle (Paleolithic cave), 84, 86–87
Perellò, E. Ripoll, 246 n45
Péricot-Garcia, Luis, 243 n3
Perugino, Pietro, 32
Petits Grotesques (Ducerceau), 68
Petronius, 28
Peyrony, D., 246 n44
Phaedrus, 178
photography, grotesque in, xxv; and mimesis, 239 n29
Piaget, Jean, 94
Picasso, Pablo, 21
Piccolomini Library (Siena cathedral), 237 n17
Pico della Mirandola, 25
Pictor in Carmine, 39, 49
Pinturicchio, 32, 45, 237 n17
Platner, Samuel Ball, 236 n1, 237 n6
Plato, 137
Pliny, 29, 237 n7, 239 n29
Poe, Edgar Allan, 141–144, 151, 153; and the grotesque, 141–144
"The Poetic Principle" (Poe), 143
Ponce, Nicolas, *3, 4,* 30
Popham, A. E., 215
Popper, Karl, xxvi, 26
Poulet, Georges, 11
Price, Uvedale, 38
Pritchett, V. S., 117
Pseudo-Dionysius, *see* Dionysius the Areopagite
pure art, 215–223

Pynchon, Thomas, 14

Rabelais, 84, 99–100, 139. See *also* Bakhtin, Mikhail
Rabelais and His World, see Bakhtin
Randall, Lilian M.C., 41, 240 n38
Random-number tables, 14
Raphael, *5, 6, 20,* 32–34, 69–71; and "The Raphael Bible,"33. *See also* Loggias, and *grotteschi*
Reformation, the, 5–6
Rickert, Margaret, 39–40
Ricoeur, Paul, 128–129, 133, 232 n36
Rilke, Rainer Maria, 140–141
Robert–Dumesnil, A.P.F., 68
Robertson, D. W., 111–112
Romano, Giulio, 242 n67
Romanesque, 113–114
Rome, 27–32
Ross, Ann, 112, 250 n7
Rousseau, Jean–Jacques, 151, 166
Rousseel, Nicasius, *18*
Rowlandson, Thomas, xxiv
Royal Chapel (Granada), 114
Ruskin, John, xxv, xxviii, 22, 35–36, 45, 97, 106, 180, 223, 234 n10, 237 n12; on sportive and terrible grotesque, 42–43, 222–224
Rutland Psalter, The, 40, 42
Ryles, Gilbert, 15

sacred uncleanness, *see* myth, and taboo
Said, Edward, 185, 256 n3, 262 n42
Sanger, Charles Percy, 121–122
Santayana, George, 18–19
Sartre, Jean Paul, 179–180

Savage, George, 242 n63
Scarlet Letter, The (Hawthorne), 26
Schapiro, Meyer, 41–42, 44, 76–77, 240 n35, 240 n42, 240 n46
Schéle, Sune, 241 n59
Schlegel, Friedrich, 249 n73
Schneidau, Herbert, 93, 247 n52
Schon, Erhard, 2, 6
Schoenberg, Arnold, 162
Schöngauer, Martin, 4, 7
Schopenhauer, Arthur, 95, 164
Schulz, J., 237 n17
Schutz, Alfred, 21
Scofield, C. I., 256 n7
Scott, Sir Walter, 97, 141
Secret Agent, The (Conrad), 185–187, 207, 212
Seneca, 137
Sense of Order, The (Gombrich), 47
Shakespeare, William, 146–148
Sheridan, Ronald, 250–251 n7
Shklovsky, Victor, 163
Sieveking, Ann, 246 n39, 246 n43
Signorelli, Luca, *10*, 32, 45–46, 77
simplicity, 178, 185–188, 258 n9
Smith, Patricia c., 142
Sober, Elliott, 258 n9
Socrates, 178
sogni dei pittori (description of the grotesque), xxiv
Sontag, Susan, 173
Sophocles, 107
"Sorcerer," the (of Les Trois Frères), *see* Les Trois Frères
Spenser, Edmund, 6, 223
Springer, Otto, 109
Stallone, Sylvester, 120
Stanza della Segnatura (Raphael), 69

Starobinski, Jean, 253 n6
Steinberg, Leo, 21
Stewart, Susan, 4
"storms" (Leonardo da Vinci), 216, 263 n4
Story of Venus and Tannhäuser, The (Aubrey Beardsley), 231
Suetonius, 28
Symonds, John Addington, 97

taboo, 4, 81–82. *See also* myth (sacred uncleanness)
Tacitus, 28
Tales of the Grotesque and Arabesque (Poe), 141–142
Tate, Allen, 142
temptation, 5, 128–129, 172
Tenniel, J., xxiv
Thomas, Dylan, 78
Thomson, Philip, 233 n4
Thrale, Mrs., 2256 n8
Tintoretto, 11, 223
Titian, 11, 69
Titus, 29
Tolstoi, Leo, 164
Trajan, 29
Transfiguration, The (Raphael), *20*, 69–71, 158–159
Treatise on Beauty (Leonardo da Vinci), 215–216
Tristram Shandy (Sterne), 26, 163, 231
Turner, J.M.W., 33
Ulysses (James Joyce), 26
Ume, Goidefroid, 68
Under Western Eyes (Joseph Conrad), 187

Valentini, Agostino, 239 n24
Valéry, Paul, 151
Van der Goes, Hugo, 128
Van der Weyden, Rogier, 238 n21

Van Gennep, Arnold, 235 n19
Van Gogh, Vincent, 11
Van Leyden, Lucas, *15*, 68, 237 n11
Vasari, Giorgio, 6–7, 30–31, 34, 36, 215, 237–238 n19
Vatican, *5, 6,* 69. *See also* Loggias
Velázquez, Diego, 11
Veneziano, Agostino, *11*
Venus of Laussel, 87
Vespasian, 29
villa di Livia, 238 n19
Virgil, 18
viscous, the, 179–180
Vitruvius, 30–31, 39, 48–49
Volpato, Giovanni, 34
Von Simson, Otto, 109
Vorlesungen über die Ästhetik (Hegel), 221

Wagner, Richard, 163
Walpole, Hugh, 263 n47
Watt, Ian, 192, 194–195, 205, 261–262 n41
Weigert, Hans, 114
Wells, H. G., 95, 185, 253 n3
Wick, Peter, 241–242 n60
Wilde, Oscar, 73
Wildridge, T. Tindall, 250 n6
Williams, William Carlos, 231
Wilson, Angus, 254 n9
Wilson, Gahan, xxv
Winckelmann, Johann, 31
Wind, Edgar, 25
Wise Blood (O'Connor), 224–228
Worringer, Wilhelm, 73
York Minster, 238 n21

Made in the USA
Lexington, KY
24 February 2017